SOCKS·SOCKS·**SOCKS**

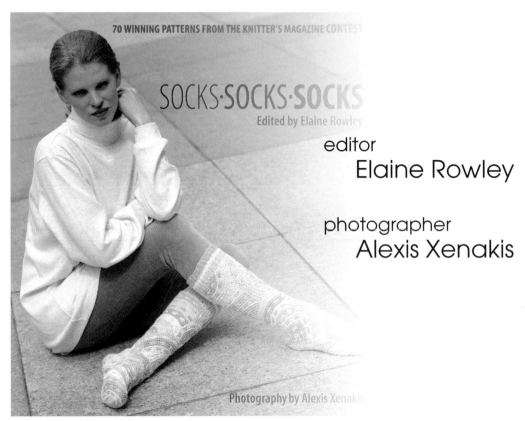

70 WINNING PATTERNS FROM THE KNITTER'S MAGAZINE CONTEST

SOCKS·SOCKS·**SOCKS**

Edited by Elaine Rowley

Photography by Alexis Xenakis

editor
Elaine Rowley

photographer
Alexis Xenakis

BOOKS

AN XRX BOOK

PUBLISHER
Alexis Yiorgos Xenakis

EDITOR
Elaine Rowley

KNITTING EDITOR
Ann Regis

INSTRUCTION EDITING
Traci Bunker
Gitta Schrade

PHOTO STYLIST
Carla Fauske

FASHION DIRECTOR
Nancy J. Thomas

PHOTOGRAPHER
Alexis Yiorgos Xenakis

PUBLISHING DIRECTOR
David Xenakis

GRAPHIC DESIGNER
Bob Natz

BOOK PRODUCTION MANAGER
Debbie Gage

DIGITAL COLOR SPECIALIST
Daren Morgan

PRODUCTION ARTISTS
Jay Reeve
Lynda Selle
Carol Skallerud

MARKETING DIRECTOR
Tad Anderson

SYSTEMS ADMINISTRATOR
Benjamin Xenakis

SIXTH PRINTING, 2003; FIRST PUBLISHED IN USA IN 1999 BY XRX, INC.
PO BOX 1525, SIOUX FALLS, SD 57101-1525

Library of Congress Catalog Card Number 99-70956

ISBN 0-9646391-5-7

Produced in Sioux Falls, South Dakota, by XRX, Inc., 605.338.2450

Printed in China

BOOKS

SOCKS·SOCKS·**SOCKS**

70
winning patterns
from the
Knitter's Magazine contest

BOOKS

64 Knitters, 70 Socks

Charlene Abrams
Lynn Adamick
Beth Morgan Adcock
Diane N. Ballerino
Judith C. Black
Beverly K. Brookhart
Patricia Brunner
Shirley Bryan
Traci Bunkers
Nell Bushby
Marilyn Buster
Nancy K. Byers
Ann Carlile
Elizabeth M. Clouthier
Dez Crawford
Cynthia Dahl
Kathleen S. Day
Debbie Drechsler
Patricia Tongue Edraos
Lorraine Ehrlinger
Dennis Elmer
Nancy Erlandson
Beverley Francis
Kathy L. Frantz
Sheri L. Franz
Kathy A. Garguilo
Lori Gayle
Judy Gibson
Dorothy S. Grubbs
Lisa Gwinner
Hildur Halldórsson
Jóhanna Hjaltadóttir
Darcy Hobgood
Darlene Joyce
Mary Kaiser
Claire Kellogg
Rita Garrity Knudson
Megan Lacey
Anna Lubiw
Katherine Matthews
Marilyn Morgan
Lucy Neatby
Debbie New
Jean Newsted
Hólmfríður Ófeigsdóttir
Lisa Parker
Guðlaug Pétursdóttir
Sharon Philbrick
Maureen E. Pratt
Margaret Radcliffe
Leslie V. Rehfield
Camille Remme
Betty Salpekar
Vivienne Shen
Kim Slad
Maude Smith
Vickie Starbuck
Nadine L. Stewart
Judith Sumner
Mary Anne Thompson
Ásthildur Thorsteinsson
Cindy Walker
Deborah F. Watson
Tricia Weatherston

When I said "Sure," I had no idea how much fun a sock contest could be! I had just gotten my feet wet at XRX when I was recruited for sock contest duty. Shortly after the word went out, the entries began to pour in. My staff and I couldn't wait for each package to arrive. It was as though we were children at Christmas. I'd open an envelope or a box and run to share what was inside. Some came with stories that touched our hearts, others made us roar with laughter, and some stopped us to marvel at a concept or a technique. But most of all, we appreciated the work that went into every one and really looked forward to the mailman's next visit.

As you turn these pages, you won't get to see all of the over-300 entries that we took to Stitches at Valley Forge that year, but you will feel the same excitement that we did. From this selection of 70 wonderful socks, you can choose a serious traditional pattern, such as the Aran Sandal Socks by Lori Gayle of Cambridge, Massachusetts, found on page 74, or a totally whimsical one, like the Licorice Socks by Debbie New of Toronto, Ontario, Canada, on page 95. Whatever your fancy, you'll find something to satisfy it. Along the way, you'll catch special insights from the knitters' comments.

If you're new to knitting socks or even to using double-pointed needles, we have great introductory instructions on page 6—I wish they had been around for my first pair! You can start with the baby-sized sock, graduate to any of the patterns marked Easy, then move on with confidence to the more complicated ones. Most socks in the first chapter, Simple Socks, beginning on page 8, are good first choices. Watch for others marked Easy or Beginner (the Slipper Socks on page 30, the Watermelon Socks on page 94, and the slippers on pages 104 and 105).

If you are a veteran sock knitter, you'll find patterns that are fun and simple to make or challenging ones that will broaden your horizons (watch for instructions marked Experienced or Adventurous). Several use techniques that may be new to you; some you may add to your regular knitting repertoire.

Look at the index of the sock knitters on page 112. You will find knitters from all over the United States and Canada, from New Zealand, and several from Iceland. (Our special thanks to Istex Ltd. and especially to Gudda Asgeirsdóttir for encouraging the Icelandic entrants and translating instructions.) And the winners? Check the sock names marked with an asterisk on p. 112 to see if you agree with the judges.

Although I am a passionate knitter, I thought sock knitting was not for me. After seeing and working with this great collection, boy, have I changed my mind. No matter what type of sock you're looking for, there's one here that will pique your interest.

May all your socks remain pairs!

Lynn McClune
Stitches Expo Director

Contents

70 SOCK PROJECTS

Six steps to sock success **6**

Simple Socks **8**

Kids Socks **20**

Lace Socks **34**

Color Socks **44**

Texture Socks **64**

Whimsical Socks **78**

Icelandic Socks **100**

Techniques & Abbreviations **106**

Colophon **110**

An Index of the Sock Knitters **112**

70 winning patterns
from the
Knitter's Magazine
contest

5

Six steps to sock success

Most socks are simple tubes with shaped heels and toes. Our six-step overview of a basic sock (Leslie Rehfield's Ragg Time from the first chapter, Simple Socks, page 18), takes the mystery out of knitting and turning heels, working gussets, and shaping toes. If you are an experienced sock knitter, a quick review of these 2 pages will introduce the approach used in our instructions. If you have not knit socks before, read this section carefully, then knit a Baby Sock. It's as easy as 1, 2, 3, 4, 5, 6!

Begin reading the following section at step 1, reading from the bottom of the page to the top.

6 Toe Decrease sts at both sides of the foot: decrease 1 stitch at end of first dpn, 1 stitch each at beg and end of 2nd dpn, and 1 stitch at beg of 3rd dpn. In our example, a decrease round alternates with a plain knit round until 16 stitches remain. Then, knit across first dpn with 3rd dpn and graft together stitches from 2nd dpn and 3rd dpn. After fastening ends, the sock is ready to wear.

5 Foot When back to the original number of stitches (60), work around on all stitches until approximately 2" less than desired length.

4 Gusset Now it is time to work around on all three dpn. With an empty dpn, pick up stitches along the side of the heel and sl them to the first dpn. With 2nd dpn, work across the stitches from the next two dpn. With 3rd dpn, pick up stitches along the other side of heel and work half the heel stitches. The beginning of the round is now at the center of the heel. The extra stitches that are picked up are decreased at each side of the foot.

3 Turn heel Continue on the heel stitches, working back and forth in short rows (for a short row, knit only part way across the dpn, leaving the rest of the stitches unworked, and turning to work back) and decreasing at the end of each short row until approximately one-third of the stitches have been decreased. The heel stitches have been *turned:* they were at the back of the heel; now they are at the bottom.

2 Heel Rearrange the stitches on the dpn: place half the stitches (30, in our example) on the first dpn and divide the rest of the stitches between the 2nd and 3rd dpn. Work back and forth on the 30 stitches of first dpn only. The other 30 stitches are for the instep (the top of the foot) and are on hold.

1 Leg Cast on, and divide the stitches on 3 double-pointed needles (dpn). Place a marker and knit a tube to the ankle. (See *Getting Started,* next page, if dpns are new to you.) Since a ring marker would fall off the end of the dpn, use a safety pin marker.

Throughout the book, little needle diagrams in the margin show the arrangement of stitches on the dpn at various stages. In our example 60 stitches are cast on and divided evenly on 3 dpn. The dpns are referred to as first, 2nd, and 3rd, indicating their position in the round. The number of stitches on the first dpn appears in red on our needle diagrams and drawings.

Other Considerations

Yarns A wide variety of yarns were used in these socks—many were spun by the knitters, others are commercial yarns that are no longer available. In the instructions, yarns are described by yardage and weight: lace-weight, fingering or sock, sport, DK, worsted, Aran, and bulky. For help categorizing an unmarked yarn, see life-size photos on p. 108. A reinforcing thread designed for socks can be used with the knitting yarn when working heels and toes.

Techniques and abbreviations See pages 106–109 for an explanation of techniques and abbreviations used.

Sizing The main adjustment required for most socks is the foot length. Most toe shapings add approximately 2" to the length of the foot, so adjust the foot length of the sock accordingly. A few patterns are written for several sizes or give suggestions for sizing. Changing the size of needles or yarn to adjust the gauge is often all that is required (larger needles and/or yarn for a larger sock, smaller for a smaller sock). Soon you will be designing socks just the way you like them.

Stitch patterns Once you understand the construction of a sock, you can begin to consider stitch or color patterns. Most often the patterning is interrupted by the heel and continues only on the top of the foot. Comfort and wear is a consideration on the heel, bottom of foot, and toe. Socks give many people an opportunity to work pattern stitches in the round—even things they may not have thought possible, such as entrelac (see p. 50 and 56) and intarsia (p. 84 and 92).

Heel stitch Most heels are worked with a chain-st selvage (slipping the first st of every row) to make picking up the gusset stitches easier. Many heels are also worked in a slip stitch pattern that adds padding and durability. If not enough stitches remain to complete last 2 rows of heel turning, just work the decreases.

Divide evenly If the number of stitches is not exactly divisible by 3, you may have an extra stitch or two on one dpn.

Beg of rnd The beginning of round is a consideration when the heel is to be worked. If the heel is centered over it, the round begins on the back of the leg. If the heel follows it, the round begins at the side of the leg. Usually after the heel is turned, the beginning of round is relocated at the center of the heel sts. This keeps it (and any jog) on the bottom of the foot and keeps it from interfering with the toe shaping.

The other 20% There are many other ways to make socks. You will find examples of seamed socks, sideways socks, tubular knit socks, socks knit Eastern-style—from toe to top . . .

Dpn Most socks are worked on double-pointed needles (dpn): needles with points at both ends. Like circular needles, dpn are designed to be used to knit circularly. They come in varying lengths and materials and in sets of four or five needles. Most instructions in this book suggest using sets of four dpn. Availability and personal preference will guide your choice, but, wood or plastic have the advantage of not being as slippery as metal.

Getting started   *Working with double-pointed needles (dpn)*

Cast stitches onto one dpn.

❶ Rearrange stitches on three dpn.

❷ Begin working in rounds as follows:

Check carefully that stitches do not twist around a dpn or between dpn. With 4th dpn, work all stitches from first dpn. Use that empty dpn to work the stitches from the 2nd dpn. Use that empty dpn to work the stitches from the 3rd dpn —one round completed. Notice that you work with only two dpn at a time. As you work the first few rounds, be careful that the stitches do not twist between the needles. If instructions recommend working with a set of five dpn, arrange the stitches on four and knit with the fifth.

Baby Socks

Try this for your first sock.

Materials A 1oz/30g (approx 100yds/110m) sport-weight yarn. **B** Set of 4 double-pointed needles (dpn) in size 4 (3.5mm), *or size to obtain gauge.*

Gauge 5½ sts to 1" over St st using size 4 (3.5mm) dpn.

Leg With larger dpn, cast on 32 sts and divide evenly over 3 dpn. Place marker, join and work 16 rnds in k2, p2 rib. K 2 rnds.

Heel Sl first 16 sts to empty dpn, next 8 sts to 2nd dpn, and rem 8 sts to 3rd dpn. Work back and forth in rows on 16 sts of first dpn: **Row 1** (RS) *Sl 1, k1; rep from*. **Row 2** Sl 1, p15. Rep last 2 rows 5 times more. K 1 row.

Turn heel Cont on 16 sts: **Row 1** (WS) P9, p2tog, p1, turn. **Row 2** Sl 1, k3, ssk, k1, turn. **Row 3** Sl 1, p4, p2tog, p1, turn. **Row 4** Sl 1, k5, ssk, k1, turn. Cont to dec in same way, working 1 more st between decs ea row until 10 sts rem, end with a RS row. Do not turn.

Gusset With empty dpn, pick up and k 8 sts along side of heel and sl to first dpn. With 2nd dpn, k next 16 sts. With 3rd dpn, pick up and k 8 sts along other side of heel, then k 5 heel sts—42 sts. Beg of rnd is now at center of heel. **Rnd 1** On first dpn, k to last 3 sts, k2tog, k1; k across 2nd dpn; on 3rd dpn, k1, ssk, k to end—2 sts dec. **Rnd 2** Knit. Rep rnds 1–2 until 32 sts rem.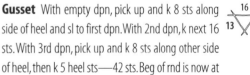

Foot K 10 rnds.

Toe Rnd 1 On first dpn, k to last 3 sts, k2tog, k1; on 2nd dpn, k1, ssk, k to last 3 sts, k2tog, k1; on 3rd dpn, k1, ssk, k to end—4 sts dec. **Rnd 2** Knit. Rep rnds 1–2 until 12 sts rem. K 3 sts of first dpn to 3rd dpn. Cut yarn, leaving a 12" tail. Graft rem 6 sts from each dpn tog.

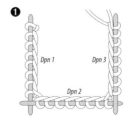 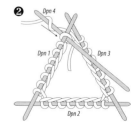

Chapter 1 Simple

10 PROJECTS

Retro Anklets	**10**
After Bertha	**11**
My Christmas Stocking	**12**
Dad's Easy Cable Socks	**13**
Autumn Leaves	**14**
Slip-st Cuffs That Won't	**15**

10

11

12

13

Golf Socks	**16**
Heart to Heart	**17**
Ragg Time	**18**
Lined Sandal Socks	**19**

Simple Socks

Retro Anklets

NANCY BYERS
KENOSHA, WISCONSIN

EASY LEVEL

A fifty-year-old pattern book and yarn purchased at a garage sale inspired these socks— period-perfect in pattern, yarn, and color.

"I knit socks constantly. They are the perfect take-along project. Socks can be made in any color or pattern, and since they don't require a lot of yarn, I can afford to use the best."

"I entered these in the contest as historical socks because I didn't think there would be many entries in that category. I like things from the 40's and 50's since they remind me of my childhood. "

"Yarns and patterns really don't age; they can still be used 50 years later— good news for people with large stashes!"

Leg Cast on 60 sts and divide evenly over 3 dpn. Place marker, join and work 1¼" in k2, p2 rib. Cont in St st until piece measures 4" from beg.

Heel Sl next 30 sts to first dpn, next 15 sts to 2nd dpn, and next 15 sts to 3rd dpn. Work back and forth in rows on 30 sts of first dpn only: **Row 1** (RS) *Sl 1, k1; rep from* across. **Row 2** Sl 1, purl across. Rep last 2 rows 12 times more.

Turn heel Cont on 30 sts: **Row 1** (RS) K19, ssk, k1, turn. **Row 2** Sl 1, p9, p2tog, p1, turn. **Row 3** Sl 1, k10, ssk, k1, turn. **Row 4** Sl 1, p11, p2tog, p1, turn. Cont to dec in same way, working 1 st more between decs on each row until 20 sts rem. **Next row** (RS) Knit. Do not turn.

Gusset With empty dpn, pick up and k 12 sts along side of heel and sl to first dpn. With 2nd dpn, k 30 sts from next 2 dpn. With 3rd dpn, pick up and k 12 sts along other side of heel, then k 10 heel sts—74 sts. Beg of rnd is at center of heel. **Rnd 1** Knit. **Rnd 2** On first dpn, k to last 3 sts, k2tog, k1; k across 2nd dpn; on 3rd dpn, k1, ssk, k to end—2 sts dec. Rep rnds 1–2 until 60 sts rem.

Foot Work even until piece measures 6" from back of heel, or 2" less than desired foot measurement.

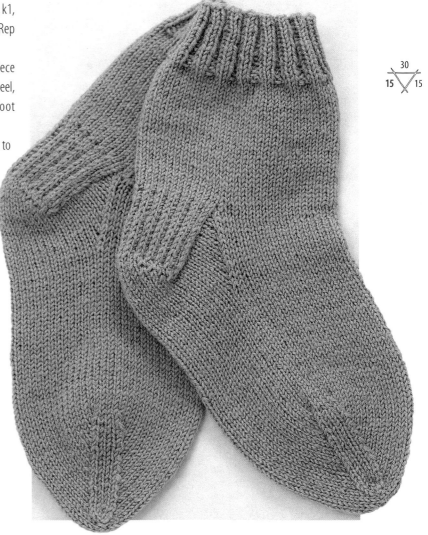

Toe Rnd 1 On first dpn, k to last 3 sts, k2tog, k1; on 2nd dpn, k1, ssk, k to last 3 sts, k2tog, k1; on 3rd dpn, k1, ssk, k to end—4 sts dec. **Rnd 2** Knit. Rep rnds 1–2 until 16 sts rem. With 3rd dpn, k 4 sts from first dpn. Cut yarn, leaving an 18" tail. Graft rem 8 sts from each dpn tog.

Size Woman's small.
Materials **A** 2oz/60g (approx 245yds/223m) sock-weight yarn. **B** Set of 4 double-pointed needles (dpn) in size 4 (3.5mm) *or size to obtain gauge.*
Gauge 7½ sts to 1" (2.5cm) in St st using size 4 (3.5mm) dpn.

After Bertha

EASY LEVEL

DIANE N. BALLERINO

SUPPLY, NORTH CAROLINA

Note For faster knitting, use worsted-weight yarn and larger needles and begin with 48 sts (or another multiple of 6).

Spiral Rib pat (6-st rep) **Rnds 1–4** *K3, p3; rep from*. **Rnds 5–8** *P1, k3, p2; rep from*. **Rnds 9–12** *P2, k3, p1; rep from*. **Rnds 13–16** *P3, k3; rep from*. **Rnds 17–20** *K1, p3, k2; rep from*. **Rnds 21–24** *K2, p3, k1; rep from*. Rep Rnds 1–24 for spiral rib pat.

Leg/Foot Cast on 66 sts and divide evenly over 3 dpn. Place marker, join and work 4" in k3, p3 rib, end at marker. Work in Spiral Rib pat until sock measures 13" from beg, or 1½" less than desired finished length.

Toe Rnds 1–2 Knit. **Rnd 3** *K4, k2tog; rep from*—55 sts. **Rnds 4–5** Knit. **Rnd 6** *K3, k2tog; rep from*—44 sts. **Rnds 7–8** Knit. **Rnd 9** *K2, k2tog; rep from*—33 sts. **Rnds 10–11** Knit. **Rnd 12** *K1, k2tog; rep from*—22 sts. **Rnds 13–14** Knit. **Rnd 15** *K2tog; rep from*—11 sts. Cut yarn, leaving an 8" tail. Run tail through rem sts twice and pull tog tightly. Fasten off.

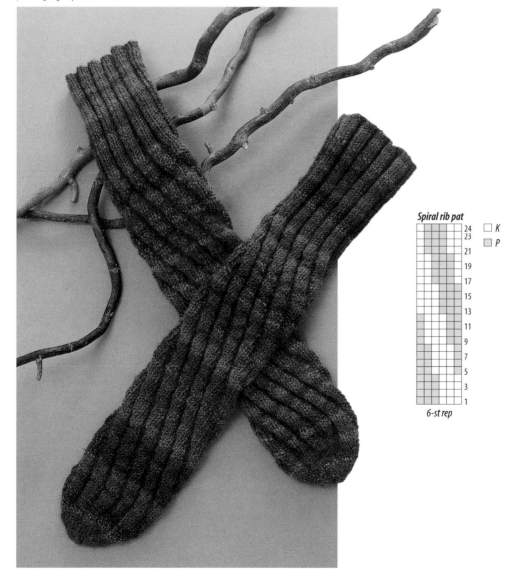

Spiral rib pat

☐ K
▨ P

24 23 21 19 17 15 13 11 9 7 5 3 1

6-st rep

The handknit version of a tube sock, spiral ribbed socks have long been considered the simplest of socks to knit: there is no heel to turn.

This pair was inspired by Garry Aney's Spiral Rib Socks in *Socks* (Interweave Press). Direction and angle of the spiral can be varied: *Mary Thomas's Knitting Book* (Dover) presents another example in which the k3, p3 rib moves 1 stitch to the right every 7th round.

"I call these my After Bertha socks because I finished them during Hurricane Bertha, which roared through here on July 12th, 1996. It was helpful to do something constructive during the long and anxious hours of waiting for the huge storm to blow itself out."

Size Woman's small to medium.

Materials A 2½oz/70g (approx 300yds/273m) fingering-weight yarn. **B** Set of 4 double-pointed needles (dpn) in size 2 (3mm) *or size to obtain gauge*.

Gauge 8½ sts to 1" (2.5cm) in Spiral Rib pat, slightly stretched, using size 2 (3mm) dpn.

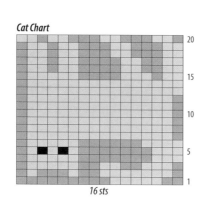

My Christmas Stocking
EASY LEVEL

CLAIRE KELLOGG
BEAVERCREEK, OREGON

Notes 1 Cuff is worked last, so use an invisible (temporary) cast-on if you prefer. **2** Pat is written for heart sock with changes for cat sock in parenthesis. **3** If using another color on toe, change color on an even row.

Leg With MC, cast on 52 sts and divide evenly over 3 dpn. Place marker, join, and work 1¾" in St st (k every rnd). **Next rnd** [K2tog, k24] twice—50 sts. Work 2½" in St st. **Next rnd** [K2tog, k23] twice—48 sts. Cont in St st until sock measures 9½" from beg.

Heel Sl first 24 sts to first dpn, next 12 sts to 2nd dpn, and last 12 sts to 3rd dpn. With CC1 (MC), work back and forth in rows on 24 sts of first dpn: **Row 1** (RS) Sl 1, k23. **Row 2** Sl 1, p 23. Rep last 2 rows 11 times more, then rep row 1. (For cat sock, after 2 rows, work Cat pat in CC2.) Change to MC.

Turn heel Cont on 24 sts of first dpn: **Row 1** (WS) P14, p2tog, p1, turn. **Row 2** Sl 1, k5, k2tog, k1, turn. **Row 3** Sl1, p6, p2tog, p1, turn. **Row 4** Sl 1, k7, k2tog, k1, turn. Cont to dec in same way, working 1 st more between decs on each row until 14 sts rem, end with a RS row. Do not turn.

Gusset With empty dpn, and MC, pick up and k 12 sts along side of heel and sl to first dpn. With 2nd dpn k 24 sts from next 2 dpn. With 3rd dpn, pick up and k 12 sts along other side of heel, then k 7 heel sts—62 sts. Beg of rnd is now at center of heel. **Rnd 1** On first dpn, k to last 2 sts, k2tog; k across 2nd dpn; on 3rd dpn, ssk, k to end—2 sts dec. **Rnd 2** Knit. Rep last 2 rnds 6 times more—48 sts.

Foot Work even for 3½" or until 2" less than desired length.

Toe Rnd 1 On first dpn, k to last 2 sts, k2tog; on 2nd dpn, ssk, k to last 2 sts, k2tog; on 3rd dpn, ssk, k to end—4 sts dec. Change to CC2 (CC1). **Rnd 2** Knit. Rep rnds 1–2 until 20 sts rem. **Next rnd** K 5 sts from first dpn onto 3rd dpn. Cut yarn, leaving an 18" tail. Graft rem 10 sts from each dpn tog.

Cuff Turn sock inside out. With CC1, pick up and k 17 sts on first dpn, 18 sts on 2nd dpn, and 17 sts on 3rd dpn—52 sts. K 1 rnd and inc 1 st at center of each dpn—55 sts. K 8 rnds, then p 6 rnds to form a roll at top of sock. K 9 rows of Heart pat with CC2 on MC; OR, if no knit-in pat, with CC1 k 4 rnds, p 4 rnds, k 2 rnds. With MC, [k 1 rnd, p 1 rnd] 4 times.

Points Work back and forth in rows on sets of 11 sts only as foll (place other sts on hold): Sl 1 as if to purl with yarn in front, k to end. ***Next (dec) row** Sl 1 as if to purl with yarn in front, k2tog, k to last 3 sts, k2tog, k1. K 3 rows even. Rep from* 3 times more. Bind off rem 3 sts, slipping rather than knitting first st.

Hanging loop With CC1, pick up and k 3 sts at top of roll and work a 3-st I-cord about 3" long. Cut yarn, leaving a 6" tail. Run tail through I-cord sts and fasten to top of sock. (Duplicate st cat's eyes in black.)

"I developed this pattern after studying early American Christmas stockings—contrasting cuff, zigzag edge, and bells were the result. I have made these to be used as Christmas stockings, but my daughter wears a pair as slippers. Noisy!"

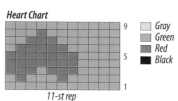

Cat Chart

20
15
10
5
1

16 sts

Heart Chart

9

5

1

11-st rep

☐ Gray
☐ Green
☐ Red
■ Black

Size Woman's medium (or one-size-fits-all Christmas stocking).

Materials A Worsted-weight wool. For each sock: 3½oz/100g (approx 230yds/210m) in gray (green) main color (MC), small amounts of contrast colors CC1 green (red), CC2 red (gray), and black. **B** Set of 4 double-pointed needles (dpn) in size 5 (3.75mm) *or size to obtain gauge.*

Gauge 5 sts to 1" (2.5cm) in St st using size 5 (3.75mm) dpn.

Dad's Easy Cable Socks

LYNN ADAMICK

INTERMEDIATE LEVEL

REDONDO BEACH, CALIFORNIA

Cable Pat (over 8 sts) **2/2 Left Cross** Sl 2 sts to cable needle, hold to front, k2; k2 from cable needle. **Rnds 1, 2, 4, 5, 6, 8** Knit. **Rnd 3** *2/2 Left Cross, k4; rep from*. **Rnd 7** *K4, 2/2 Left Cross; rep from*. Rep rnds 1–8 for Cable pat.
Note Stretch sock slightly when measuring for length of foot.

Cuff With size 5 dpn, cast on 48 sts and divide evenly over 3 dpn. Place marker, join and work 1" in k1, p1 rib.

Leg Change to size 8 dpn. Work in Cable pat until sock measures 8" from beg, end with rnd 8.

Heel Sl next 24 sts to first dpn, next 12 sts to 2nd dpn, and next 12 sts to 3rd dpn. Using optional heel reinforcement, work back and forth in rows on 24 sts of first dpn only: **Row 1** (RS) *Sl 1, k1; rep from* across. **Row 2** Sl 1, p23. Rep last 2 rows 10 times more, then rep row 1.

Turn heel Cont on 24 sts: **Row 1** (WS) P14, p2tog, p1, turn. **Row 2** Sl 1, k5, k2tog, k1, turn. **Row 3** Sl 1, p6, p2tog, p1, turn. **Row 4** Sl 1, k7, k2tog, k1, turn. Cont to dec in same way, working 1 st more between decs on each row until 14 sts rem, end with a RS row. Do not turn. Cut reinforcement yarn.

Gusset With empty dpn, pick up and k 12 sts along side of heel and sl to first dpn. With 2nd dpn, cont established cable pat over 24 sts from next 2 dpn. With 3rd dpn, pick up and k 12 sts along other side of heel, then k 7 heel sts—62 sts. Beg of rnd is now at center of heel. **Rnd 1** On first dpn, k to last 3 sts, k2tog, k1; on 2nd dpn, work in cable pat; on 3rd dpn, k1, ssk, k to end—2 sts dec. **Rnd 2** K and work Cable pat as est. Rep rnds 1–2 until 48 sts rem.

Foot Work even for 4", or until 2" less than desired length.

Toe Change to size 6 dpn. Add optional toe reinforcement. **Rnd 1** On first dpn, k to last 3 sts, k2 tog, k1; on 2nd dpn, k1, ssk, k to last 3 sts, k2tog, k1; on 3rd dpn, k1, ssk, k to end. **Rnd 2** Knit. Rep rnds 1–2 until 20 sts remain. K 5 sts of first dpn onto 3rd dpn. Graft rem 10 sts from each dpn tog.

"These heavy men's socks, made especially for my dad, can be worn with boots, Birkenstocks, or moccasins. Since I can't imagine my dad, or any man I know, handwashing a pair of socks, I used machine-washable wool. They are the perfect socks for cold climates."

Size Man's medium.

Materials **A** 5¼oz/150g (approx 275yds/251m) chunky-weight yarn. **B** One set each of 4 double-pointed needles (dpn) in sizes 5, 6, and 8 (3.75, 4, and 5mm) *or size to obtain gauge.* **C** Cable needle. **D** Optional reinforcement yarn for heel and toe.

Gauge 5 sts to 1" (2.5cm) over Cable Pat using size 8 (5mm) dpn.

Cable pat

8
7
5
3
1

8-st repeat

☐ K

⟋ 2/2 Left cross

Autumn Leaves

EASY LEVEL

DARCY HOBGOOD

NORTH BERWICK, MAINE

"Being a practical and frugal New Englander, I wanted to knit socks which would be worn and worn a lot! Nothing terribly time consuming or fussy. Easy-care, go-with-anything, no-fuss, warm and comfortable socks would fit the bill.

Because the yarn for these socks would be hand spun and dyed, I wanted to make just enough. 'Waste not, want not.'

Having exactly eight ounces of yarn and not being quite sure how far it would go, I started my socks just above the heel with an invisible cast on. By knitting both feet first, dividing the remaining yarn in two, and picking up stitches to knit the cuffs from bottom to top, I could maximize cuff length and still eliminate any fear of running short of yarn.

The half-stitch jog in ribbing worked both directions isn't apparent with a variegated yarn and on a sock that's meant to be cuffed. The ribbed instep ensures a perfect fit with no puckers at the ankle."

Our instructions for this very basic sock begin at the cuff and end at the toe.

Size Woman's medium.

Materials A 8oz/225g (approx 650yds/592m) DK-weight wool. **B** Set of 4 double-pointed needles (dpn) in size 4 (3.5mm), *or size to obtain gauge.*

Gauge 6½sts to 1" (2.5cm) in St st using size 4 (3.5mm) dpn.

Leg Cast on 60 sts and divide evenly over 3 dpn. Place marker, join and work 6" in k2, p2 rib.

Heel Sl next 30 sts to first dpn, next 15 sts to 2nd dpn, and next 15 sts to 3rd dpn. Work back and forth in rows on 30 sts of first dpn only: **Row 1** (RS) *Sl 1, k1; rep from* across. **Row 2** Sl 1, p29. Rep last 2 rows 13 times more, then rep row 1.

Turn heel Cont on 30 sts: **Row 1** (WS) P17, p2tog, p1, turn. **Row 2** Sl 1, k5, k2tog, k1, turn. **Row 3** Sl 1, p6, p2tog, p1, turn. **Row 4** Sl 1, k7, k2tog, k1, turn. Cont to dec in same way, working 1 st more between decs on each row until 18 sts rem, end with a RS row. Do not turn.

Gusset With empty dpn, pick up and k 15 sts along side of heel and sl to first dpn. With 2nd dpn, cont rib pat across 30 sts of next 2 dpn. With 3rd dpn, pick up and k 15 sts along other side of heel, then k 9 heel sts—78 sts. Beg of rnd is now at center of heel. **Rnd 1** On first dpn, k to last 3 sts, k2tog, k1; work rib pat across 2nd dpn; on 3rd dpn, k1, ssk, k to end—2 sts dec. **Rnd 2** K and work rib pat as established. Rep rnds 1–2 until 60 sts rem.

Foot Work 4" even, or until 2" less than desired length.

Toe Rnd 1 On first dpn, k to last 3 sts, k2 tog, k1; on 2nd dpn, k1, ssk, k to last 3 sts, k2tog, k1; on 3rd dpn, k1, ssk, k to end—4 sts dec. **Rnd 2** Knit. Rep rnds 1–2 until 16 sts rem. K 4 sts from first dpn onto 3rd dpn. Cut yarn, leaving an 18" tail. Graft rem 8 sts from each dpn tog.

Spin/dye your own "I started with superwash merino lambswool roving. The wool was spun using a worsted technique to give a tightly spun, durable yarn, slightly finer than a worsted weight. Dyeing in the yarn stage would give the speckled look I was after. Cushing's old gold, khaki drab, and terra cotta dyes were each mixed in a concentrated solution (a tablespoon of dye to a cup of water) in pancake syrup containers (the plastic spout is ideal for controlling the flow of dye). After the yarn was mordanted in a vinegar/water solution, squeezed dry, and placed on a plastic sheet outside (this can be a messy method), dye was sprinkled on in spots until most of the yarn had some color. After steaming on a rack over boiling water for 20 minutes, the yarn was placed in a second dyebath of diluted old gold to mellow the colors and fill in any remaining white areas."

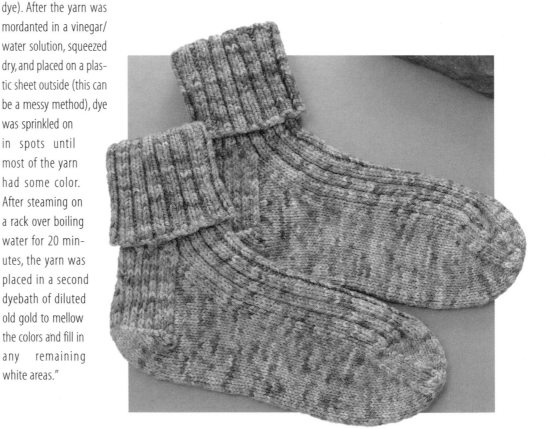

Slip-st Cuffs That Won't

INTERMEDIATE LEVEL

LORRAINE EHRLINGER
CLEVELAND HEIGHTS, OHIO

Mosaic chart notes **1** Each chart row consists of knit stitches and slipped stitches. On each row, stitches to be knit are indicated at the right of the chart. All other stitches in that row are slipped purlwise with yarn in back. **2** Work each chart row twice, knitting and slipping the same sts on 2nd row as on the previous row, slipping purlwise with yarn in front.

Cuff With straight needle and MC, cast on 54 sts. Work 3 rows in k1, p1 rib. With MC and CC, work 44 rows of Mosaic chart.

Leg With WS of cuff facing, divide sts evenly onto 3 dpn. Place marker, join and with MC work 2" in k1, p1 rib. K until piece is 1½" after rib.

Heel K next 14 sts onto first dpn; sl next 13 sts to 2nd dpn, next 13 sts to 3rd dpn, and next 14 sts to first dpn. Work back and forth in rows on 28 sts of first dpn only: **Row 1** (RS) *Sl 1, k1; rep from*. **Row 2** Sl 1, purl across. Rep last 2 rows 13 times more.

Turn heel Cont on 28 sts: **Row 1** (RS) K16, ssk, k1, turn. **Row 2** Sl 1, p5, p2tog, p1, turn. **Row 3** Sl 1, k6, k2tog, k1, turn. **Row 4** Sl 1, p7, p2tog, p1, turn. Cont to dec in same way, working 1 st more between decs on each row until 16 sts rem, end with a RS row. Do not turn.

Gusset With empty dpn, pick up and k 14 sts along side of heel and sl to first dpn. With 2nd dpn k 26 sts from 2nd and 3rd dpn. With 3rd dpn, pick up and k 14 sts along other side of heel, then k 8 heel sts—70 sts. Beg of rnd is at center of heel. Sl last st on first dpn and first st on 3rd dpn to 2nd dpn. **Rnd 1** On first dpn, k to last 3 sts, k2tog, k1; k across 2nd dpn; on 3rd dpn, k1, ssk, k to end—2 sts dec. **Rnd 2** Knit. Rep rnds 1–2 until 56 sts rem.

Foot Work even until foot measures 7½" or 2" less than desired finished length.

Toe **Rnd 1** On first dpn, k to last 3 sts, k2tog, k1; on 2nd dpn, k1, ssk, k to last 3 sts, k2tog, k1; on 3rd dpn, k1, ssk, k to end—4 sts dec. **Rnd 2** Knit. Rep rnds 1–2 until 16 sts rem. K 4 sts of first dpn onto 3rd dpn. Cut yarn, leaving an 18" tail. Graft rem 8 sts from each dpn tog. Seam cuff.

For years, the only socks Lorraine knit were Christmas socks. Now she even knits socks to match her green bowling shirt! This pair earns compound interest with a patterned cuff: both the knitter and the viewer benefit. This mosaic cuff can be knit back and forth as written, or worked around on dpn. To work circularly, the 2nd time you work each chart row, *purl* and slip the stitches purlwise with yarn in back. And Lorraine's secret to the sock's tidy fit? The cuff folds down over an equal expanse of k1, p1 ribbing.

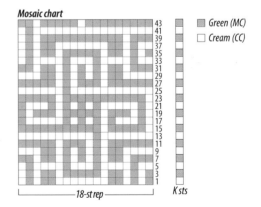

Mosaic chart

Green (MC)
Cream (CC)

18-st rep   K sts

Size Women's medium.

Materials A 1¾oz/50g (approx 215yds/196m) sock yarn: green (MC), small amount cream (CC) **B** One pair 10" straight needles and set of 4 double-pointed needles (dpn) in size 2 (2.75mm), *or size to obtain gauge.*

Gauge 8 sts to 1" (2.5cm) in St st using size 2 (2.75mm) dpn.

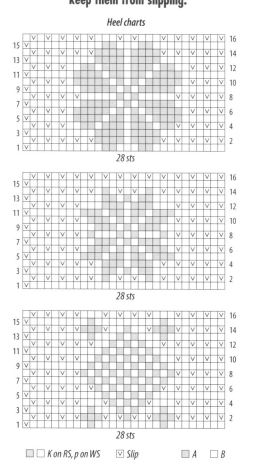

"I started to knit in high school in 1927.
When I learned to play golf in the 50's,
I began to knit socks like these.
The rolled edges work better than a pompon to
keep them from slipping."

Heel charts

(charts, 28 sts each, with row numbers 1–16)

☐ ☐ K on RS, p on WS   ☑ Slip   ▨ A   ☐ B

Size Small (medium, large).

Materials **A** 1¾oz/50g skeins (approx 215yds/196m each) fingering-weight sock yarn: small amount in Cream (A) and 2 skeins Blue Heather (B). **B** Set of 5 double-pointed needles (dpn) in size 2 (2.75mm) *or size to obtain gauge.*

Gauge 8 sts to 1" (2.5cm) in St st using size 2 (2.75mm) dpn.

Golf Socks

INTERMEDIATE LEVEL

DOROTHY S. GRUBBS

LEBANON, NEW HAMPSHIRE

Note Needle diagrams show stitch numbers for small size. Heel charts show the 28 stitches of small heel; for sizes medium and large, center heel motif and work extra stitches in pattern.

Ankle With A, cast on 28 (32, 36) sts. Work 1" in St st (k on RS, p on WS) and cast on 28 (32, 36) sts at beg of last RS row. Do not turn. Place marker, join and *k14 (16, 18) sts onto first dpn; rep from* onto 3 more dpn—56 (64, 72) sts. K for ½" more. Change to B and k 3 rnds more.

Heel K across 28 (32, 36) sts of first and 2nd dpn, turn and work back and forth in rows on these sts (place rem sts on hold) as foll: **Row 1** (WS) Sl 1, p27 (31, 35), turn. **Row 2** *Sl 1, k1; rep from* across, turn. Rep last 2 rows once. Then select one of the Heel charts and work rows 1–16 of chart. **Next row** (WS) Sl 1, p27 (31, 35), turn. **Next row** *Sl 1, k1; rep from* across, turn. Rep last 2 rows once.

Turn heel Cont on 28 (32, 36) sts: **Row 1** (WS) Sl 1, p15 (17, 19) sts, p2tog, p1. **Row 2** Sl 1, k5, ssk, k1, turn. **Row 3** Sl 1, p6, p2tog, p1, turn. **Row 4** Sl 1, k7, ssk, k1, turn. Cont to dec in same way, working 1 st more between decs on each row until 16 (20, 22) sts rem, end with a RS row. Do not turn.

Gusset With empty dpn and B, pick up and k 14 sts along side of heel and sl to first dpn, k across 14 (16, 18) sts each of next 2 dpn, pick up and k 14 sts along other side of heel, then k rem 8 (10, 11) sts—72 (80, 86) sts. Beg of rnd is at center of heel. **Rnd 1** On first dpn, k to last 3 sts, k2tog, k1; k across 2nd and 3rd dpns; on 4th dpn, k1, ssk, k to end—2 sts dec. **Rnd 2** Knit. Rep rnds 1–2 until there are 14 (16, 18) sts on each of 4 dpn.

Foot Work even until foot measures 2" less than desired length to toe.

Toe **Rnd 1** On first dpn, k to last 3 sts, k2tog, k1; on 2nd dpn, k1, ssk, k across; on 3rd dpn, k to last 3 sts, k2tog, k1; on 4th dpn, k1, ssk, k across—4 sts dec. **Rnds 2–3** Knit. **For size large only**, rep last 3 rnds once. **For all sizes**, rep rnds 1–2 until 4 sts rem on each dpn. Cut yarn, leaving a 12" tail. Sl sts from first dpn to 2nd dpn. Sl sts from 3rd dpn to 4th dpn. Graft rem 8 sts from each dpn tog.

Heart to Heart

EASY LEVEL

BEVERLY BROOKHART

BROADWAY, NORTH CAROLINA

Leg With smaller dpn and A, cast on 60 sts and divide evenly over 3 dpn. Place marker, join and work 2½" in k1, p1 rib. Change to larger dpn and k 3 rows. Cont to k each rnd in colors as foll: 4 rnds B, 4 rnds C, 4 rnds B, 4 rnds A. Beg Heart pat: Work 8 rnds of chart with B on A. K 4 rnds A, 4 rnds B, 4 rnds C, 4 rnds B, 8 rnds A, and 2 rnds C. Sock measures approx 9" from beg.

Heel With C, k next 15 sts onto first dpn, sl next 15 sts to 2nd dpn, next 15 sts to 3rd dpn, and next 15 sts to first dpn. Work back and forth in rows on 30 sts of first dpn only: **Row 1** (WS) Sl 1, purl across. **Row 2** *Sl 1, k1; rep from*. Rep last 2 rows 11 times more.

Turn heel Cont on 30 sts with C: **Row 1** (WS) P19, p2tog, p1, turn. **Row 2** Sl 1, k9, ssk, k1, turn. **Row 3** Sl 1, p10, p2tog, p1, turn. **Row 4** Sl 1, k11, ssk, k1, turn. Cont to dec in same way, working 1 st more between decs on each row until 20 sts rem, end with a RS row.

Gusset With empty dpn and C, pick up and k 12 sts along side of heel and sl to first dpn. With 2nd dpn, k 30 sts from next 2 dpn. With 3rd dpn, pick up and k 12 sts along other side of heel, then k 10 heel sts—74 sts. Beg of rnd is now at center of heel. **Rnd 1** Knit. **Rnd 2** On first dpn, k to last 3 sts, k2tog, k1; k across 2nd dpn; on 3rd dpn, k1, ssk, k to end—2 sts dec. Rep rnds 1–2 until 60 sts rem.

Foot K 15 rnds A, 10 rnds B, 4 rnds C, 7 rnds B, 6 rnds A.

Toe Work foll 2 rnds with A: **Rnd 1** On first dpn, k to last 3 sts, k2tog, k1; on 2nd dpn, k1, ssk, k to last 3 sts, k2tog, k1; on 3rd dpn, k1, ssk, k to end — 4 sts dec. **Rnd 2** Knit. With C, rep last 2 rnds until 16 sts rem. K 4 sts of first dpn onto 3rd dpn. Cut yarn, leaving a 20" tail. Graft rem 8 sts from each dpn tog.

The handspun yarn for these socks, half mohair, half Romney wool, was dyed in three colors: periwinkle blue from indigo and cochineal, pink from cochineal, and yellow from zinnias. Even if you are not involved in color from the ground up, you can try re-coloring these socks in bright or rich hues.

The hearts are optional but not for Beverly. She uses hearts in her knitting as often as she can. Sock tops need to stretch to fit over the heel as they are pulled on and off. Be careful to allow for this as you work a fairisle pattern, even a little one such as these hearts.

Heart pat

□ Pink (B)
▩ Blue (A)

12-st rep

Size Women's large.

Materials **A** 1¾oz/50g (approx 165 yds/150m) sport weight yarn each in blue (A), pink (B), and yellow (C). **B** One set each of 4 double-pointed needles (dpn) in sizes 3 and 4 (3.25 and 3.5mm) *or size to obtain gauge.*

Gauge 7 sts to 1" (2.5cm) in St st using size 4 (3.5mm) dpn.

Ragg Time

EASY LEVEL

LESLIE REHFIELD

JUNEAU, ALASKA

The color changes on this sock highlight the
different sections of the sock:
from the leg in ragg-blend,
through the orange and white striped heel,
the gray gusset continuing into the striped foot,
ending at the ragg-blend toe.
Along the way, lengthening stripes of orange and
white reveal the turn of the heel.

Leg With larger dpn and A, cast on 60 sts and divide evenly on 3 dpn. Place marker, join and work in k1, p1 rib as foll: 3 rnds A, 4 rnds B, 3 rnds C. Change to D and work 32 rnds in k2, p2 rib, end last rnd 15 sts before marker. Piece measures approx 4" from beg.

Heel Sl next 30 sts to first dpn, next 15 sts to 2nd dpn, and next 15 sts to 3rd dpn. Change to smaller dpn. Work back and forth in rows in St st (k on RS, p on WS) on 30 sts of first dpn only (sl first and last st of each knit row): 1 row B, then *2 rows C, 2 rows B; rep from* 4 times more—21 rows completed, end with a k row.

Turn heel Cont on 30 sts and alternate 2 rows C and 2 rows B, beginning with C: **Row 1** (WS) P18, p2tog, p1, turn. **Row 2** Sl 1, k7, ssk, k1, turn. **Row 3** Sl 1, p8, p2tog, p1, turn. **Row 4** Sl 1, k9, ssk, k1, turn. Cont to dec in same way, working 1 st more between decs on each row until 18 sts rem, end with a RS row. Do not turn.

Gusset Change to larger dpn and A. With empty dpn, pick up and k 11 sts along side of heel and sl to first dpn. With 2nd dpn, k 30 sts from 2nd and 3rd dpn. With 3rd dpn, pick up and k 11 sts along other side of heel, then k 9 heel sts—70 sts. Beg of rnd is now at center of heel. **Rnd 1** On first dpn, k to last 3 sts, k2tog, k1; k across 30 sts of 2nd dpn; on 3rd dpn, k1, ssk, k to end—2 sts dec. **Rnd 2** Knit. Rep rnds 1–2 until 60 sts rem.

Foot Work 20 rnds A, then 20 rnds D.

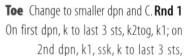

Toe Change to smaller dpn and C. **Rnd 1** On first dpn, k to last 3 sts, k2tog, k1; on 2nd dpn, k1, ssk, k to last 3 sts, k2tog, k1; on 3rd dpn, k1, ssk, k to end—4 sts dec. **Rnd 2** Knit. Rep rnds 1–2 (working 2 rows with B, 2 rows with D) until 16 sts rem. K 4 sts from first dpn to 3rd dpn. Graft rem 8 sts on each dpn tog.

Size Woman's medium.

Materials **A** 3-ply sport-weight yarn in 4 colors: 1oz/30g (approx 100yds/91m) each in gray (A), white (B) and orange (C); 2oz/60g (approx 200yds/182m) ragg-type in gray/white/orange (D). **B** One set each of 4 dpn in sizes 1 and 2 (2.25 and 2.75mm), *or size to obtain gauge.*

Gauge 7 sts to 1" (2.5cm) in St st using size 2 (2.75mm) dpn.

Lined Sandal Socks

INTERMEDIATE LEVEL

JUDITH C. BLACK

SLOANSVILLE, NEW YORK

Note A k2, p1 rib is used throughout this sock, including the heel flap and turn, the gusset, the sole, and the toe. Try knitting and lining a swatch before making these socks: Cast on 38 sts; work k2, p1 rib for 3". Follow lining steps 1–3.

Leg With A, cast on 108 sts and divide evenly over 3 dpn. Place marker, join, and work 8" in k2, p1 rib.

Heel Sl 53 sts to first dpn, next 27 sts to 2nd dpn, and rem 28 sts to 3rd dpn. Work back and forth in rows on 53 sts of first dpn: **Row 1** (RS) Sl 1, k1, *p1, k2; rep from*. **Row 2** Sl 1, p1, *k1, p2; rep from*. Rep last 2 rows 17 times more, then rep row 1.

Turn heel Cont on 53 sts of first dpn: **Row 1** (WS) Work 30, p2tog, p1, turn. **Row 2** Sl 1, work 8, k2tog, k1, turn. **Row 3** Sl 1, work 9, p2tog, p1, turn. **Row 4** Sl 1, work 10, k2tog, k1, turn. Cont to dec in same way, working 1 st more between decs on each row until 29 sts rem, end with a RS row. Do not turn.

Gusset With empty dpn, pick up and k 21 sts along side of heel and sl to first dpn. With 2nd dpn, work 55 sts from next 2 dpn. With 3rd dpn, pick up and k 21 sts along other side of heel, then k 15 heel sts—126 sts. Beg of rnd is now at center of heel. **Rnd 1** Work in rib pat. **Rnd 2** On first dpn, work to last 3 sts, k2tog, k1; cont pat across 2nd dpn; on 3rd dpn, k1, ssk, work to end—2 sts dec. Rep rnds 1–2 until 108 sts rem.

Foot Work even until 2" less than desired length.

Toe Rnd 1 On first dpn, work in pat to last 3 sts, k2tog, k1; on 2nd dpn k1, ssk, work in pat to last 3 sts, k2tog, k1; on 3rd dpn, k1, ssk, work in pat to end—4 sts dec. **Rnd 2** Work even. Rep rnds 1–2 for 1", then rep rnd 1 until 48 sts rem. (**Note** Foot length should be about ½" shorter than normal because the lining lengthens the sock.) With 3rd dpn, k 12 sts from first dpn. Cut yarn, leaving a 24" tail. Graft rem 24 sts from each dpn tog.

Lining Turn sock inside out. Thread a tapestry needle with 30" of B. ❶ Stitch under both sides of first knit st at cuff, then wrap yarn around the size 3 needle. ❷ Working along the same column of knit sts, stitch under 2nd knit st and then wrap yarn around the needle. ❸ Cont along the column from cuff to toe. As the needle fills with wraps, simply slide it in the direction of the unwrapped sts. Rep for every column of knit sts. Tuck the ends into the wrap "tubes", tugging to lock the first and last wraps into place.

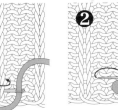 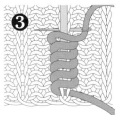

These sumptuous socks develop in two stages. First, knit a fine k2, p1 ribbed sock. Then stitch an ingeniously-simple looped lining. Handspun mohair makes it luxurious and resilient. Judith adapted the technique used by Robin Hansen in the Kennebunkport Wooly Bear Mittens in *Homespun, Handknit*.

Size Women's large.

Materials A 3½oz/100g (approx 430yds/392m) sock yarn. (*Spinner's note* 70% Merino, 30% kid mohair; 20 wraps per inch/ 2600 yds per lb.) **B** 4oz/120g (approx 175 yds/160m) worsted weight yarn for lining. (*Spinner's note* 100% kid mohair; 12 wraps per inch, approx 700 yds per lb.) **C** Set of 4 double-pointed needles (dpn) in size 1 (2.25mm) *or size to obtain gauge*. **D** One size 3 (3.25mm) knitting needle to use as a gauge for the lining.

Gauge 12 sts to 1" (2.5cm), in k2, p1 rib, lined and slightly stretched.

Chapter 2

Kids

10 PROJECTS

Baby Socks **22**

Gumball Boot Socks **23**

Crazy Crayons **24**

First Lace **26**

Multicolored Sockies **27**

Shell Lace **28**

22

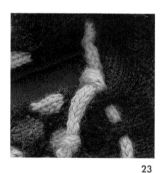

23

24

26

My Little Angel **29**

Slipper Socks **30**

Brendan's Vine Socks **31**

Dragon Socks **32**

Kids Socks

27

28

29

30

31

32

SOCKS

21

These chubby little socks are a great way
to sample 2-color knitting.
Try a few short rounds in ribbing and stockinette.
Just make sure to carry the color
not being worked loosely.

Size Infant. Finished length, heel to toe, is 4".

Materials A Sport to DK-weight yarn: small amounts in 4 colors: light green (A), dark tweed (B), light turquoise (C), dark turquoise (D). **B** Set of 4 double-pointed needles (dpn) in sizes 3 and 4 (3.25 and 3.5mm) *or size to obtain gauge.*

Gauge 5½ sts to 1" (2.5cm) in St st using size 4 (3.5mm) dpn.

Baby Socks

EASY LEVEL

SHIRLEY BRYAN

TACOMA, WASHINGTON

Leg With larger dpn and A, cast on 32 sts and divide evenly over 3 dpn. Place marker, join and p 1 rnd. Work 5 rnds in rib as foll: *K2 B, p2 A; rep from* around. Cut A and B. With C, k 1 rnd and inc 4 sts evenly around—36 sts. With C, p 2 rnds. With B and C, work 6 rnds in Color Pat. Cut B. With C, k 1 rnd and dec 4 sts evenly around—32 sts. Cut C. With A, k 1 rnd, then p 2 rnds.

Heel Sl first 16 sts to empty dpn, next 8 sts to 2nd dpn, and rem 8 sts to 3rd dpn. With A, work back and forth in rows on 16 sts of first dpn only: **Row 1** (RS) *Sl 1, k1; rep from*. **Row 2** Sl 1, p15. Rep last 2 rows 5 times more. K 1 row.

Turn heel Cont on 16 sts: **Row 1** (WS) P9, p2tog, p1, turn. **Row 2** Sl 1, k3, ssk, k1, turn. **Row 3** Sl 1, p4, p2tog, p1, turn. **Row 4** Sl 1, k5, ssk, k1, turn. Cont to dec in same way, working 1 st more between decs on each row until 10 sts rem, end with a RS row. Do not turn.

Gusset Change to smaller dpn. With empty dpn, pick up and k 8 sts along side of heel and sl to first dpn. With 2nd dpn, k 16 sts from next 2 dpn. With 3rd dpn, pick up and k 8 sts along other side of heel, then k 5 heel sts—42 sts. Beg of rnd is now at center of heel. Change to D. **Rnd 1** On first dpn, k to last 3 sts, k2tog, k1; k across 2nd dpn; on 3rd dpn, k1, ssk, k to end—2 sts dec. **Rnd 2** Knit. Rep rnds 1–2 until 32 sts rem.

Foot K 3 rnds. Cut D.

Toe Change to B. **Rnd** 1 On first dpn, k to last 3 sts, k2tog, k1; on 2nd dpn, k1, ssk, k to last 3 sts, k2tog, k1; on 3rd dpn, k1, ssk, k to end—4 sts dec. **Rnd 2** Knit. Rep rnds 1–2 until 12 sts rem. K 3 sts of first dpn to 3rd dpn. Cut yarn, leaving a 12" tail. Graft rem 6 sts from each dpn tog

Color Pat

6
5

1

6-st rep
◻ B   ◻ C

Gumball Boot Socks

MARY ANNE THOMPSON

EASY LEVEL

BOISE, IDAHO

Leg With smaller dpn and MC, cast on 36 sts and divide over 3 dpn as foll: 11 sts on first dpn, 14 sts on 2nd dpn, and 11 sts on 3rd dpn. Place marker, join and work 6 rnds in k1, p2 rib. Change to larger dpn. **Rnds 1–2** With MC, k 1 rnd, then p 1 rnd. Do not cut MC. **Rnds 3–8** With A, work 6 rnds as foll: *K4, sl 2; rep from*. Carry MC by twisting it around A as you work each rnd. Cut A. **Rnds 9–10** With MC, rep rnds 1–2. **Rnds 11–16** With B, work 6 rnds as foll: K1, *sl 2, k4; rep from*, end sl 2, k3. Cut B. **Rnds 17–32** Rep rnds 1–16, using C for rnds 3–8 and B for rnds 11–16. **Rnds 33–40** Rep rnds 1–8, using A for rnds 3–8. Cont with MC only: **Rnds 41–42** Rep rnds 1–2. **Rnd 43** (eyelet rnd) *K1, yo, k2tog; rep from*. **Rnds 44–48** Knit.

Instep K across 11 sts of first dpn; with empty dpn, k next 14 sts, turn and p same 14 sts. Working back and forth on these 14 sts only, work 11 more rows in St st, end with a k row.

Foot With empty dpn, pick up and k 11 sts along side of instep and k next 11 sts; with 3rd dpn, k next 11 sts, then pick up and k 11 sts along other side of instep—58 sts. Beg of rnd is at beg of instep. Place marker and work in garter st as foll: **Rnds 1–2** P 1 rnd, then k 1 rnd. **Rnd 3** P3, [p2tog] 4 times, p around—54 sts. **Rnd 4** Knit. **Rnd 5** On first dpn, p1, p2tog, p4, p2tog, p1; on 2nd dpn, p19, p2tog, p1; on 3rd dpn, p1, p2tog, p19—50 sts. **Rnd 6** Knit. **Rnd 7** On first dpn, p1, p2tog, p2, p2tog, p1; on 2nd dpn, p18, p2tog, p1; on 3rd dpn, p1, p2tog, p18—46 sts. **Rnd 8** Knit. **Rnd 9** On first dpn, p1, [p2tog] twice, p1; on 2nd dpn, p17, p2tog, p1; on 3rd dpn, p1, p2tog, p17—42 sts. **Rnds 10–11** Rep rnds 1–2. Cut yarn, leaving a 12" tail. Divide rem sts evenly onto 2 dpn and graft tog. Fasten off.

Finishing With a contrast color, make a 12" tie (a 3-st I-cord or a crochet chain works well). Using photo as guide, weave tie through eyelet row of each sock.

Reminiscent of red gumball machines, these warm, colorful socks are as much fun to knit as they are to wear. All this color and you never work with more than one color in a round.

"My grandkids kick off their wet boots at the door and hop into these colorful socks for indoor wear. The lace tie keeps the boots in place on active little feet. Or, discard the tie and use them as warm liners inside those boots. "

Size In sport weight yarn, sock will fit 1–2 yr old. In worsted weight yarn, sock will fit 2–3 yr old.

Materials A In sport or worsted weight yarn: 1¾oz/50g (approx 115yds/105m) Main Color (MC) and approx 10 yds each of 3 contrasting colors (A, B, and C). **B** Set of 4 double-pointed needles (dpn) in sizes 3 and 5 (3.25 and 3.75mm), *or size to obtain gauge*.

Gauge In St st using size 5 (3.75mm) dpn: 5 sts to 1" in worsted-weight yarn; 6 sts to 1" in sport-weight yarn.

Crazy Crayons

INTERMEDIATE LEVEL

**Lisa's socks begin at the bottom
of the crayon rib.
This rib is worked from bottom to top, allowing
each crayon to decrease to a sharp point.
The stitches at the beginning of the ribbing are
then picked up and the foot worked circularly.
Read our notes on the next page to familiarize
yourself with circular intarsia.**

Note 1 Stitches are temporarily cast on at the ankle. The cuff is worked up from the ankle, then stitches are picked up from the cast on edge and the sock is worked down to the toe. *2* To reduce bulk and tangling, I found it helpful to wind only the colored yarns (7 yds each) onto bobbins. I wound 3 yd lengths of the white into butterflies. The 1 yd lengths of black didn't need winding.

Leg With scrap yarn, cast on 60 sts. Beg with row 1, work 30 sts of Crayon Rib chart twice, twisting colors to prevent holes. Work through chart row 13, then rep rows 1–13 until piece measures approx 3½" from beg. Turn work inside out and cont chart pat by working row 14 to top of chart. As you work last row, bind off the purl (white) sts. Make crayon tips across each knit (colored) section as foll: **Row 1** With RS facing and matching color, ssk, k3, k2tog. **Row 2** Purl. **Row 3** Ssk, k1, k2tog. **Row 4** Purl. **Row 5** Sl 2- k1-p2sso. Fasten off.

Heel With MC and dpn, pick up sts from scrap yarn. K 3 rnds, end at marker. Sl 30 sts to first dpn, next 15 sts to 2nd dpn and rem 15 sts to 3rd dpn. Work back and forth in rows on 30 sts of first dpn: **Row 1** (RS) Sl 1, k29. **Row 2** Sl 1, p29. Rep last 2 rows 11 more times.

Turn heel Cont on 30 sts: **Row 1** K17, ssk, k1, turn. **Row 2** Sl 1, p5, p2tog, p1, turn. **Row 3** Sl 1, k6, ssk, k1, turn. **Row 4** Sl 1, p7, p2tog, p1, turn. Cont to dec in same way, working 1 st more between decs on each row until 16 sts rem. K 1 row.

Gusset With RS facing and empty dpn, pick up and k 12 sts along side of heel and sl to first dpn. With 2nd dpn, k 30 sts from next 2 dpn. With 3rd dpn, pick up and k 12 sts along other side of heel, then k 8 heel sts—70 sts. Beg of rnd is at center of heel. **Rnd 1** On first dpn, k to last 3 sts, k2tog, k1; k across 2nd dpn; on 3rd dpn, k1, ssk, k to end—2 sts dec. **Rnd 2** Knit. Rep rnds 1–2 until 60 sts rem.

Foot K 8 rnds. K 2 rnds C, 6 rnds MC, 2 rnds A, 6 rnds MC, 2 rnds B, end k 9 rnds MC.

Toe **Rnd 1** On first dpn, k to last 3 sts, k2tog, k1; on 2nd dpn, k1, ssk, k to last 3 sts, k2tog, k1; on 3rd dpn, k1, ssk, k to end. **Rnd 2** Knit. Rep rnds 1–2 until 30 sts rem. Rep rnd 1 until 16 sts rem. Cut yarn, leaving a 6" tail. Run tail through rem sts, pull tog tightly and fasten off.

Finishing As you weave in ends for crayon tips, pull so that the last st is in back. Block socks. Fold cuff and if desired, tack crayon points to socks, using matching colors for each point.

Size Child's shoe size 1–2. Finished length from heel to toe is 7½".

Materials **A** Sock-weight yarn: 2oz/60g (approx 215yds/196m) light tweed (MC); 1oz/30g each yellow (A), red (B), and blue (C); small amount of black. **B** Set of 4 double-pointed needles (dpn) size 1 (2.25mm), or *size to obtain gauge.* **C** Small amount of scrap yarn. **D** Bobbins.

Gauge 8 sts to 1"/2.5cm in St st using size 1 (2.25mm) dpn.

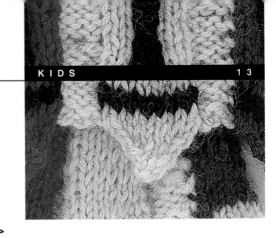

Our instructions are for working
the intarsia cuff in the round as Lisa did.
Intarsia in the round?
Yes, although the intarsia is worked
by knitting, turning, and purling back,
"rounds" are formed by twisting yarns
from beginning and end sections.

"Once you understand this technique for intarsia,
these socks knit quickly."

Begin working
in middle of first
blue strand.

①

②

③

④

Arrow indicates direction of
work. Arrowhead also
indicates where yarn end is
after working row.

"Round" 1
① At end of RS row, white twists
with one strand of blue.
② At end of WS row, change to
other strand of blue.

"Round" 2
③ At end of RS row, white twists
with other strand of blue.
④ At end of WS row, change to
first strand of blue.

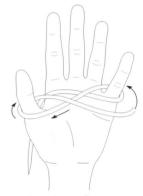

To make a butterfly, wrap yarn
around thumb and little finger in
figure-8 fashion. Fasten end around
center of 8; pull beginning strand.

Intarsia in the round

After casting on the 60 sts, divide them evenly over 3 dpn.
Place marker, join and beg with row 1, work Crayon Rib
chart as follows: For the first blue section, work from the
middle of your length of yarn. You will be working from
both ends of this strand (indicated by solid and dotted blue
lines), alternating ends each "round." At the end of the row,
twist blue and white, turn, and work back (2 in our illustra-
tion). For the next round; pick up end of white that you
twisted with blue, work ribbing as established. *The tube is
formed when you twist the strand from the last rev St st
section with the strand from the first St st section.*

Crayon rib

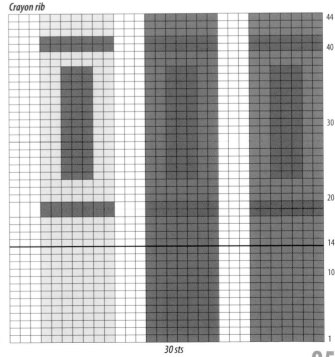

Rows 1-13
☐ rev St st
▨ ■ ■ St st
Rows 14-44
☐ St st
▨ ■ ■ rev St st

30 sts

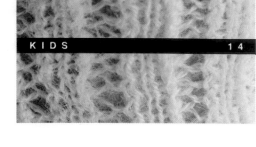

First Lace

BEVERLEY FRANCIS

INTERMEDIATE LEVEL   WHITBY, WELLINGTON, NEW ZEALAND

"I began to knit doll clothes when I was six. No pattern, I just cast on and knit, shaping as I went. I love to spin lace-weight yarns. These tiny socks are knit in yarn left over from a lace jabot and cuffs knit to commemorate the 250th anniversary of the Battle of Culloden where my Scots ancestors fought."

Note 1 This 2-needle pattern is adapted from *Paragon Baby Book No. 2.* **2** Size the sock up by working with sock-weight yarn and larger needles, adding length to rib, leg, heel, and foot. **3** If you prefer working socks circularly, cast on 48 sts and work Circular Lace pat: Mult of 4 sts. **Rnd 1** *K2tog, yo, k2; rep from*. **Rnd 2** K1, *yo, ssk, k2; rep from*, end yo, ssk, k1. Rep rnds 1–2 for Circular Lace pat. Follow Shell Lace Sock (page 28) for heel and toe shaping.

Lace Pat Multiple of 4 sts plus 3. **Row 1** (RS) K2, *k2tog, yo, k2; rep from*, end k2tog, yo, k3. **Row 2** P2 *p2tog, yo, p2; rep from*, end p2tog, yo, p3. Rep rows 1–2 for Lace pat.

Leg Cast on 46 sts. Work ½" in k1, p1 rib, inc 1 st on last row—47 sts. Work in Lace pat until piece measures 1½" from beg, end with a WS row.

Heel Work first half of heel flap: **Row 1** K12, turn. **Row 2** Sl 1, p to last st, k1. Rep last 2 rows 6 times more. Turn half heel: **Row 1** K3, k2tog, k1, turn. **Rows 2, 4, and 6** Sl 1, p to last st, k1. **Row 3** K4, k2tog, k1, turn. **Row 5** K5, k2tog, k1, turn. **Row 7** K6, k2tog, k1, then pick up and k 7 sts along side of heel flap, work next 23 sts in pat, k12.

Work 2nd half of heel flap: **Row 1** K1, p11, turn. **Row 2** Sl 1, k to end. Rep last 2 rows 6 times more. Turn half heel: **Row 1** P3, p2tog, p1, turn. **Rows 2, 4, and 6** Sl 1, k to end. **Row 3** P4, p2tog, p1, turn. **Row 5** P5, p2tog, p1, turn. **Row 7** P6, p2tog, p1, pick up and p 7 sts along side of heel flap, work next 23 sts in pat, p15—53 sts.

Gusset Row 1 K12, k2tog, k1, cont pat over 23 sts, k1, ssk, k to end. **Rows 2 and 4** K1, cont pats to last st, k1. **Row 3** K11, k2tog, k1, cont pat over 23 sts, k1, ssk, k to end. **Row 5** K10, k2tog, k1, cont pat over 23 sts, k1, ssk, k to end—47 sts. Work even in pats for 1", end with a WS row.

Toe Row 1 K9, k2tog, k2, ssk, k17, k2tog, k2, ssk, k9. **Row 2 and all WS rows** K1, p to last st, k1. **Row 3** K8, k2tog, k2, ssk, k15, k2tog, k2, ssk, k8. **Row 5** K7, k2tog, k2, ssk, k13, k2tog, k2, ssk, k7. In same way, cont to dec 4 sts on all RS rows, working 1 st less before first dec, 1 st less after last dec, and 1 st less at center until 19 sts rem. Graft rem sts tog.

Finishing Block piece. Sew leg, foot, and toe.

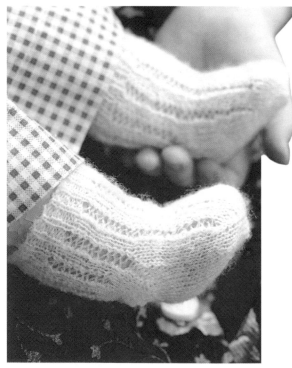

Size Newborn.

Materials A ⅛oz/2g (approx 60yds/55m) lace-weight yarn. *Spinner's note* Handspun Merino 2-ply worsted was used. **B** Size 0 (2mm) needles, *or size needed to obtain gauge.*

Gauge 12 sts to 1" (2.5cm) over St st using size 0 (2mm) needles.

Multicolored Sockies

EASY LEVEL

MAUDE SMITH

SAN FRANCISCO, CALIFORNIA

Note Change gauge and yarn weight to make other sizes.

Sole Cast on 10 sts. K 36 rows—18 garter stitch ridges.

Foot With 2nd dpn, pick up and k 18 sts along side of sole. With 3rd dpn, pick up and k 10 sts along cast-on edge of sole. With 4th dpn, pick up and k 18 sts along other side of sole—56 sts. Place marker, join and *p 4 rnds, then k 4 rnds; rep from* once. P 4 rnds.

Instep Work back and forth in rows on 10 sts of first dpn only: **Row 1** (RS) K to last st, k last st tog with first st on 2nd dpn. Turn. **Row 2** P to last st, p last st tog with first st on 4th dpn. Rep last 2 rows 7 times more—40 sts, 10 on each dpn.

Leg K 5 rnds. **Next (eyelet) rnd** *K2, yo, k2tog; rep from* around. K around for 1". Work 1" in k2, p2 rib. Bind off loosely in rib. Make 12" laces of ribbon, crocheted chain, or I-cord (as shown here). Thread laces through eyelets.

```
18  ╲╱  10
    ╳
10  ╱╲  18
```

```
10  ╲╱  10
    ╳
10  ╱╲  10
```

These sockies (a cross between socks and booties) are another version of footwear knitted from bottom to top. "I cannot recall where I first read of booties with ridged knitting near the sole. This is my interpretation of another's long-remembered and long-cherished idea."

Size Infant.

Materials A 1oz/28g (approx 125yds/114m) fingering weight yarn. **B** Set of 5 double-pointed needles (dpn) in size 3 (3.25mm), *or size to obtain gauge.*

Gauge 8 sts to 1"/2.5cm over St st using size 3 (3.25mm) dpn.

The well-shaped legs on these charming stockings are accomplished simply by not working a few yarn overs in the lace pattern.

Size 3–4 year old child.

Materials **A** 2oz/60g (approx 200 yds/182m) sock-weight yarn in white. **B** Set of 4 double-pointed needles (dpn) in sizes 2 and 3 (2.75 and 3.25mm) *or size to obtain gauge.*

Gauge 6 sts to 1"/2.5cm in St st using size 3 (3.25mm) dpn.

Shell Lace

INTERMEDIATE LEVEL

JÓHANNA HJALTADÓTTIR

REYKJAVIK, ICELAND

Lace pat 8-st rep **Rnd 1** *K2, k3tog, k2, yo, k1, yo; rep from*. **Rnd 2** *K5, p3; rep from*. **Rnd 3** *Yo, k1, k3tog, k1, yo, k3; rep from*. **Rnd 4** P1, k3, p4; rep from*. **Rnd 5** *K1, yo, k3tog, yo, k4; rep from*. **Rnd 6** *P2, k1, p5; rep from*. **Rnd 7** Knit. Rep rnds 1–7 for Lace pat.

Leg With smaller dpn, cast on 48 sts and divide evenly on 3 dpn. Place marker, join, and work 7 rnds in k1, p1 rib. Change to larger dpn. Working 8-st rep of chart pat, work rows 1–7 of chart 5 times. Cont chart pat and dec 2 sts each on rnds 1 and 3 by not working yo's on first rep—12 sts on first dpn. Work through rnd 7, then rep rnds 1–7 once more—49 chart rows from beg.

Heel Sl 8 sts from 3rd dpn to first dpn; sl 4 sts from 2nd dpn to 3rd dpn. Work back and forth in rows on 20 sts of first dpn: *K 1 row, then p 1 row; rep from* 8 more times.

Turn heel Cont on 20 sts: **Row 1** (RS) K10, k2tog, k1; turn. **Row 2** Sl 1, p1, p2tog, p1, turn. **Row 3** Sl 1, k4, k2tog, k1, turn. **Row 4** Sl 1, p5, p2tog, p1, turn. Cont to dec in same way, working 1 more st between decs, until there are 10 sts, end with a RS row. Do not turn.

Gusset With RS facing and empty dpn, pick up and k 10 sts along side of heel and sl to first dpn. With 2nd dpn, cont pat across 24 sts of next 2 dpn. With 3rd dpn, pick up and k 10 sts along other side of heel, then k 5 heel sts—54 sts. Beg of rnd is at center of heel. **Rnd 1** On first dpn, k to last 3 sts, k2tog, k1; cont pat across 2nd dpn; on 3rd dpn, k1, ssk, k to end. **Rnd 2** Work even. Rep last 2 rnds 4 times more—44 sts.

Foot Cont pat across 2nd dpn and k every rnd on first and 3rd dpns until 4 complete pat reps have been worked from gusset.

Toe **Rnd 1** On first dpn, k to last 3 sts, k2tog, k1; on 2nd dpn, k1, ssk, k to last 3 sts, k2tog, k1; on 3rd dpn, k1, ssk, k to end—4 sts dec. **Rnd 2** Knit. Rep last 2 rnds until 8 sts rem. Cut yarn, pull through rem sts and fasten off.

Lace pat

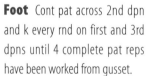

□ K
□ P
◉ Yo
▲ K3tog

8-st rep

My Little Angel

INTERMEDIATE LEVEL

DARLENE R. JOYCE

DES PLAINES, ILLINOIS

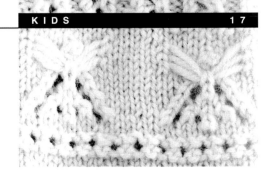

Tip For a looser cast-on, use 2 needles held together.

Lace Rib (5-st rep) **Rnd 1** *K3, p2; rep from*. **Rnd 2** *K1, yo, ssk, p2; rep from*. **Rnd 3** *K3, p2; rep from*. **Rnd 4** *K2tog, yo, k1, p2; rep from*. Rep rnds 1–4 for Lace rib pat.

Angel (13-st rep) Make bobble (MB) K in front, back, front of st (3 sts from 1), turn. P 3, turn. K 3, sl first 2 sts over last k st. **Rnds 1, 3 and 6** *K3, sl 7 sts with yarn in front (wyif), k3; rep from*. **Rnds 2, 4, 8, and 10** Knit. **Rnd 5** *K6, MB, k6; rep from*. **Rnd 7** *K6, sl dpn under 3 strands and k next st, k6; rep from*. **Rnd 9** *K4, k2tog, yo, k1, yo, ssk, k4; rep from*. **Rnd 11** *K3, k2tog, yo, k3, yo, ssk, k3; rep from*. **Rnd 12** Knit. **Rnd 13** *K2, [k2tog, yo] twice, k1, [yo, ssk] twice, k2; rep from*.

Horizontal Lace (2-st rep) **Rnd 1** Purl. **Rnd 2** *Yo, k2tog; rep from*. **Rnd 3** Purl.

Leg Cast on 50 sts and divide on 3 dpn as foll: 20 sts on first dpn, 15 sts each on 2nd and 3rd dpn. Place marker, join, and work 1½" in Lace Rib pat, end with rnds 1 or 3. K 1 rnd, inc 2 sts evenly spaced—52 sts. K 3 rnds. Rearrange sts as foll: sl 26 sts to first dpn, 13 sts each to 2nd and 3rd dpn. *Work 13 rnds of Angel pat. K 3 rnds. Work 3 rnds of Horizontal Lace pat. Rep from * twice more.

Heel Work back and forth in rows on 26 sts of first dpn: Beg Heel Flap chart: **Row 1** P1, k1, p1, k9, k2tog, k9, p1, k1, p1—25 sts. Work through chart row 19.

Turn heel Row 1 (WS) K1, p1, k1, p12, p2tog, p1, turn. **Row 2** Sl 1, k6, ssk, k1, turn. **Row 3** Sl 1, p7, p2tog, p1, turn. **Row 4** Sl 1, k8, ssk, k1, turn. **Row 5** Sl 1, p9, p2tog, p1, turn. **Row 6** Sl 1, k10, ssk, k1, turn. Cont to dec in same way, working 1 more st between decs, until all sts have been worked, AT SAME TIME, on last row inc 1 st in center (16 sts), end with a RS row.

Gusset With empty dpn, pick up and k 11 sts along left side of heel and sl to first dpn; k across next 26 sts with 2nd dpn; with 3rd dpn, pick up and k 11 sts along other side of heel, then k first 8 heel sts—64 sts. **Rnd 1** On first dpn, k to last 3 sts, k2tog, k1; k across 2nd dpn; on 3rd dpn, k1, ssk, k to end—2 sts dec. **Rnd 2** Knit. Shape gusset and work foot simultaneously as foll: Dec 2 sts every other rnd 5 times more—52 sts, then k every rnd across first and 3rd dpns, AT SAME TIME, on 2nd dpn, k 1 rnd, then work *Angel pat, k 3 rnds, Horizontal Lace pat*, k 3 rnds, rep between *'s once.

Toe Rnd 1 On first dpn, k to last 3 sts, k2tog, k1; on 2nd dpn, k1, ssk, k to last 3 sts, k2tog, k1; on 3rd dpn, k1, ssk, k to end. **Rnd 2** Knit. Rep rnds 1–2 until 36 sts rem. Rep rnd 1 until 16 sts rem. K 4 sts of first dpn onto 3rd dpn. Cut yarn, leaving a 12" tail. Graft 8 sts from each dpn tog.

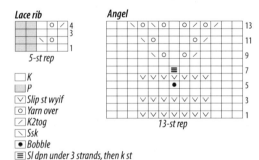

Lace angels and seed stitch hearts—girls of all ages find these stockings irresistible.

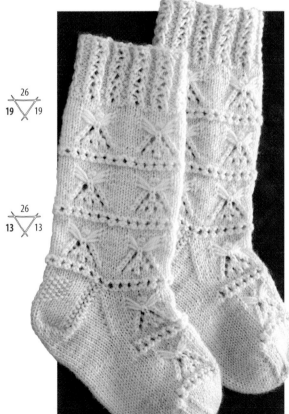

15 / 15 / 20

13 / 13 / 26

26 / 19 / 19

26 / 13 / 13

Lace rib

o / 4
3
\ o 2
1

5-st rep

Angel

13-st rep

☐ K
☐ P
▽ Slip st wyif
o Yarn over
╱ K2tog
╲ Ssk
● Bobble
≡ Sl dpn under 3 strands, then k st

Heel Flap

25 sts

Size 4–5 year old child.

Materials A 1¾oz/50g fingering weight yarn (approx 215yds/196m). **B** Set of 4 double-pointed needles (dpn) in size 1 (2.5mm), *or size needed to obtain gauge.*

Gauge 8½ sts to 1" (2.5cm) in St st using size 1 (2.5mm) dpn.

Slipper Socks

BEGINNER LEVEL

GUÕLAUG PÉTURSDÓTTIR

PÓRSHÖFN, ICELAND

Guõlaug lives and knits in a fishing village
on the north-eastern coast of Iceland.
A single purl stitch along each side of the foot
gives grown-up definition to the soles
of her easy-to-knit, easy-to-wear slippers.

Foot Cast on 32 sts. Work back and forth in rows on 2 dpn as foll: **Row 1** (RS) Knit. **Row 2** K10, p1, k10, p1, k10. Rep last 2 rows until piece measures 3" from beg, end with row 2. Work in rnds as foll: With empty dpn, *k1, p1; rep from* 4 times more; with 2nd dpn, *k1, p1; rep from* 4 times more, k1; on 3rd dpn, *p1, k1; rep from* 4 times more, p1—32 sts on 3 dpn. Place marker, join and work around in k1, p1 rib as established until piece measures 5½" from beg, end at joining marker.

Toe Next 2 rnds K2tog around. Cut yarn, pull through rem sts and fasten off.

Finishing Fold piece in half and sew back seam. **Picot edge** With crochet hook, RS facing and contrast color, join yarn, ch 2, work 1 sc into edge*, ch 3 and sl st to first ch (picot), work 2 sc into edge; rep from* evenly around, sl st to beg ch 2. Fasten off.

11 11
10

Size 2–3 yr old.

Materials **A** 1¾oz/50g (approx 115yds/105m) worsted-weight yarn in green. Small amount of white for crochet trim. **B** Set of double-pointed needles (dpn) in size 7 (4.5mm) needles, *or size to obtain gauge.* **C** Size F/5 crochet hook

Gauge 5 sts to 1" (2.5cm) in St st using size 7 (4.5mm) dpn.

Brendan's Vine Socks

LISA GWINNER

INTERMEDIATE LEVEL   ROCHESTER, NEW YORK

Note These are Turkish-style socks knit in the round from cuff to toe rather than the traditional toe to cuff.

Leg With A, cast on 54 sts using backward loop cast-on and divide over 3 dpn as foll: 27 sts to first dpn, 14 to 2nd dpn, and 13 sts to 3rd dpn. Place marker, join and with A and C, *k1 A, k1 C; rep from* around.

Work 2-color braid: Next rnd With both yarns in front, p1 A, *pick up C under A and p1 C, pick up A under C and p1 A; rep from* around. **Next rnd** *Pick up A over C and p1 A, pick up C over A and p1 C; rep from* around. Work rows 1–28 of Brendan's Vine Socks' chart.

Heel placement Rnd 29 K27 sts. Cut B, leaving an 8" tail. Place next 27 sts on hold. With A and backward-loop cast-on, cast on 27 sts, holding dpn very snugly against first dpn when you beg casting-on to minimize hole. Sl first 14 cast-on sts to 2nd dpn and rem 13 sts to 3rd dpn. Leaving an 8" tail, join B and k chart rnds 30–52.

Toe Rnd 53 On first dpn, k1 A, k2tog with B, k to last 3 sts, ssk with B, k1 A; on 2nd dpn, k1 A, k2tog with B, k to end; on 3rd dpn, k to last 3 sts, ssk with B, k1 A. **Rnds 54–60** Cont with A and C, working decs as for Rnd 53 with C. Sl sts from 2nd dpn to 3rd dpn. With A, graft rem sts from each dpn tog.

Heel Sl sts from waste yarn to first dpn. With A and B, foll Pickup row on Heel Chart and k sts for bottom of heel, working into cast-on: 14 sts on 2nd dpn and 13 sts on 3rd dpn. Work chart rnds 1–9. Complete as for toe.

Finishing Use tails to close holes where heel was knitted on and weave in all ends so little toes don't get tangled in them.

I never really noticed until my son was born that babies' feet are wedge-shaped. A pointed toe looks silly and doesn't really fit on them. So I've designed these socks to accommodate them. The pattern for the sock bottom can be found in Anna Zilboorg's *Fancy Feet;* the vine pattern is my own design.

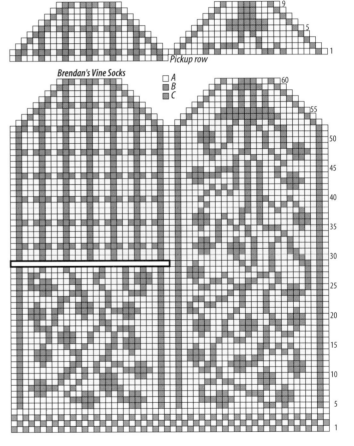

Heel Chart

Pickup row

Brendan's Vine Socks
□ A
▨ B
■ C

Size To fit infants' feet up to 4" long, 5½" around.

Materials A Fingering-weight yarn: 1oz/28g (approx 127yds/116m) each light gray (A) and teal (B); small amount plum (C). **B** Set of 4 double-pointed needles (dpn) in size 3 (3.25mm), *or size to obtain gauge.*

Gauge 9 sts to 1" (2.5cm) in color pat using size 3 (3.25mm) dpn.

Dragon Socks

INTERMEDIATE LEVEL

"These socks are for my son Arlo. I wanted to do something with the roundness of socks, hence the tail circling the leg. Inspiration for the dragon came from a beautiful book of my mother's on old Icelandic embroidery that I pored over as a child."

This elaborate, kid-pleasing design is very simple to knit. The colors are knit in only on the cuff and heel. Even the dragons are no menace: they are duplicate-stitched on after the socks are knitted.

Size Child's medium. Finished length, heel to toe, is 7".
Materials A 1¾oz/50g (approx 215yds/196m) sock-weight yarn in red; small amounts of gold, purple, turquoise, and green. **B** Set of 4 double-pointed needles (dpn) in size 2 (2.75mm), *or size needed to obtain gauge.* **C** Tapestry needle.
Gauge 15 sts to 2" in St st using size 2 (2.75mm) dpn.

Leg With red, cast on 48 sts and divide evenly over 3 dpn. Place marker, join and work in k1, p1 rib as foll: 2 rnds red; 2 rnds purple; 1 rnd red; 1 rnd turquoise; 3 rnds k1 gold, p1 turquoise; 1 rnd turquoise; 3 rnds red; 2 rnds green. K every rnd in colors as foll: **Rnd 1** K with red. **Rnd 2** *K3 turquoise, k1 red; rep from*. **Rnds 3–4** K1 red, *k1 turquoise, k3 red; rep from*, end k1 turquoise, k2 red. **Rnd 5** *K3 red, k1 gold; rep from*. With red, k 25 rnds, end 12 sts before end of rnd.

Heel Sl next 24 sts onto empty dpn; sl next 12 sts to 2nd dpn and next 12 sts to 3rd dpn. Work back and forth in rows on 24 sts of first dpn only: **Row 1** Sl 1, [k1 gold, k1 red] 5 times, k 1 gold, M1 with red, [k1 gold, k1 red] 5 times, k1 gold, sl 1. **Row 2** P the red sts and sl the gold sts, carrying the gold yarn back with you. **Row 3** Sl 1, *k1 gold, k1 red; rep from*, end k1 gold, sl 1. Rep rows 2–3 a total of 9 times, then rep row 2 once. Cut gold.

Turn heel Cont on 24 sts with red: **Row 1** K14, ssk, k1, turn. **Row 2** Sl 1, p5, p2tog, p1, turn. **Row 3** Sl 1, k6, ssk, k1, turn. **Row 4** Sl 1, p7, p2tog, p1, turn. Cont to dec in same way, working 1 more st between decs, until 15 sts rem, end with a RS row. Do not turn.

Gusset With empty dpn, pick up and k 10 sts along side of heel and sl to first dpn; k next 24 sts onto 2nd dpn; with 3rd dpn, pick up and k 10 sts along other side of heel, then k first 8 heel sts. Beg of rnd is at center of heel. **Rnd 1** On first dpn, k to last 3 sts, k2tog, k1; k across 2nd dpn; on 3rd dpn, k1, ssk, k to end. **Rnd 2** Knit. Rep rnds 1–2 until 49 sts rem.

Foot With red, k 54 rnds.

Toe Rnd 1 On first dpn, k to last 3 sts, k2tog, k1; on 2nd dpn, k1, ssk, k to last 3 sts, k2tog, k1; on 3rd dpn, k1, ssk, k to end. **Rnd 2** Knit. Rep rnds 1–2 until 25 sts rem. Rep rnd 1 until 9 sts rem. Cut yarn, leaving a 6" tail. Draw tail tightly through rem sts and fasten off.

Finishing Foll chart and work dragon chart 1 in duplicate st. On 2nd sock, work dragon chart 2.

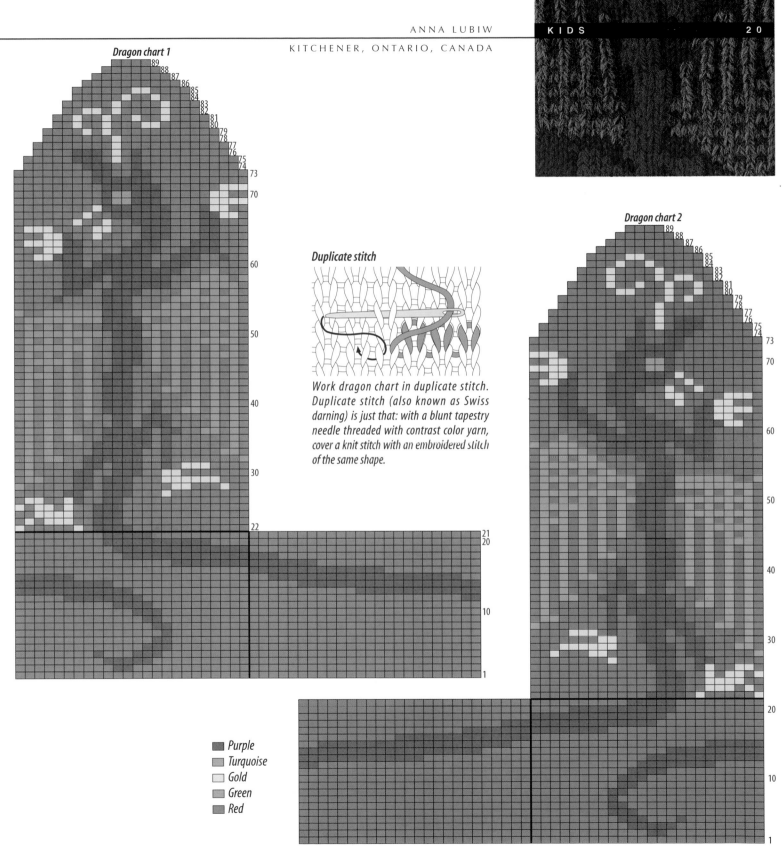

Dragon chart 1

Dragon chart 2

Duplicate stitch

Work dragon chart in duplicate stitch. Duplicate stitch (also known as Swiss darning) is just that: with a blunt tapestry needle threaded with contrast color yarn, cover a knit stitch with an embroidered stitch of the same shape.

■ Purple
■ Turquoise
□ Gold
■ Green
■ Red

Chapter 3　　　Lace

Leaf Socks **36**

Feather & Fan **38**

Gull Wings **39**

Purl Lace Socks **40**

Tipsy Knitter Socks **41**

Tiger Eyes **42**

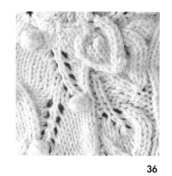
36

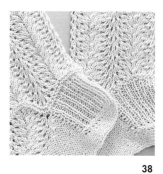
38

39

Vine Lace Socks **43**

Lace Socks

Leaf Socks

EXPERIENCED LEVEL

The leaf pattern is used three ways
on these delightful socks:
as a panel running along the wheat pattern,
as a border on the top of the sock,
and as a single leaf tab at the end
of the overlapping border.

"These socks were my first venture into lace
knitting, although my swatch was so large
that perhaps the socks really count
as my second lace-knit item.
I always knit swatches
that could almost pass as scarves
as I try stitch variations and different needle
sizes to get just the right effect.
This star toe is the only toe shaping
I have mastered."

Special abbreviations inc1k inc 1 st knitwise. **inc1p** inc 1 st purlwise. **MLB** Make large bobble: (k1, yo, k1, yo, k1) in one st, turn; k5, turn; p5, turn; k1, sl1-k2tog-psso, k1, turn; p3tog. **MSB** Make small bobble: k1, [k1 into st just worked] 4 times to make a 4-chain st, k main st and last chain st together through the back loop (tbl).

Leaf pattern (over 7 sts) **Rnd 1** K1, [yo, k1] twice, p4. **Rnd 2** Inc1k, k4, p2, p2tog. **Rnd 3** P1, k2, [yo, k1] twice, ssk, p2. **Rnd 4** Inc1p, k7, p2. **Rnd 5** P2, k3, [yo, k1] twice, k1, ssk, p1. **Rnd 6** Inc1p, p1, k9, p1. **Rnd 7** P3, ssk, k4, k2tog, k1, p1. **Rnd 8** Inc1p, p2, k7, p1. **Rnd 9** P1, k1, p2, ssk, k2, k2tog, k1, p1. **Rnd 10** P1, k1, inc1p, p1, k5, p1. **Rnd 11** P1, k1, p3, ssk, k2tog, k1, p1. **Rnd 12** P1, k1, inc1p, p2, k3, p1. **Rnd 13** P1, k1, p4, sl1-k2tog-psso, p1. **Rnd 14** P1, k1, p2tog, p4. Rep rnds 1–14 for Leaf pat.

Right Sock

Leg Cast on 62 sts and divide over 3 dpn as foll: 22 sts to first dpn, 20 sts to 2nd dpn, 20 sts to 3rd dpn. Place marker (pm), join and work Field of Wheat and Leaf pats as foll: **Rnd 1** [K1, MLB, k2, yo, k1, yo, k4, k2tog] 3 times; pm; work rnd 1 of Leaf pat across next 7 sts; pm; [k1, MLB, k2, yo, k1, yo, k4, k2tog] twice. **Rnd 2** [K1, k1 tbl, k8, k2tog] 3 times; work Leaf pat as established; [k1, k1 tbl, k8, k2tog] twice. **Rnd 3** [K5, yo, k1, yo, k3, k2tog] 3 times; work Leaf pat; [k5, yo, k1, yo, k3, k2tog] twice. **Rnds 4, 6, 8, and 10** [K10, k2tog] 3 times; work Leaf pat; [k10, k2tog] twice. **Rnd 5** [K6, yo, k1, yo, k2, k2tog] 3 times; work Leaf pat; [k6, yo, k1, yo, k2, k2tog] twice. **Rnd 7** [K7, (yo, k1) twice, k2tog] 3 times; work Leaf pat; [k7, (yo, k1) twice, k2tog] twice. **Rnd 9** [K8, yo, k1, yo, k2tog] 3 times; work Leaf pat; [k8, yo, k1, yo, k2tog] twice. **Rnd 11** [Ssk, k4, yo, k1, yo, k2 MLB, k1] 3 times; work Leaf pat; [ssk, k4, yo, k1, yo, k2 MLB, k1] twice. **Rnd 12** [Ssk, k8, k1 tbl, k1] 3 times; work Leaf pat; [ssk, k8, k1 tbl, k1] twice. **Rnd 13** [Ssk, k3, yo, k1, yo, k5] 3 times; work Leaf pat; [ssk, k3, yo, k1, yo, k5] twice. **Rnds 14, 16, 18, and 20** [Ssk, k10] 3 times; work Leaf pat; [ssk, p10] twice. **Rnd 15** [Ssk, k2, yo, k1, yo, k6] 3 times; work Leaf pat; [ssk, k2, yo, k1, yo, k6] twice. **Rnd 17** [Ssk, (k1, yo) twice; k7] 3 times; work Leaf pat; [ssk, (k1, yo) twice; k7] twice. **Rnd 19** [Ssk, yo, k1, yo, k8] 3 times; work Leaf pat; [ssk, yo, k1, yo, k8] twice. Cont pats as established until 50 rnds have been completed (ending with rnd 10 of Field of Wheat pat and rnd 8 of Leaf pat)—67 sts.

Divide for heel Sl next 33 sts to first dpn, next 17 sts to 2nd dpn, next 17 sts to 3rd dpn. Work back and forth in rows on 33 sts of first dpn only: **Row 1** (RS) *Sl 1 knitwise, k1; rep from* across end sl 1 knitwise. **Row 2** Purl. Rep last 2 rows until heel measures 2", end with a WS row.

Turn heel Cont on 33 sts: **Row 1** (RS) K18, ssk, k1, turn. **Row 2** Sl 1, p4, p2tog, p1, turn. **Row 3** Sl 1, k5, ssk, k1, turn. **Row 4** Sl 1, p6, p2tog, p1, turn. Cont to dec in same way, working 1 st more between decs on each row until 19 sts rem. K 1 row. Do not turn.

20 / 20 / 22

17 / 17 / 33

Size Woman's medium.

Materials A 3 oz/84g (approx 375yds/342m) sock-weight yarn. **B** Set of 4 double-pointed needles (dpn) in size 2 (2.75 mm) *or size to obtain gauge.*

Gauge 8½ sts to 1" (2.5cm) over St st using size 2 (2.75mm) dpn.

Gusset With empty dpn, pick up and k 18 sts along side of heel and sl to first dpn. With 2nd dpn, cont pat over 34 sts of next 2 dpn (rnd 9 of Leaf pat, rnd 11 of Field of Wheat pat). With 3rd dpn, pick up and k 18 sts along other side of heel, then k 19 heel sts—89 sts. Beg of rnd is at center of heel. **Rnd 1** K across first dpn; cont pats on 2nd dpn; k across 3rd dpn. **Rnd 2** On first dpn, k to last 3 sts, k2tog, k1; work pat across 2nd dpn; on 3rd dpn, k1, ssk, k to end—2 sts dec. Rep rnds 1–2 until there are a total of 31 sts on dpns 1 and 3. Pat conts on 2nd dpn.

Foot Work even (working MSB instead of MLB) until 112 rnds of Field of Wheat pat and 8 reps of Leaf pat have been completed—60 sts. Piece measures approx 7½" from back of heel, or 2" less than desired foot measurement.

Toe **Rnd 1** [K13, k2tog] 4 times—4 sts dec. **Rnd 2** Work even. Rep last 2 rnds, working 1 st less every dec rnd between k2tog's until 32 sts rem. Then dec every row until 8 sts rem. **Next rnd** [K2tog] 4 times. Cut yarn, leaving an 18" tail. Run tail through rem sts, pull tog tightly and fasten off.

Left Sock

Leg Cast on 62 sts and divide over 3 dpn as foll: 22 sts to first dpn, 20 sts to 2nd dpn, 20 sts to 3rd dpn. Pm for beg of rnd, join and work in Field of Wheat and Leaf pats as foll: **Rnd 1** [K1, MLB, k2, yo, k1, yo, k4, k2tog] 5 times, pm, work rnd 1 of Leaf pat across next 7 sts. **Rnd 2** [K1, k1 tbl, k8, k2tog] 5 times, work Leaf pat as established. Cont pats, shape and complete as for Right Leg.

Leaf Border With 2 dpn, cast on 5 sts. **Row 1** (RS) P2, k1, [yo, k1] twice. **Row 2** P5, k2. **Row 3** P1, inc1p, k2, yo, k1, yo, k2. **Row 4** P7, k3. **Row 5** P2, inc1p, k3, yo, k1, yo, k3. **Row 6** P9, k4. **Row 7** P3, inc1p, ssk, k4, k2tog, k1. **Row 8** P7, k5. **Row 9** P3, k1, inc1p, ssk, k2, k2tog, k1. **Row 10** P5, k2, p1, k3. **Row 11** P3, k1, p1, inc1p, sl1 k2tog psso, k2. **Row 12** Bind off 5 sts in pat, p1, k3—5 sts. Rep last 12 rows 7 times more. Work overlapping leaf: **Row 13** (RS) Bind off 2, [yo, k1] twice. **Row 14** P5. **Row 15** K2, yo, k1, yo, k2. **Row 16** P7. **Row 17** K3, yo, k1, yo, k3. **Row 18** P9. **Row 19** Ssk, k4, k2tog, k1. **Row 20** P7. **Row 21** Ssk, k2, k2tog, k1. **Row 22** P5. **Row 23** Sl1-k2tog-psso, k2tog. **Row 24** P2tog. Cut yarn and fasten off.

Using photo as guide, sew 8 leaves evenly around cast-on edge of sock, overlapping by approx 2 sts. Slip stitch overlapping leaf into place (facing downwards on Leaf panel of sock).

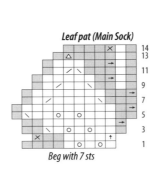

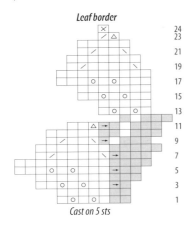

Leaf border

24
23
21
19
17
15
13
11
9
7
5
3
1

Cast on 5 sts

Field of Wheat pat

20
19
17
15
13
11
9
7
5
3
1

Beg with 11 sts

Leaf pat (Main Sock)

14
13
11
9
7
5
3
1

Beg with 7 sts

Symbol	Meaning	Symbol	Meaning
☐	K	☑ K2tog	→ Inc 1 purlwise
▨	P	◹ Ssk	↑ Inc 1 knitwise
⊙	Yo	◪ K1 tbl	△ Sl1-k2tog-psso
B	Make bobble: MLB on leg, MSB on foot		☒ P2tog

Feather & Fan

INTERMEDIATE LEVEL

JUDITH SUMNER

KNOXVILLE, TENNESSEE

Leg Cast on 64 sts and divide over 3 dpn as foll: 32 sts to first dpn, 16 sts to 2nd dpn, and 16 sts to 3rd dpn. Place marker, join and [k 1 rnd, p 1 rnd] 3 times. K 1 rnd.
Work Feather and Fan pat: **Rnd 1** *Yo, [k1, yo] twice, [ssk] twice, sl 2-k1-p2sso, [k2tog] twice, [yo, k1] 3 times, rep from* around. **Rnds 2–4** Knit. Rep rnds 1–4 until piece measures 5½" from beg, end with rnd 2. [P 1 rnd, k 1 rnd] twice.

$\triangle$ 16 / 16 \\ 32

Heel Work back and forth in rows on 32 sts of first dpn only: **Row 1** (RS) *K1, p1; rep from*, end k2. **Row 2** P2,* k1, p1; rep from*. Rep last 2 rows 9 times more.

$\triangle$ 16 / 16 \\ 32

Turn heel Cont on 32 sts: **Row 1** (RS) K21, ssk, turn. **Row 2** Sl 1, p10, p2tog, turn. **Row 3** Sl 1, k10, ssk, turn. **Row 4** Sl 1, p10, p2tog, turn. Rep last 2 rows 8 times more—12 sts. **Next row** Sl 1, k across. Do not turn.

Gusset With empty dpn, pick up and k 12 sts along side of heel and sl to first dpn. With 2nd dpn, k32 sts from next 2 dpn. With 3rd dpn, pick up and k 12 sts along other side of heel, then k 6 heel sts—68 sts. Beg of rnd is at center of heel. **Rnd 1** Knit. **Rnd 2** (dec rnd) On first dpn, k to last 3 sts, ssk, k1; on 2nd dpn, work rnd 1 of Feather & Fan pat across 32 sts; on 3rd dpn, k1, k2tog, k to end—2 sts dec. Cont Feather & Fan pat across 32 sts of 2nd dpn and dec as foll: **Rnds 3, 4, 6, and 7** Work even. **Rnds 5 and 8** Rep dec rnd—62 sts.

32 / \\ 18 \/ 18

Foot Work even in St st across first and 3rd dpn and cont Feather and Fan pat across 2nd dpn until piece measures approx 7½" from back of heel, or 2" less than desired foot measurement.

32 / \\ 15 \/ 15

Toe Sl 1 st from 2nd dpn to 3rd dpn. **Rnd 1** On first dpn, k to last 3 sts, ssk, k1; on 2nd dpn, k1, k2tog, k to last 3 sts, ssk, k1; on 3rd dpn, k1, k2tog, k to end—4 sts dec.
Rnds 2–4 Work even. Rep rnds 1–4 until 38 sts rem, end with rnd 1. Rep rnd 1 until 18 sts rem. K sts from first dpn onto 3rd dpn. Cut yarn, leaving an 18" tail. Graft rem 9 sts from each dpn tog.

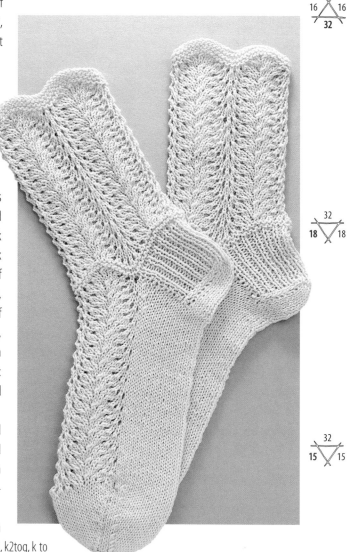

"After knitting a baby sweater, I realized that the feather and fan pattern on its border would provide a scalloped edge on socks.
Since I was using cotton yarn, I decided to rib the heel flap to prevent the bunching at the back of the heel that happens when putting on a shoe. I have also made a pair of these socks in black cashmere with sparkly heels and toes."

A Dutch heel shaping is used: decreases are worked each side of a 10-stitch center band.

Feather and Fan

																4
																3
																2
	○		○		○	╱	╱	△	╲	╲	○		○		○	1

16-st rep

□ K   ╱ K2tog   △ Sl 2-k1-p2sso
○ Yo   ╲ Ssk

Size Woman's medium.

Materials **A** 3oz/84g (approx 375yds/342m) sock-weight yarn. **B** Set of 4 double-pointed needles (dpn) in size 1 (2.5mm) *or size to obtain gauge.*

Gauge 7½ sts to 1" (2.5cm) over St st using size 1 (2.5mm) dpn.

Gull Wings

INTERMEDIATE LEVEL

VIVIENNE SHEN

HOUSTON, TEXAS

Leg Cast on 54 sts and divide evenly over 3 dpn. Place marker, join and work 2" in k1, p1 rib. **Foundation rnd** [P1, k7, p1] 6 times. Work in Lace pat as foll: **Rnds 1, 3** [P1, k7, p1] 6 times. **Rnd 2** [P1, k1, k2tog, yo, k1, yo, ssk, k1, p1] 6 times. **Rnd 4** [P1, k2tog, yo, k3, yo, ssk, p1] 6 times. Rep rnds 1–4 until piece measures 5½" from beg.

Heel Sl 27 sts to first dpn, next 14 sts to 2nd dpn and next 13 sts to 3rd dpn. Work back and forth in rows on 27 sts of first dpn only as foll: **Row 1** (RS) K1 through the back loop (tbl), k25, sl 1. **Row 2** P1 tbl, p25, sl 1. Rep last 2 rows until heel measures 2", end with a WS row.

Turn heel Cont to work on 27 sts of first dpn: **Row 1** (RS) K 14, ssk, k1, turn. **Row 2** Sl 1, p2, p2tog, p1, turn. **Row 3** Sl 1, k3, ssk, k1, turn. **Row 4** Sl 1, p4, p2tog, p1, turn. Cont to dec in same way, working 1 st more between decs on each row until 15 sts rem. K 1 row. Do not turn.

Gusset With empty dpn, pick up and k 15 sts along side of heel and sl to first dpn; with 2nd dpn, cont Lace pat over next 27 sts; with 3rd dpn pick up and k 15 sts along other side of heel, then k 8 heel sts—72 sts. Beg of rnd is at center of heel. **Rnd 1** K across first dpn; cont Lace pat across 2nd dpn; k across 3rd dpn. **Rnd 2** On first dpn, k to last 3 sts, k2tog, k1; cont Lace pat across 2nd dpn; on 3rd dpn, k1, ssk, k to end—2 sts dec. Rep last 2 rnds 8 times more—54 sts.

Foot Work even until piece measures approx 7½" from back of heel, or 2" less than desired foot measurement.

Toe **Rnd 1** On first dpn, k to last 3 sts, k2tog, k1; on 2nd dpn, k1, ssk, k to last 3 sts, k2tog, k1; on 3rd dpn, k1, ssk, k to end—4 sts dec. **Rnd 2** Work even. Rep rnds 1–2 until 10 sts rem. K sts from first dpn onto 3rd dpn. Cut yarn, leaving an 10" tail. Graft rem 5 sts from each dpn tog.

"This sock pattern was my first design!
I chose this lace because it is simple,
yet elegant, and looks good 'up side up'
or 'up side down.'"

Gull Wing Lace Rib

9-st rep

☐ K
▨ P
☉ Yo
▱ K2tog
◺ Ssk

Size Woman's medium.

Materials **A** 1¾oz/50g (approx 215yds/196m) sock-weight yarn. **B** Set of 4 double-pointed needles (dpn) in size 2 (2.75 mm) *or size to obtain gauge.*

Gauge 8 sts to 1" (2.5cm) over St st using size 2 (2.75mm) dpn.

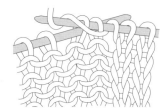

"There is no need to carry a written pattern, row counter, or ruler when making these socks: the stitch pattern is easily memorized, and the second sock is matched in length by counting pattern repeats—thus making this the perfect portable project for me. The small repeat allows sizing up or down or adjusting for gauge easily by adding or deleting full repeats. The repeat can be expanded to 7 or 8 stitches by adding an extra purl or two between the decreases."

K, yo, p2tog: Knit, bring yarn under the needle to the front, then back under the needle to the front before you purl the next two stitches together.

P2tog, yo, k: Purl two stitches together, the yarn is already to the front of the needle so simply bring it back over the needle; it is in position to knit the next stitch.

Size Woman's medium.

Materials A 3½oz/100g (approx 430yds/392m) sock-weight yarn. **B** Set of 4 double-pointed needles (dpn) in sizes 1 and 2 (2.25 and 2.75 mm) *or size to obtain gauge.*

Gauge 8 sts to 1" (2.5cm) over St st using size 2 (2.75mm) dpn.

Purl Lace Socks

INTERMEDIATE LEVEL

SHERI FRANZ

PITTSBURGH, PENNSYLVANIA

Leg With smaller dpn, cast on 60 sts and divide evenly over 3 dpn. Place marker, join and work 1¼" in k1, p1 rib. Change to larger dpn. Work in Lace pat as foll: **Rnd 1** *K1, yo, p2tog, p1, p2tog, yo; rep from* around. **Rnds 2–4** Knit. Rep rnds 1–4 until piece measures 6" from beg, end with rnd 2.

Heel K next 15 sts onto first dpn; sl next 15 to 2nd dpn, next 15 to 3rd dpn, and next 15 to first dpn. Work back and forth in rows on 30 sts of first dpn only: **Row 1** (WS) *Sl 1, p1; rep from* across. **Row 2** Sl 1, k across. Rep last 2 rows until heel is 2", end with a WS row.

Turn heel Cont to work on 30 sts of first dpn only: **Row 1** (RS) K 17, ssk, k1, turn. **Row 2** Sl 1, p5, p2tog, p1, turn. **Row 3** Sl 1, k6, ssk, k1, turn. **Row 4** Sl 1, p7, p2tog, p1, turn. Cont to dec in same way, working 1 st more between decs on each row until 18 sts rem. K 1 row. Do not turn.

Gusset With empty dpn, pick up and k 15 sts along side of heel, k2tog from Lace dpn, and sl these 16 sts to first dpn; with 2nd dpn, k1, cont Lace pat over next 24 sts, k1; with 3rd dpn, ssk last 2 sts from Lace dpn, pick up and k15 sts along other side of heel and k 9 heel sts—76 sts. Beg of rnd is at center of heel. **Rnd 1** K across first dpn; cont Lace pat across 2nd dpn; k across 3rd dpn. **Rnd 2** On first dpn, k to last 2 sts, k2tog; on 2nd dpn, cont Lace pat; on 3rd dpn, ssk, k to end—2 sts dec. Rep rnds 1–2 until 54 sts rem.

Foot Work even as established until piece measures approx 7½" from back of heel, or 2" less than desired foot measurement.

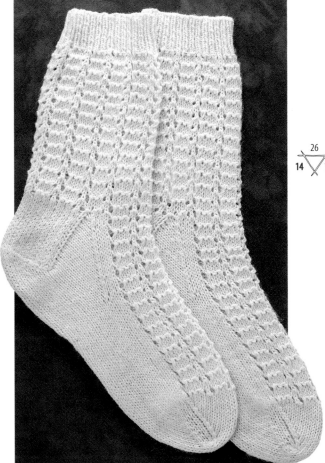

Toe Sl last st from first dpn to 2nd dpn. **Rnd 1** On first dpn, k to last 3 sts, k2tog, k1; on 2nd dpn, k1, ssk, k to last 3 sts, k2tog, k1, on 3rd dpn, k1, ssk, k to end—4 sts dec. **Rnd 2** Work even. Rep rnds 1–2 until 18 sts rem. K sts from first dpn to 3rd dpn. Cut yarn, leaving an 18" tail. Graft rem 9 sts from each dpn tog.

Lace pat

6-st rep

☐ K
▨ P
⊡ Yo
⧄ P2tog

Tipsy Knitter Socks

INTERMEDIATE LEVEL

TORONTO, ONTARIO, CANADA

Special abbreviations **2/2LC** Sl 2 sts to cable needle, hold to front, k2; k2 from cable needle. **2/2RC** Sl 2 sts to cable needle, hold to back, k2; k2 from cable needle.

Leg Cast on 66 sts and divide over 3 dpn as foll: 18 sts to first dpn, 30 sts to 2nd dpn, 18 sts to 3rd dpn. Place marker, join and work in Cable Rib: **Rnds 1–4** *K4, p2; rep from*. **Rnd 5** *2/2LC, p2; rep from*. **Rnds 6–10** Rep rnds 1–5. **Rnds 11–12** Rep rnd 1. **Next rnd** K63, k2tog, k1—65 sts. Work Tilting Ladder pat: **Rnds 1 and 13** [K5, p1, k5, p2] 5 times. **Rnd 2** [K1, (yo, k2tog) twice, p1, k5, p2] 5 times. **Rnds 3, 5, 7, 9, and 11** [K4, p2, k5, p2] 5 times. **Rnd 4, 8, and 12** [K1 (yo, k2tog) twice, p2, k4, p2] 5 times. **Rnds 6 and 10** [K1, (yo, k2tog) twice, p2, 2/2 RC, p2] 5 times. **Rnds 14, 16, 20, and 24** [K4, p2, (ssk, yo) twice, k1, p2] 5 times. **Rnds 15, 17, 19, 21, and 23** [K5, p2, k4, p2] 5 times. **Rnds 18 and 22** [2/2 LC, p2, (ssk, yo) twice, k1, p2] 5 times. Rep Rnds 1–24 once more.

Heel Sl next 32 sts to first dpn, next 15 sts to 2nd dpn, next 18 sts to 3rd dpn. Work back and forth in rows on 32 sts of first dpn only as foll: **Row 1** (RS) *Sl 1 knitwise, k1; rep from*. **Row 2** Sl 1, purl. Rep last 2 rows until heel measures 2", end with a WS row.

Turn heel Cont to work on 32 sts of first dpn only: **Row 1** (RS) K18, ssk, k1, turn. **Row 2** Sl 1, p5, p2tog, p1, turn. **Row 3** Sl 1, k6, ssk, k1, turn. **Row 4** Sl 1, p7, p2tog, p1, turn. Cont to dec in same way, working 1 st more between decs on each row until 18 sts rem, end with a WS row. K 1 row. Do not turn.

Gusset With empty dpn, pick up and k 17 sts along side of heel, and sl to first dpn; with 2nd dpn, pick up and p 2 sts between last st and next st, cont Lace pat over 33 sts from next 2 dpn—35 sts; with 3rd dpn, pick up and k 17 sts along other side of heel, k 9 heel sts—87 sts. Beg of rnd is at center of heel. **Rnd 1** K across first dpn; beg and end with p2, cont Lace pat across 35 sts on 2nd dpn; k across 3rd dpn. **Rnd 2** On first dpn, k to last 4 sts, k2tog, k2; cont Lace pat across 2nd dpn; on 3rd dpn, k2, ssk, k to end—2 sts dec. Rep rnds 1–2 until 69 sts rem.

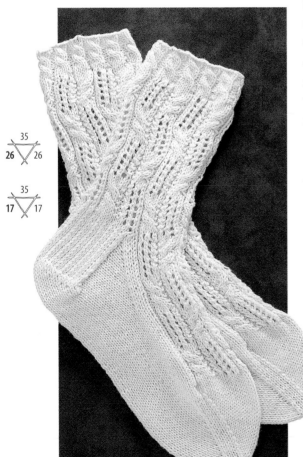

Foot Work even as established until piece measures approx 7½" from back of heel, or 2" less than desired length and 24-rnd rep of Lace pat has been worked 4 times, end with rnd 12 or 24.

Toe **Rnd 1** On first dpn, k to last 3 sts, k2tog, k1; on 2nd dpn, k1, ssk, k to last 3 sts, k2tog, k1, on 3rd dpn, k1, ssk, k to end—4 sts dec. **Rnd 2** Work even. Rep last 2 rnds 9 times more. Cont to dec every row until 9 sts rem. Cut yarn, leaving an 8" tail. Thread yarn through rem sts, pull tightly, and fasten off.

"When I read what Barbara G. Walker wrote about this pattern—'. . . gay and fascinating in any kind of yarn, for any kind of garment.'— I knew I had to try it. I decided to knit a cable cuff—my thinking being that since cables tend to pull in, the cuff might have a better chance of staying up. It works on my leg!"

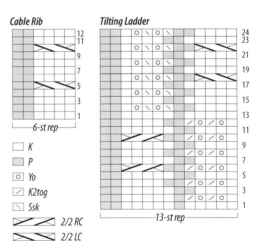

Cable Rib *Tilting Ladder*

□ K
▨ P
◦ Yo
⟋ K2tog
⟍ Ssk
⬛ 2/2 RC
⬛ 2/2 LC

Size Woman's medium.

Materials **A** 3½oz/100g (approx 430yds/392m) sock-weight yarn. **B** Set of 4 double-pointed needles (dpn) in size 2 (2.75 mm) *or size to obtain gauge.*

Gauge 7½ sts to 1" (2.5cm) over St st using size 2 (2.75mm) dpn.

· SOCKS · SOCKS · SOCKS ·

Tiger Eyes

EXPERIENCED LEVEL

MARGARET RADCLIFFE

BLACKSBURG, VIRGINIA

"This sock is knit from the toe up with the Tiger Eye pattern on the front from toe to top and the sole in stockinette. Lace mock cable on the back of the leg insures that the socks stay up. The heel is a standard round heel, just worked 'upside down.'"

Tiger Eye

panel incs & decs from 25 to 33 to 25 sts

Lace Mock Cable

5-st rep

☐ K	☐ P (shaded)
⟋ K2tog	◹ K3tog
⟍ Ssk	■ No stitch
◺ Sl1-k2tog-psso	⌒ Sl, k2, psso
⊙ Yo	

Size Woman's medium. For a smaller size, work on size 0 or 1 needles. For a larger size, add stitches at the toe, in stockinette and in mock cable pat, with a proportionally wider and longer heel flap.

Materials **A** 1¾oz/50g (approx 215yds/196m) sock-weight yarn. **B** Set of 4 double-pointed needles (dpn) in size 2 (2.75mm) *or size to obtain gauge.* **C** Size B/1 (2mm) crochet hook.

Gauge 7½ sts to 1" (2.5cm) over St st using size 2 (2.75mm) dpn.

Lace Mock Cable **Rnd 1** P2, *sl 1, k2, psso, p2; rep from*. **Rnd 2** P2, *k1, yo, k1, p2; rep from*. **Rnds 3–4** P2, *k3, p2; rep from*. Rep these 4 rnds for lace mock cable pat.

Toe Cast on 8 sts. **Row 1** (RS) K8. **Row 2** Turn knitting upside down. Using 2nd dpn, pick up and k 7 sts across the bottom of cast-on row; k 4 sts from first dpn to 3rd dpn—15 sts. Place marker and work in rnds: **Rnd 1** On first dpn, k to last 2 sts, inc 1 by k into front, then p into back of same st, k1; on 2nd dpn, inc 1, k to last 2 sts, inc 1, k1; on 3rd dpn, inc 1, k to end—19 sts. **Rnds 2–3** Rep rnd 1—27 sts. **Rnd 4** Knit. **Rnd 5** Rep rnd 1. Rep rnds 4–5 until there are 51 sts.

Foot Work as foll (working Tiger Eye pat on 2nd dpn): **Rnd 1** Knit. **Rnd 2** K13; on 2nd dpn, k2, [yo, k2tog] twice, k1, [yo] 4 times, k1, [k2tog, yo] twice, k1, [yo, ssk] twice, k1, [yo] 4 times, k1, [ssk, yo] twice, k2 (33 sts on 2nd dpn); on 3rd dpn k13. **Rnd 3** K13; k7 [k1, p1] twice into 4 yo's from rnd 2, k11, [k1, p1] twice into 4 yo's from rnd 2, k7; k13. **Rnd 4** K13; k2, [yo, k2tog] twice, k4, k3tog, yo, k2tog, yo, k3, yo, ssk, yo, sl1-k2tog-psso, k4, [ssk, yo] twice, k2, (31 sts on 2nd dpn); k13. **Rnds 5, 7, 9, 11, 13, and 15** Knit. **Rnd 6** K13; k2, [yo, k2tog] twice, k2, k3tog, yo, k2tog, yo, k5, yo, ssk, yo, sl1-k2tog-psso, k2, [ssk, yo] twice, k2, (29 sts on 2nd dpn); k13. **Rnd 8** K13; k2, [yo, k2tog] twice, k3tog, yo, k2tog, yo, k3, yo, ssk, k2, yo, ssk, yo, sl1-k2tog-psso, [ssk, yo] twice, k2, (27 sts on 2nd dpn); k13. **Rnd 10** K13; k2, yo, k2tog, k3tog, yo, k2tog, yo, k2, k2tog, yo, k1, yo, ssk, k2, yo, ssk, yo, sl1-k2tog-psso, ssk, yo, k2, (25 sts on 2nd dpn); k13. **Rnd 12** K13; k3, [k2tog, yo] twice, k2, k2tog, yo, k3, yo, ssk, k2, [yo, ssk] twice, k3; k13. **Rnd 14** K13; k2, [k2tog, yo] twice, k2, k2tog, yo, k1, yo, sl1-k2tog-psso, yo, k1, yo, ssk, k2, [yo, ssk] twice, k2; k13. **Rnd 16** K13; k1, [k2tog, yo] twice, k4, yo, sl1-k2tog-psso, yo, k1, yo, k3tog, yo, k4, [yo, ssk] twice, k1; k13. Rep rnds 1–16 until foot measures desired length to beg of heel, end with rnd 16.

Heel With 3rd dpn, k13 from first dpn (26 sts on dpn); sl next 13 sts of Tiger Eye pat to first dpn; 12 sts of Tiger Eye pat rem on 2nd dpn. Work back and forth in rows on 26 sts of 3rd dpn only: **Next row** (WS) Sl 1, p25. **Next row** Sl 1, k24, p1. Rep last 2 rows 12 times more, then work 1 more WS row.

Turn heel Cont on 26 sts: **Row 1** (RS) Sl 1, k14, ssk, k1, turn. **Row 2** Sl 1, p5, p2tog, p1, turn. **Row 3** Sl 1, k6, ssk, k1, turn. **Row 4** Sl 1, p7, p2tog, p1, turn. Cont to dec in same way, working 1 st more between decs on each row until 16 sts rem. K 1 row. Do not turn.

Gusset With empty dpn, pick up and k 14 sts along side of heel (pick up last st in row below last edge st) and sl to 3rd dpn. With first dpn, cont Tiger Eye pat across 25 sts of next 2 dpn. With 2nd dpn, pick up and k 14 sts along other side of heel, then k 8 heel sts—69 sts. Beg of rnd is at end of heel. **Next rnd** Cont Tiger Eye pat across first dpn; on 2nd dpn, k1, k2tog, k across; on 3rd dpn, k to last 3 sts, ssk, k1—2 sts dec. Work 1 rnd even, taking care to keep Tiger Eye pat correct. Rep last 2 rnds 7 times more, AT SAME TIME, dec 1 extra st at end of 2nd dpn (13 sts on 2nd dpn).

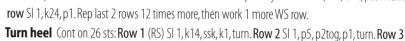

Leg Work Tiger Eye pat on first dpn and Lace Mock Cable pat on 2nd and 3rd dpns for approx 5½", end with an odd-numbered rnd of Tiger Eye pat. Do not cut yarn. Turn.

Picot Edging With crochet hook, and WS of leg showing, bind off by working 1 sl stitch in each knitted stitch, taking sts off dpn. Sl st to join and turn. With RS facing, work picot edge: Sl st into next 4 sts, *ch 5 and sl st into first ch (picot), sl st into next 3 sts; rep from* around. Fasten off.

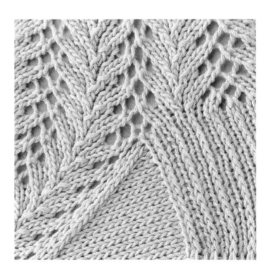
Vine Lace Socks

INTERMEDIATE LEVEL

KATHY GARGUILO

SALEM, OREGON

Leg With smaller dpn, cast on 68 sts and divide evenly over 3 dpn. Place marker, join and work 1½" in k1, p1 rib. Change to larger dpn. Work 1 dec rnd as foll: K1, k2tog, [k3, k2tog] 13 times—54 sts. Work in Vine Lace pat as foll: **Rnd 1** [K1, yo, k2, ssk, k2tog, k2, yo] 6 times. **Rnds 2, 4** Knit. **Rnd 3** [Yo, k2, ssk, k2tog, k2, yo, k1] 6 times. Rep rnds 1–4 until piece measures 5½" from beg.

Heel Sl 27 sts to first dpn, next 14 sts to 2nd dpn, next 13 sts on 3rd dpn. Work back and forth in rows on 27 sts of first dpn only: **Row 1** (RS) *Sl 1 knitwise, k1; rep from* across, end sl 1 knitwise. **Row 2** Purl. Rep last 2 rows until heel measures 2", end with a WS row.

Turn heel Cont on 27 sts: **Row 1** (RS) K14, ssk, k1, turn. **Row 2** Sl 1, p2, p2tog, p1, turn. **Row 3** Sl 1, k3, ssk, k1, turn. **Row 4** Sl 1, p4, p2tog, p1, turn. Cont to dec in same way, working 1 st more between decs on each row until 15 sts rem. K 1 row. Do not turn.

Gusset With empty dpn, pick up and k 14 sts along side of heel and sl to first dpn; with 2nd dpn, M1, and cont Lace pat over 27 sts of next 2 dpn, M1—29 sts; with 3rd dpn, pick up and k 14 sts along other side of heel, then k 8 heel sts—72 sts. Beg of rnd is at center of heel. **Rnd 1** K across first dpn; on 2nd dpn, k1, cont pat across 27 sts, k1; k across 3rd dpn. **Rnd 2** On first dpn, k to last 2 sts, k2tog; cont Lace pat across 2nd dpn; on 3rd dpn, ssk, k to end—2 sts dec. Rep last 2 rnds 8 times more—54 sts.

Foot Work even until piece measures approx 7½" from back of heel, or 2" less than desired length.

Toe Sl first st from 2nd dpn to first dpn; sl last st from 2nd dpn to 3rd dpn. **Rnd 1** On first dpn, k to last 3 sts, k2tog, k1; on 2nd dpn, k1, ssk, k to last 3 sts, k2tog, k1, on 3rd dpn, k1, ssk, k to end—4 sts dec. **Rnd 2** Work even. Rep last 2 rnds 5 times more—30 sts. Rep rnd 1 until 10 sts rem. K sts from first dpn to 3rd dpn. Cut yarn, leaving a 10" tail. Graft rem 5 sts from each dpn tog.

"Most of my knitting is done as gifts for friends and family. This easy, beautiful sock is the perfect gift project. The patterning results from two identical rows merely offset by one stitch and separated by a 'work even' row."

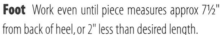
Vine Lace

9-st rep

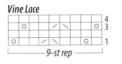
☐ K
⊙ Yo
◿ K2tog
◺ Ssk

Size Woman's medium.

Materials A 2oz/56g (approx 250yds/228m) sock-weight yarn. **B** Set of 4 double-pointed needles (dpn) in sizes 1 and 2 (2.25 and 2.75 mm) *or size to obtain gauge.*

Gauge 8 sts to 1" (2.5cm) over St st using size 2 (2.75mm) dpn..

Chapter 4   Color

17 PROJECTS

2 Socks, 2 Ways   **46**

Gray Progression   **48**

Tweed Socks   **49**

Harlequin Socks   **50**

Rainbows   **51**

Travelling Socks   **52**

Free-Form Socks   **53**

46   48   49   50

Toe-tally Reversible Toasty Toes   **54**

False Flame Crew Socks   **55**

Entrelac Socks   **56**

Harry's Socks   **57**

Best Of Show Socks   **58**

Wedgwood Socks   **59**

Stained Glass Bubble Socks   **60**

Tile Socks   **61**

Bob's Socks   **62**

Salsa Socks   **63**

57

58

Color Socks

52
53
54
55
56
59
60
61
62
63

2 Socks, 2 Ways

INTERMEDIATE LEVEL

These two machine-knit socks are so appealing
that we are also presenting directions
for hand knitters.
A standard heel worked on 24 sts
could be substituted for the Eastern-style heel
we have inserted.

Hand knitting directions

Set of 4 double-pointed needles (dpn) in size 6 (4mm) *or size to obtain gauge.*

For Black sock

Leg With MC, cast on 48 sts and divide on 4 dpn as foll: 24 on first dpn, 12 on 2nd dpn, and 12 on 3rd dpn. Place marker, join, and k 4 rnds. **Next rnd** *K2tog, yo; rep from*. K4 rnds. Work rnds 1–13 of Chart B. Rep last 4 rnds 7 more times, then work rnds 14–16 .

Foot With waste yarn, k 24 sts and sl back to left-hand dpn. With MC, k 36 rnds.

Toe **Rnd 1** With C, on first dpn, k1, ssk, k to last 3 sts, k2tog, k1; on 2nd dpn, k1, ssk, k to end; on 3rd dpn, k to last 3 sts, k2tog, k1. **Rnd 2** Knit. Rep last 2 rnds until 16 sts rem. Sl 4 sts of 2nd dpn to 3rd dpn. Cut yarn, leaving a 12" tail. Graft 8 sts from each dpn tog.

Heel Remove waste yarn and sl 23 sts each to 2 dpn. Rearrange on 4 dpn: 23 on first dpn, 12 on 2nd, and 11 on 3rd. With C, k 1 rnd, picking up an extra st at end of first dpn and at end of 3rd dpn—48 sts. Shape and finish heel as for toe.

Finishing Fold top along picot edge and st to inside.

For Yellow sock Change colors and work Chart A. Repeat chart 1 time more, then work rnds 1–10.

Chart A

21
20

10

1
└ 4-st rep ┘

Chart B

16

13

10

1
└ 4-st rep ┘

Color Key
■ Black (MC)
■ Purple (A)
□ Turquoise (B)
■ Raspberry (C)

Color Key
■ Raspberry (MC)
■ Purple (A)
□ Yellow (B)
■ Turquoise (C)
■ Terra cotta (D)

Stitch Key
□ K   ⊟ P

Size Woman's medium.

Materials: Worsted-weight yarn: *For yellow sock* 1¾oz/50g (approx 115yds/105m) in raspberry (MC), yellow (B); 1oz/25g each in purple (A), turquoise (C), terra cotta (D). *For black sock* 1¾oz/50g in black (MC); 1oz/25g each in purple (A), turquoise (B), and raspberry (C).

Gauge 5 sts to 1" (2.5cm) over St st.

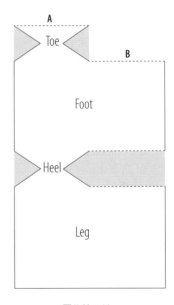

Machine knitting directions
Mid-gauge machine

Stitch Size: 6.1

For Black sock
Left Sock
Leg Using e-wrap method, cast on 48 sts in MC. Knit 4 rows. Beg with 3rd st from right, transfer every other st to its neighbor; leave empty needles in work. Knit 4 rows. Work rnds 1–13 of Chart B. Rep last 4 rows 7 more times, then work rows 14–16 .

Heel With carriage on right side, place all needles left of 0 to hold position. With C, *knit 1 row and do yarn wrap under first needle in hold. Place 1 needle opposite the carriage to hold. Rep from* until only 8 needles remain in work. *Return one needle to upper-work position on carriage side. Knit 1 row and wrap yarn under first needle in hold. Rep from* until all right side needles are working. With carriage at right, set it to knit all needles.

Foot With MC, knit 36 rows over all needles.

Toe With carriage on right, place all needles at left of 0 to hold position. With C, shape toe as for heel. Scrap off 24 sts right of 0. Scrap off 24 sts left of 0 separately.

Finishing Foll diagram, graft the A toe sts together with the B sts. Fold top along picot edge and sew to inside. Sew side seam.

Right Sock
Work as for left sock, reversing all shaping.

For Yellow sock
Change colors and work Chart A. Rep chart once more, then work rows 1–10 once. Complete as for Black sock.

☐ *Hold position*

On this simple and elegant sock,
chevrons blend the bands of color.
With a progression of eight colors,
none repeats from top to toe.
The heel is worked at the end, as a thumb
on a mitten.

Gray Progression

INTERMEDIATE LEVEL

MAUREEN PRATT

RADNOR, PENNSYLVANIA

Note Arrange colors in an order (here, from light to dark) and call them A (lightest), B, C, etc., to H (darkest).

Leg With A, cast on 42 sts. Sl 10 sts to first dpn, 11 sts to 2nd dpn, 10 sts to 3rd dpn and 11 sts to 4th dpn. Place marker, join and work 2 rnds in k1, p1 rib. **Rnds 1–7** With A and B, work chart rnds 1–3 (using A as old color, B as new color), then k 4 rnds with B. **Rnds 8–16** With B and C, work 3 chart rnds, then k 6 rnds with C. **Rnds 17–27** With C and D, work 3 chart rnds, then k 8 rnds with D. **Rnds 28–38** With D and E, work 3 chart rnds, then k 8 rnds with E. **Rnds 39–40** K 21 sts with waste yarn and sl back to left-hand needle. With E, k 2 rnds. **Rnds 41–55** With E and F, work 3 chart rnds, then k 12 rnds with F. **Rnds 56–72** With F and G, work 3 chart rnds, then k 14 rnds with G. **Rnds 73–75** With G and H, work 3 chart rnds. Cont with H only.

Toe **Next rnd** On first dpn, k1, ssk, k to end; on 2nd dpn, k to last 3 sts, k2tog, k1; on 3rd dpn, k1, ssk, k to end; on 4th dpn, k to last 3 sts, k2tog, k1. **Next rnd** Knit. Rep last 2 rnds until 22 sts rem. **Next rnd** On first dpn, k5; on 2nd dpn, k to last 3 sts, k2tog, k1; on 3rd dpn, k5; on 4th dpn, k to last 3 sts, k2tog, k1—20 sts. K 5 sts of first dpn onto 4th dpn. Sl 5 sts of 2nd dpn to 3rd dpn. Cut yarn, leaving a 12" tail. Graft rem 10 sts from each dpn tog.

Heel Remove waste yarn and sl 20 sts each to 2 dpn. Rearrange sts by sl 10 each onto 4 dpn. With E, k around for 1". **Next rnd** On first dpn, k1, ssk, k to end; on 2nd dpn, k to last 3 sts, k2tog, k1; on 3rd dpn, k1, ssk, k to end; on 4th dpn, k to last 3 sts, k2tog, k1. Rep last rnd until 12 sts rem. K 3 sts of first dpn onto 4th dpn. Sl 3 sts of 2nd dpn onto 3rd dpn. Cut yarn, leaving a 12" tail. Graft rem 6 sts from each dpn tog.

Old Color
New Color
6-st rep
3
2
1

Size Adult small.

Materials **A** DK-weight yarn: 1¾oz/50g (approx 140yds/128m) in black (H); small amounts of 8 colors (in this case, white and 6 grays, A–G). **B** Set of 5 double-pointed needles (dpn) in size 4 (3.5mm) *or size to obtain gauge*.

Gauge 5½ sts to 1" (2.5cm) over St st using size 4 (3.5mm) dpn.

Tweed Socks

INTERMEDIATE LEVEL

MARILYN MORGAN

OLATHE, KANSAS

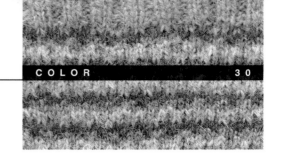

Tweed pat (Multiple of 3 sts) Slip sts as if to purl and with yarn in back (wyib). **Rnd 1** *K2, sl 1; rep from*. **Rnds 2, 4, 6** Knit. **Rnd 3** *K1, sl 1, k1; rep from*. **Rnd 5** *Sl 1, k2; rep from*.

Leg With A, cast on 68 sts and divide evenly over 3 dpn. Place marker, join and work 1½" in k2, p2 rib, inc 1 st on last rnd—69 sts. With A, k 1 rnd. Work Tweed pat in colors as foll: *2 rnds each with B, C, D, then A; rep from* in Tweed pat until piece measures 7" from beg, end with row 2, 4, or 6 in A.

Heel With empty dpn and A, k 17 sts on first dpn, sl next 17 sts to 2nd dpn, sl next 18 sts to 3rd dpn and rem 17 sts to first dpn. Work back and forth in rows on 34 sts of first dpn only: **Row 1 (RS)** *Sl 1, k1; rep from*. **Row 2** Sl 1, p across. Rep last 2 rows 13 more times, end with a RS row.

Turn heel Cont on 34 sts: **Row 1** (WS) P19, p2tog, p1, turn. **Row 2** Sl 1, k5, ssk, k1, turn. **Row 3** Sl 1, p6, p2tog, p1, turn. **Row 4** Sl 1, k7, ssk, k1, turn. **Row 5** Sl 1, p8, p2tog, p1, turn. In same way, cont to dec, working 1 st more between decs, until 20 sts rem, end with a RS row. Do not turn.

Gusset With empty dpn and B, pick up and k 14 sts along left side of heel and sl to first dpn. With 2nd dpn, work Tweed pat as established over 35 sts from next 2 dpn; with 3rd dpn, pick up and k 14 sts along right side of heel, then k 10 heel sts—83 sts. Beg of rnd is now at center of heel. Cont Tweed and color pat (ready for 2nd rnd of B and an even-numbered rnd of Tweed pat), AT SAME TIME, shape as foll: **Next rnd** On first dpn, work to last 3 sts, k2tog, k1; work across 2nd dpn; on 3rd dpn, k1, ssk, pat to end. **Next rnd** Work even. Rep last 2 rnds until 69 sts rem.

Foot Work even until piece measures 10" from beg or 2" less than desired length. Dec 1 st on 2nd dpn—68 sts.

Toe Cont with A only. **Rnd 1** On first dpn, k to last 3 sts, k2tog, k1; on 2nd dpn, k1, ssk, k to last 3 sts, k2tog, k1; on 3rd dpn, k1, ssk, k to end—4 sts dec. **Rnd 2** Knit. Rep rnds 1–2 until 12 sts rem. K 3 sts of first dpn onto 3rd dpn. Cut yarn, leaving a 12" tail. Graft 6 sts from each dpn tog.

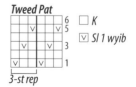

Tweed Pat

☐ K
☑ Sl 1 wyib

3-st rep

Size Woman's large or Man's medium. Foot measures 9½" from heel to toe.

Materials A Sport-weight yarn: 2 skeins moss green (A); 1 skein each cranberry (B), light gray (C), and dark gray (D). **B** Set of 4 double-pointed needles (dpn) size 2 (2.75mm), or size to obtain gauge.

Gauge 7 sts to 1" (2.5cm) over Slip St pat using size 2 (2.75mm) dpn.

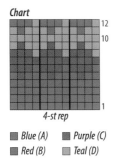

Harlequin Socks

TRICIA WEATHERSTON

EXPERIENCED LEVEL

EAST STROUDSBURG, PENNSYLVANIA

*"First and foremost I am a spinner.
The fiber is a space-dyed merino top, so in order
to get the individual colors, I had to separate
them before spinning.
I spun a bit variegated, as it comes off
the top, and used that to knit the
ribbing, under the cuff."*

*"The trick to knitting entrelac in the round
is to reverse the direction of knitting
at the end of each round.
Nine ridges of garter stitch make a nice neat
square, while the equivalent rows in the other
patterns make anything but a square.
I dealt with this by knitting 3tog on the 2nd
and 7th rows or the equivalent in psso blocks.
This is not a fast sock to knit!"*

Chart

4-st rep

■ Blue (A)   ■ Purple (C)
■ Red (B)   ☐ Teal (D)

Size Woman's medium.

Materials A Sock-weight yarn: 1oz/28g (approx 130 yds/118m) each in blue (A), red (B), purple (C), and teal (D). **B** Set of 4 double-pointed needles (dpn) sizes 0 and 1 (2 and 2.5mm) *or size to obtain gauge.*

Gauge 9½ sts to 1" (2.5cm) over Chart pat using size 1 (2.5mm) dpn.

Leg BASE: FIRST RND (garter st) (left-leaning squares) *With smaller dpn and A, cast on 9 sts. K 18 rows. Cut yarn and leave square on spare needle; rep from* 6 times more. **2ND RND (rev St st)** (right-leaning squares) Sl one square each to left hand (LH) and right hand (RH) needle. With B and RH needle, pick up and k 9 sts up the outer right edge of LH square, turn. Work in rows as foll: **Row 1** (WS) K8, k2tog, turn. **Row 2** Sl 1, p8, turn. In same way, cont until 9 sts on RH needle are used up, end with row 17. Do not turn. Sl next 9-st square to RH needle and work as for previous square. Rep until all 7 squares have been worked, adding dpn as necessary, join rnd. **3RD RND (seed st)** With C, pick up and k 9 sts along square on RH needle, turn. **Row 1** (WS) K2tog, [p1, k1] 4 times, turn. **Row 2** Sl 1, [p1, k1] 4 times, turn. **Row 3** K2tog, k1, [p1, k1] 3 times, turn. In same way, cont until 9 sts on LH needle are used up, end with row 17. Do not turn. In same way, work across all squares with C. **4TH RND (sand st)** With D, work right-leaning squares as foll: k1, p1 across RS rows and k across WS rows. **5TH RND (garter st)** With A, work left-leaning squares and k every row. **6TH RND (St st triangles)** With B, pick up and k 9 sts, turn. **Row 1** (WS) P8, p2tog, turn. **Row 2** Sl 1, k7, turn. **Row 3** Sl 1, p6, p2tog, turn. **Row 4** Sl 1, k6, turn. **Row 5** Sl 1, p5, p2tog, turn. **Row 6** Sl 1, k5, turn. **Row 7** Sl 1, p4, p2tog, turn. **Row 8** Sl 1, k4, turn. **Row 9** Sl 1, p3, p2tog, turn. **Row 10** Sl 1, k3, turn. **Row 11** Sl 1, p2, p2tog, turn. **Row 12** Sl 1, k2, turn. **Row 13** Sl 1, k1, p2tog, turn. **Row 14** Sl 1, k1, turn. **Row 15** Sl 1, p2tog, turn. **Row 16** K1, turn. **Row 17** P2tog, turn. In same way, work around—63 sts. **NEXT RND** Purl. With C, k 3 rnds, inc 13 sts evenly across last rnd—76 sts. Turn work inside out. Work 3" in k2, p2 rib. Change to larger dpn and work 4-st rep of chart rnds 1–9.

21 ╱╲ 21
    ‾‾
    21

Heel With D, k first 19 sts onto first dpn, sl next 19 sts to 2nd dpn, next 19 sts to 3rd dpn, and last 19 sts to first dpn. Work back and forth on 38 sts of first dpn only: **Row 1** (WS) Sl 1, purl across. **Row 2** *Sl 1, k1; rep from* across. Rep last 2 rows until heel measures 2¼", end with WS row.

19 ╱╲ 19
    ‾‾
    38

Turn heel Cont on 38 sts of first dpn: **Row 1** (RS) With D, k21, ssk, k1, turn. **Row 2** Sl 1, p5, p2tog, p1, turn. **Row 3** Sl 1, k6, ssk, k1, turn. **Row 4** Sl 1, p7, p2tog, p1, turn. Cont to dec in same way, working 1 st more between decs on each row until 22 sts rem. K 1 row. Do not turn.

Gusset With empty dpn and D, pick up and k 18 sts along side of heel and sl to first dpn. With 2nd dpn, work chart rnd 10 across 38 sts from next 2 dpn; with 3rd dpn, pick up and k 18 sts along other side of heel, then k 10 heel sts—96 sts. Beg of rnd is 2 sts before center of heel. Cont chart pat (ready for rnd 11), AT SAME TIME, shape as foll: **Next rnd** Work even. **Next (dec) rnd** On first dpn, k to last 2 sts, k2tog; k across 2nd dpn; on 3rd dpn, ssk, k to end—94 sts. Rep last 2 rnds until 80 sts rem.

        38
30 ╲╱ 28

Foot Work even until foot measures 5¾", or 2" less than desired length, end with chart rnd 3.

Toe Sl 1 st from end of first dpn to 2nd dpn, 1 st from beg of 3rd dpn to 2nd dpn and 1 st from beg of first dpn to 3rd dpn: 20 sts each on first and 3rd dpns, 40 sts on 2nd dpn. **Next rnd** With B, on first dpn, cont pat to last 3 sts, k2tog, k1; on 2nd dpn, k1, ssk, cont pat to last 3 sts, k2tog, k1; on 3rd dpn, k1, ssk, cont pat to end. Cont to dec 4 sts every other rnd until 16 sts rem. K sts from first dpn to 3rd dpn and graft rem 8 sts on each dpn tog.

        40
20 ╲╱ 20

Rainbows

CAMILLE REMME

INTERMEDIATE LEVEL

ETOBICOKE, ONTARIO, CANADA

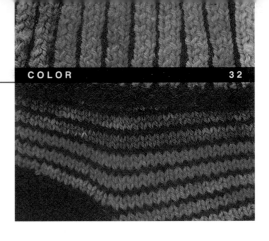

Note For vertical stripes, cut 1½ yd lengths of 24 colors plus 24 lengths in black. Work each stripe with separate strands; do not carry yarns across WS. Arrange B colors in rainbow sequence: red-purples, reds, oranges, yellows, greens, blues, and blue-purples. Use photo as guide for color placement.

Cuff With straight needles and A, cast on 72 sts. K 3 rows. Using B colors in sequence, work as foll: **Row 1** (RS) *K2 B, p1 A; rep from* across. **Row 2** *K1 A, p2 B; rep from* across. Rep last 2 rows until piece measures 2" from beg, end with a WS row. With A, k 1 row and dec 8 sts evenly across—64 sts.

Leg Sl 20 sts to first dpn, 24 sts to 2nd dpn and 20 sts to 3rd dpn. Place marker, join and with A, work 24 rnds in k1, p1 rib. Turn work inside out. *With A, k 1 rnd. With B, k 2 rnds. Working B colors in same sequence as for cuff, rep from* 5 times more.

Heel With A, k first 16 sts onto first dpn, sl next 16 sts to 2nd dpn, next 16 sts to 3rd dpn, and next 16 sts to first dpn. Work back and forth in rows on 32 sts of first dpn only: **Row 1** (WS) Sl 1, p across. **Row 2** Sl 1, k across. Rep last 2 rows until heel measures 2", end with a WS row..

Turn heel Cont on 32 sts of first dpn: **Row 1** (RS) K18, ssk, k1, turn. **Row 2** Sl 1, p5, p2tog, p1, turn. **Row 3** Sl 1, k6, ssk, k1, turn. **Row 4** Sl 1, p7, p2tog, p1, turn. Cont to dec in same way, working 1 st more between decs on each row until 18 sts rem. K 1 row. Do not turn.

Gusset With empty dpn and A, pick up and k 12 sts along side of heel and sl to first dpn; with 2nd dpn k 32 sts from next 2 dpn; with 3rd dpn, pick up and k 12 sts along other side of heel, then k 9 heel sts—74 sts. Beg of rnd is at center of heel. Cont strip pat, work as foll: **Rnd 1** Knit. **Rnd 2** On first dpn, k to last 3 sts, k2tog, k1; k across 2nd dpn; on 3rd dpn, k1, ssk, k to end—72 sts. Rep rnds 1–2 until 64 sts rem.

Foot Work even until foot measures 4", or 2" less than desired length, end with 2nd rnd of B.

Toe Rearrange sts as foll: Sl 3 sts each from 2nd dpn to first and 3rd dpn—19 sts each on first and 3rd dpns, 26 sts on 2nd dpn. **Next rnd** Keeping colors correct, [k6, k2tog] 8 times—56 sts. Work 5 rnds even. **Next rnd** Keeping colors correct, [k5, k2tog] 8 times—48 sts. Cont with A as foll: K 4 rnds. **Next rnd** [K4, k2tog] 8 times—40 sts. K 3 rnds. **Next rnd** [K3, k2tog] 8 times—32 sts. K 3 rnds. **Next rnd** [K2, k2tog] 8 times—24 sts. K 1 rnd. **Next rnd** [K1, k2tog] 8 times—16 sts. **Next rnd** [K2tog] 8 times—8 sts. Cut yarn, leaving a 6" tail. Draw tail through rem sts, pull tightly and secure. Sew cuff seam.

Camille dyed white yarn in 24 colors for these— the first pair of socks she has ever knitted! Even in a more limited palette, this combination of vertical stripes and horizontal bands of color divided by fine black lines would be effective.

Size Woman's small.

Materials **A** Sock-weight yarn: 1¾ oz/50g (approx 215yds/196m) in black (A); a total of 3½oz/100g in 24 colors (B). **B** Set of 4 double-pointed needles (dpn) size 1 (2.5mm), *or size to obtain gauge.* **C** One pair straight needles size 0 (2mm) for cuff.

Gauge 8 sts to 1" (2.5cm) over St st, using size 1 (2.5mm) dpn.

Travelling Socks

EXPERIENCED LEVEL

LUCY NEATBY

DARTMOUTH, NOVA SCOTIA, CANADA

Designed as "dashboard knitting" for a summer's travels around Nova Scotia, these socks are carefree knitting: use any small repeat, not worrying about what happens at the join. A needle threaded through the three balls kept the yarn from flying out of the van window and allowed Lucy to concentrate on knitting many happy memories into these socks.

Size Woman's medium.

Materials A Sock-weight yarn: 1¾oz/50g (220yds/201m) each in variegated (A), fuchsia (B), and yellow (C). **B** Set of 4 double-pointed needles (dpn) size 1 (2.5mm), *or size to obtain gauge.*

Gauge 8½ sts to 1" (2.5cm) over St st using size 1 (2.5mm) dpn.

Note Chart repeats may not match at end of rnd.

Leg With A, cast on 80 sts and divide over 3 dpn as foll: 20 sts each on first and 3rd dpns, 40 sts on 2nd dpn. Place marker, join and work 1¾" in k1, p1 rib. Work 40 rnds of chart 1 or 2.

Heel With A, k first 20 sts to first dpn, sl next 20 sts to 2nd dpn, next 20 sts to 3rd dpn, and rem 20 sts to first dpn. Work back and forth in rows on 40 sts of first dpn only: **Row 1** (RS) *Sl 1 knitwise, k1; rep from*. **Row 2** Sl 1, p across. Rep last 2 rows 21 times more, end with a WS row.

Turn heel Cont on 40 sts of first dpn: **Row 1** (RS) K22, ssk, k1, turn. **Row 2** Sl 1, p5, p2tog, p1, turn. **Row 3** Sl 1, k6, ssk, k1, turn. **Row 4** Sl 1, p7, p2tog, p1, turn. Cont to dec in same way, working 1 st more between decs on each row until 22 sts rem, end with a RS row. Do not turn.

Gusset With empty dpn and C, pick up and k 22 sts along side of heel; with 2nd dpn, work chart rnd 41 over 40 sts from next 2 dpn; with 3rd dpn, pick up and k 22 sts along other side of heel, then k 22 heel sts—106 sts. Beg of rnd is at end of heel. **Next (dec) rnd** (chart rnd 42) On first dpn, pat to last 3 sts, k2tog, k1; on 2nd dpn, pat across; on 3rd dpn, k1, ssk, pat to end—2 sts dec. **Next rnd** (chart rnd 43) Work chart pat across to last 22 heel sts, k22. In same way, cont chart pat, always working last 22 sts in knit, and dec 2 sts every other rnd until 80 sts rem.

Foot Sl last 11 sts from 3rd dpn to first dpn—20 sts each on first and 3rd dpn, 40 sts on 2nd dpn. Work even in chart pat (cont to k 22 heel sts and on chart rnds 79 to 89, alternate 1 B st and 1 C st and work through chart rnd 98.

Toe Rnd 1 With A, on first dpn, k to last 3 sts, k2tog, k1; on 2nd dpn, k1, ssk, k to last 3 sts, k2tog, k1; on 3rd dpn, k1, ssk, k to end—4 sts dec. **Rnd 2** Work even. Rep last 2 rnds 14 times more—20 sts. K sts from first dpn to 3rd dpn. Using 3-needle bind-off, bind off all sts.

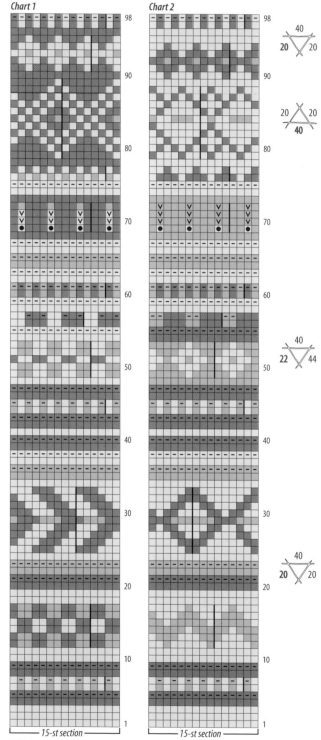

Chart 1   Chart 2

Color key A B C

Stitch key – P ⊙ K1, yo, yo ☑ Sl2, drop yo's off dpn

Note Repeat lengths vary. Repeats are marked with a heavy black line.

Left slipper *Note* Use as much yarn variety as available, chosen from two contrasting color groups. Yarn weights and types can be mixed in the slipper top. All can be knitted on the same needle. Finer yarns can be used if surrounded by sections in DK or heavier weights.

Leg Using larger needle, knit a small shape. Bind off. With new yarn, pick up along an edge and add another small shape. Bind off. Place this piece on your foot to determine where you want to add to it next. Continue to add shapes, always picking up with RS facing and using a variety of stitches to highlight the textural interest of multi-directional knitting. (Avoid using much stocking stitch because of its wish to curl.) The top can be built right around the back and to the sole and top of leg without seaming. Seam in places if you feel the need.

Ribbing With RS facing, 3 dpn and black DK yarn, pick up and k 52 sts evenly around top of leg piece. **Rnd 1** *K2, p2; rep from*. **Rnd 2** With contrasting DK yarn, *k2 black, k2 color; rep from*. **Rnds 3–6** *K2 black, p2 color; rep from*. **Rnd 7** Rep rnd 2. **Rnd 8** Rep rnd 1. Bind off in pat.

Sole Mark the position of the center back and the inside tip of the big toe on the knitted piece. With RS facing, circular needle and black DK yarn, pick up and k 53 sts evenly from heel to toe, then pick up and k 69 sts from toe to heel—122 sts. Work 2 rows in reverse St st. **Foll chart:** For the colored sections use a selection of hard-wearing DK yarns from the color group to be used in the right sock top. Some cheating on the yarn weight is allowed in the smallest patches. Cut short lengths for small sections to avoid tangles. The rest of the sole is worked in St st back and forth in rows on circular needles, except for the first two rounds which are knit circularly. **Rnd 1** K with black DK, dec where marked and adding markers as indicated. **Rnd 2** K in colors indicated, twisting the yarns at color changes. **Row 3** Turn work for purl row. At the beg of this and every row, twist the yarn with the first yarn on the other end of the row even though it will be in the wrong position. It can be pulled tight after knitting the next row. Cont working the chart back and forth. Partial, or short, rows are at the center. Turn at these spots and sl the first st on the next row. Leave the stitches on hold for grafting.

Right slipper Work as for left slipper. When picking up for sole, pick up 69 sts from heel to toe, then 53 from toe to heel. Foll graph in reverse.

Finishing Graft the center sole in the appropriate colors. Fasten ends.

"These socks were designed to fit over other socks for cosy sitting. The tops were made by free-form knitting—adding small pieces, casting off, picking up, and adding again. My feet were my models, and I built up pieces to cover them as far as the sole (a gymnastic challenge) then added ribbing and soles."

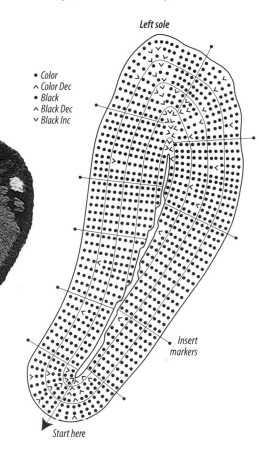

Left sole

- • Color
- ∧ Color Dec
- • Black
- ∧ Black Dec
- ∨ Black Inc

Insert markers

Start here

Size Women's medium.

Materials A DK-weight yarn: small amounts of assorted colors and black. **B** 24"/60cm circular needle in size 6 (4mm), *or size to obtain gauge.* **C** Set of 4 double-pointed needles (dpn) in size 4 (3½mm).

Gauge 8 sts to 1" (2.5cm) over St st using size 6 (4mm) needle.

Toe-tally Reversible Toasty Toes

KIM SLAD

EXPERIENCED LEVEL

RAMONA, CALIFORNIA

> "Since double knitting offers twice the warmth, cushion, and creative space as regular knitting, it's a natural choice for toasty, trendy bed socks. This balanced (no-roll) fabric eliminates the need for ribbing or hem, allowing one to begin the pattern immediately."
>
> By working this pattern at different gauges (from 5.5 sts to 8 sts to the inch), Kim can make bed socks that measure from 10" around to 7" around.

Double knitting Double knitting is a k1, p1 rib in which the knit stitches form a pattern on one side and the purl stitches form a pattern on the other. A purl stitch in the opposite color must follow every knit stitch represented on the chart. For example, rnd 1 of chart 1 shows 28 squares, or stitches, but actually represents 56 sts. After k1 A, you would p1 B (not shown on chart). Carry yarns together, forward and back, between sts. Rnd 2 would be k1 B (the first square), followed by p1 A (not shown); then k1 A (the 2nd square), followed by p1 B (not shown).

Leg With A, cast on 112 sts and divide evenly over 4 dpn. Place marker, join and work 9 rnds of Chart 1 around. Work 18 rnds of Chart 2 a total of 3 times.

Heel Sl 28 sts from 2nd dpn to first dpn—56 sts. Leave rem 56 sts on hold. Work back and forth in rows on 56 sts of first dpn only (reversing colors on WS rows) as foll: Work rows 1–9 of Chart 3, working decs over first and last 4 sts as foll: sl 1 k st to right hand (RH) needle, sl next p st to spare needle and hold to back, sl next k st to RH needle, then sl p st on spare needle back to left hand (LH) needle, sl 2 k sts back to LH needle; k2tog, p2tog—4 sts dec each row, 20 sts rem after completing row 9. Fold heel along row 9 with WS tog. Work rows 10–17 of Chart 3, working incs at beg and end of rows as foll: At beg of row 10, sl first 2 sts from row 8 onto LH needle and k1, p1; work across in pat, then sl last 2 sts from row 8 onto LH needle and k1, p1—24 sts. In same way, cont to inc by picking up sts from each previously worked row (row 11 picks up from row 7, row 12 picks up from row 6, etc.)—52 sts after working row 17.

Rearrange these heel sts onto 2 dpn. Work rnd 1 of Chart 2 across sts on hold, M1 (for each strand) to create first st of rnd 1 of Chart 2; cont rnd 1 across heel sts, M1 (for each strand) at end of rnd. Work 18 rnds of Chart 2 a total of 3 times.

Toe Rep rnds 1–9 of Chart 3, dec at both edges of both sides of sock as for heel.

Finishing Close toe by drawing yarn through purl sts. Cut both strands, leaving an 8" tail in each color. With A, graft the knit sts tog, then secure and pull end between sock layers. Turn inside out. With B, graft rem sts tog, then secure and pull end between layers.

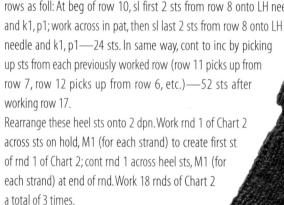

Chart 1, Cuff

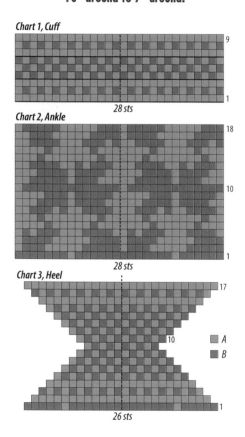

28 sts

Chart 2, Ankle

28 sts

Chart 3, Heel

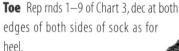

☐ A
■ B

26 sts

Size Woman's small, bed sock measures approx 9" around.

Materials **A** 3½oz/100g (approx 350yds/319m) fingering- to sport- weight each in: variegated red (A) and variegated green (B). **B** Set of 5 double-pointed needles (dpn) size 1 (2.5mm), *or size to obtain gauge.*

Gauge 6½ sts to 1" (2.5cm) over double knitting using size 1 (2.5mm) dpn.

False Flame Crew Socks

CYNTHIA DAHL

OLATHE, KANSAS

INTERMEDIATE LEVEL

False Flame Multiple of 4 sts **Rnd 1** Knit. **Rnd 2** *K1 wrapping yarn twice around needle, k3; rep from* across. **Rnd 3** *Sl 1 with yarn in back (wyib), dropping extra wrap; k1, k into stitch 2 rows below next st and pull up a loop, k next st on LH needle and pass loop over stitch just knit, k1; rep from* around. **Rnd 4** *Sl 1 wyib, k3; rep from* around. Rep rnds 1–4 for pat, changing colors as foll: 2 rnds MC; *4 rnds B, 4 rnds A, 4 rnds MC; rep from*.

Leg With MC, cast on 48 sts and divide evenly over 3 dpn. Place marker, join and work 2" in k2, p2 rib. Work in False Flame pat until piece measures 7" from beg, end with 3rd rnd of MC.

Heel Sl 4 sts from first and 3rd dpn to 2nd dpn. Sl rem 12 sts from 3rd dpn to first dpn, then divide 24 sts from 2nd dpn to 2 empty dpn. With MC, work back and forth in rows on 24 sts of first dpn only: **Row 1** (RS) *Sl 1, k1; rep from* across. **Row 2** (WS) *Sl 1, purl across. Rep last 2 rows until heel measures 2¼", end with a WS row.

Turn heel With MC, cont pat as established over 24 sts of first dpn: **Row 1** (RS) Work 14 sts, ssk, k1, turn. **Row 2** Sl 1, p5, p2tog, p1, turn. **Row 3** Sl 1, pat 6, ssk, k1, turn. **Row 4** Sl 1, p7, p2tog, p1, turn. Cont to dec in same way, working 1 st more between decs on each row until 14 sts rem, end with a RS row. Do not turn.

Gusset With empty dpn and MC, pick up and k 13 sts along side of heel and sl to first dpn; with 2nd dpn, cont pat across 24 sts of next 2 dpn; with 3rd dpn, pick up and k 13 sts along other side of heel, then k 7 heel sts—64 sts. Beg of rnd is at center of heel. **Rnd 1** On first dpn, k to last 2 sts, k2tog; cont pat across 2nd dpn; on 3rd dpn, ssk, k to end—62 sts. **Rnd 2** Work even, working pat st across 2nd dpn and using same color to k across first and 3rd dpn. Rep last 2 rnds until 48 sts rem.

Foot Work even until foot measures 5" or 2" less than desired length, end with 3rd rnd in A—12 sts each on first and 3rd dpn, 24 sts on 2nd dpn.

Toe Cont with MC as foll: **Rnd 1** On first dpn, cont pat to last 3 sts, k2tog, k1; on 2nd dpn, k1, ssk, cont pat to last 3 sts, k2tog, k1; on 3rd dpn, k1, ssk, cont pat to end. **Rnd 2** Work even. Rep last 2 rnds until 24 sts rem. Rep rnd 1 until 12 sts rem. K sts from first dpn to 3rd dpn. Cut yarn, leaving a 12" tail. Graft rem 6 sts from each dpn tog.

This rich zigzag pattern does not require you to work with more than one color at a time. A glance at the bottom of the foot reveals it to be a simple 4-row stripe sequence. It zigs by lengthening some stitches; it zags by working others into stitches two rows below.

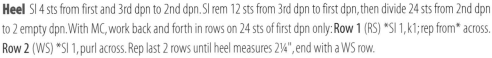

Size Woman's medium.

Materials A Worsted-weight yarn: 3½oz/100g (approx 230yds/210m) in bright red (MC); 1¾oz/50g each in dark red (A) and light red (B). **B** Set of 4 double-pointed needles (dpn) size 4 (3.5 mm), *or size to obtain gauge.*

Gauge 5½ sts to 1" (2.5cm) over False Flame Stitch pat, using size 4 (3.5mm) dpn.

Entrelac Socks

EXPERIENCED LEVEL

VICKIE STARBUCK
COLUMBUS, OHIO

"My goal was a sock knit in entrelac all the way from toe to cuff."

Note Recommended for knitters with experience knitting entrelac.

Triangle A (TA) (1-st dec) **Row 1** (RS) K2tog, k1, turn. **Row 2** Sl 1, p1, turn. **Row 3** Sl 1, k2, turn. **Row 4** Sl 1, p2, turn. **Row 5** Sl 1, k3, turn. **Row 6** Sl 1, p3, turn. **Row 7** Sl 1, k4.

Triangle B (TB) (2-st dec) **Row 1** K2tog, k1, turn. **Row 2** Sl 1, p1, turn. **Row 3** Sl 1, k2, turn. **Row 4** Sl 1, p2, turn. **Row 5** Sl 1, k2, k2tog, turn. **Row 6** Sl 1, p 3, turn. **Row 7** Sl 1, k4.

Right-leaning rectangle (RRT) With WS, pick up and p 4 sts down next triangle, p next st, turn. **Rows 1, 3, 5, 7** (RS) Sl 1, k4, turn. **Rows 2, 4, 6** (WS) Sl 1, p3, p2tog, turn. **Row 8** Sl 1, p3, p2tog.

Left-leaning rectangle (LRT) With RS, pick up and k 4 sts down next RRT, k next st, turn. **Rows 1, 3, 5, 7** (WS) Sl 1, p4, turn. **Rows 2, 4, 6** (RS) Sl 1, k3, ssk, turn. **Row 8** Sl 1, k3, ssk.

Left-leaning heel triangle (LHT) Pick up and k 4 sts down RRT, ssk; turn. **Row 1** (WS) Sl 1, p4, turn. **Row 2** Sl 1, k3, ssk, turn. **Row 3** Sl 1, p3, turn. **Row 4** Sl 1, k2, ssk, turn. **Row 5** Sl 1, p2, turn. **Row 6** Sl 1, k1, ssk.

Toe With MC, cast on 4 sts. Work 6 rows in St st. Do not turn. With first dpn, pick up and k 2 sts down left edge; with 2nd dpn, pick up and k 2 sts down left edge, then pick up and k 2 sts along cast on edge; with 3rd dpn pick up and k 2 sts along cast on edge, then 2 sts up right edge; with 3rd dpn, pick up and k 2 sts along right edge and sl onto first dpn. Do not turn—16 sts (8 sts on first dpn, 4 sts each on 2nd and 3rd dpn). Rnd starts at beg of first dpn. With A, work as foll: **Rnd 1** On first dpn, k2, M1, k4, M1, k2; on 2nd dpn, k2, M1, k2; on 3rd dpn, k2, M1, k2—20 sts. **Rnd 2** On first dpn, k3, M1, k5, M1, k2; on 2nd dpn, k3, M1, k2; on 3rd dpn, k3, M1, k2—24 sts. In same way, cont to inc 4 sts, equally spaced, every rnd until there are 44 sts. Inc every other rnd until there are 64 sts. K 10 rnds.

Foot Sl 13 sts from beg of first dpn to end of 3rd dpn; sl 3 sts from beg of 3rd dpn to end of 2nd dpn—19 sts each on first and 2nd dpns, 26 sts on 3rd dpn. **Establish base: Rnd 1** *Work [TA, TB] twice, work TA once; rep from* once, turn. Sl 1, p4—50 sts (10 triangles, each with 5 sts). **Rnd 2** Work 10 RRT; turn. Sl 1, k4. **Rnd 3** Work 10 LRT; turn. Sl 1, p4. Rep last 2 rnds 5 times more, then work rnd 2 once.

Heel Work 5 LHT (25 sts); place rem sts on hold, turn. Join A and p25 sts just worked and inc 7 sts evenly across—32 sts. Turn. With scrap yarn, chain cast-on 32 sts. Rearrange sts as foll: Sl 32 heel sts to first dpn; sl 16 cast-on sts to 2nd dpn and rem 16 cast-on sts to 3rd dpn—64 sts. K 9 rnds. **Next rnd** On first dpn, k1, ssk, k to last 3 sts, k2tog, k1; on 2nd dpn, k1, ssk, k to end; on 3rd dpn, k to last 3 sts, k2tog k1—60 sts. **Next rnd** Knit. Rep last 2 rnds until 44 sts rem, then dec every rnd until 20 sts rem. Work back and forth in rows as foll: K2, turn. Cont with A as foll: **Next row** (WS) Sl 1, p2, p2tog, turn. **Next row** (RS) Sl 1, k2, k2tog, turn. Rep last 2 rows until 8 sts rem. Cut yarn, leaving a 10" tail. Graft last 4 sts worked with rem (unworked) 4 sts.

Leg With MC, pick up and k 32 sts from chain cast-on (open chain st-by-st and pick up loops). **Next rnd** On first dpn, work [TA, TB] twice, then TA once, turn. Sl 1, p4—25 sts. Sl 15 sts from holder to 2nd dpn and rem 10 sts from holder to 3rd dpn—50 sts total. **Next rnd** Work 10 RRT; turn, sl 1, k4. **Next rnd** Work 10 LRT; turn, sl 1, p4. Rep last 2 rnds 7 times more, then work first rnd once. Work 1 rnd LLT as for heel to end leg. **Next rnd** K and inc 14 sts evenly across—64 sts. Work 2½" in k2, p2 rib, then work 3 rnds in k1, p1 rib. Bind off, using tubular bind-off technique.

Size Woman's medium.

Materials **A** Sport-weight yarn: 3½oz/100g (approx 350yds/319m) in variegated (MC); 1¾oz/50g in lilac (A). Scrap yarn. **B** Set of 4 double-pointed needles (dpn) size 0 (2mm) *or size to obtain gauge.*

Gauge 9 sts to 1" (2.5cm) over St st using size 0 (2mm) dpn. Entrelac squares measure ½" from side to side.

Harry's Socks

EXPERIENCED LEVEL

VICKIE STARBUCK

COLUMBUS, OHIO

Right Sock

Toe **With A, cast on 6 sts. Work 9 rows in St st. Do not turn. With first dpn, pick up and k 2 sts down left edge; with 2nd dpn, pick up and k 2 sts down left edge, then pick up and k 3 sts along cast-on edge; with 3rd dpn pick up and k 3 sts along cast on-edge and 2 sts up right edge, then pick up and k 2 sts along right edge and sl to first dpn. Do not turn— 20 sts (10 sts on first dpn, 5 sts each on 2nd and 3rd dpns). Rnd starts at beg of first dpn. **Rnd 1** On first dpn, k2, M1, k6, M1, k2; on 2nd dpn, k2, M1, k3; on 3rd dpn, k3, M1, k2—24 sts. **Rnd 2** On first dpn, k3, M1, k6, M1, k3; on 2nd dpn, k3, M1, k3; on 3rd dpn, k3, M1, k3—28 sts. **Rnd 3** On first dpn, k4, M1, k6, M1, k4; on 2nd dpn, k4, M1, k3; on 3rd dpn, k3, M1, k4—32 sts. In same way, cont to inc until there are 44 sts.**

Next rnd On first dpn, k8, M1, k6, M1, k to end of rnd—46 sts. Work 1 rnd even. **Next rnd** On first dpn, k9, M1, k6, M1, k to end of rnd—48 sts. In same way, cont to inc every other rnd until there are 60 sts. Work 1 rnd even.

Foot Work 21 rnds of Chart A around for 5½" (end with rnd 8, 9, or 10). **Next rnd** On first dpn, cont pat across 19 sts, join scrap yarn and k to end of dpn; on 2nd dpn, k 11 sts in scrap yarn; on 3rd dpn, cont chart pat across—30 sts worked on scrap yarn and 30 sts in chart pat.

Leg **Next rnd** Cont chart pat over 60 sts for approx 2½", end with chart rnd 16, 17, or 18. Cont with variegated yarn only and work 6" in k2, p2 rib, then work 1 rnd in k1, p1 rib. In k1, p1 rib, work 2 rnds with B, then 1 rnd with A. With A, bind off using tubular bind-off technique.

Heel With A, pick up and k 30 sts above scrap yarn and 30 sts below scrap yarn—60 sts. Carefully remove scrap yarn and rearrange sts as foll: 30 sts on first dpn from foot; 15 sts each (from leg) on 2nd and 3rd dpns. **Next rnd** On first dpn, pick up and k 1 st, k30, pick up and k 1 st; on 2nd dpn, pick up and k 1 st, k15; on 3rd dpn, k15, pick up and k 1 st—64 sts. **Next rnd** On first dpn, k2tog, k to last 2 sts, ssk; on 2nd dpn, k2tog, k to end; on 3rd dpn, k to last 2 sts, ssk—60 sts. K 1 rnd even. Work Socks chart rnds 1–5, beg with st 15. With A, k 3 rnds. Cont with A as foll: **Next (dec) rnd** On first dpn, k1, ssk, k to last 3 sts, k2tog, k1; on 2nd dpn, k1, ssk, k to end; on 3rd dpn, k to last 3 sts, k2tog, k1—56 sts. **Next rnd** Knit. Rep last 2 rnds until 44 sts rem, then dec every rnd until 20 sts rem. Work back and forth in rows as foll: K2, turn. **Next row** (WS) Sl 1, p2, p2 tog, turn. **Next row** Sl 1, k2, k2tog, turn. Rep last 2 rows until 8 sts rem. Cut yarn, leaving a 10" tail. Graft last 4 sts worked with rem (unworked) 4 sts.

Left Sock

Work as for Right Sock from ** to **. **Next rnd** K across first dpn; on 2nd dpn, k8, M1, k3; on 3rd dpn, k3, M1, k around—46 sts. Work 1 rnd even. **Next rnd** K across first dpn; on 2nd dpn, k9, M1, k3; on 3rd dpn, k3, M1, k around—48 sts. Cont to inc every other rnd until there are 60 sts. Work 1 rnd even. Cont as for Right Sock, taking care to place 2nd half of sts from first dpn on waste yarn for heel.

Chart A

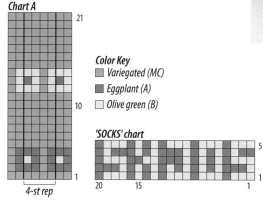

21

10

1

4-st rep

Color Key
- Variegated (MC)
- Eggplant (A)
- Olive green (B)

'SOCKS' chart

5

1

20   15   1

Size Men's medium.

Materials **A** Sport-weight yarn: 3½oz/100g (approx 350yds/319m) in variegated (MC); 1¾oz/50g each in eggplant (A) and olive green (B). Scrap yarn. **B** Set of 4 double-pointed needles (dpn) size 2 (3mm) *or size to obtain gauge.* **Gauge** 7 sts to 1" (2.5cm) over Chart A using size 2 (3mm) dpn.

Best Of Show Socks

DEBBIE DRECHSLER

EXPERIENCED LEVEL

SANTA ROSA, CALIFORNIA

"My inspiration came from an Anatolian sock on page 26 of Priscilla Gibson-Roberts' Ethnic Socks and Stockings. I wanted to try carrying three yarns. Until I found the new rhythm, I hated it. I was also interested in using the design to achieve shaping. "

Leg With one strand each of A and B held tog, cast on 96 sts and divide evenly over 3 dpn. Place marker, join and work 9 rnds in k1, p1 rib as foll: k1 A, p1 B. With B, k 1 rnd. Work 17 rnds of Chart A. With B, k 1 rnd. With A, k 1 rnd and dec 1 st on 3rd dpn—95 sts. Work 12 rnds of Chart B once, then rep rnds 1-5. **Next rnd** Work chart rnd 6 and dec 10 sts by k sts 2 and 3 and sts 9 and 10 tog every rep—85 sts. Work 12 rnds of Chart C twice.

Heel Sl 7 sts from first dpn and 6 sts from 3rd dpn to 2nd dpn. Sl rem 22 sts from 3rd dpn to first dpn. Divide 42 sts from 2nd dpn onto 2 empty dpn for instep. Work back and forth in rows on 43 sts of first dpn only: **Row 1** (RS) Work row 1 of Chart D across, end k1 A. **Row 2** P1 A, work row 2 of Chart D across. Work through chart row 5. **Beg stripe pat: Next row** (RS) K1 A; *k1 C, k1 A; rep from* across. **Next row** P1 A; *p1 C, p1 A; rep from* across. Rep last 2 rows until heel measures 2½", end with a WS row.

Turn heel Cont in 2-color stripe pat as established over 43 sts of first dpn: **Row 1** (RS) Work 25 sts, ssk, k1, turn. **Row 2** Sl 1, work 8 sts, p2tog, p1, turn. **Row 3** Sl 1, work 9 sts, ssk, k1, turn. **Row 4** Sl 1, work 10 sts, p2tog, p1, turn. Cont to dec in same way, working 1 st more between decs on each row until 25 sts rem, end with a RS row. Do not turn.

Gusset With empty dpn and C, pick up and k 18 sts along side of heel and sl to first dpn; with 2nd dpn, work rnd 1 of Chart C across 42 sts from next 2 dpn; with 3rd dpn, pick up and k 18 sts along other side of heel, then k 13 heel sts—103 sts. Beg of rnd is at center of heel. **Next rnd** On first dpn, work rnd 2 of Chart C over 21 sts, [k1 A, k1 B] 4 times, k1 A; on 2nd dpn, work rnd 2 of Chart C; on 3rd dpn, [k1 A, k1 C] 4 times, k1 A; work rnd 2 of Chart C (beg with st 13 of chart) to end. **Next rnd** On first dpn, work rnd 3 of Chart C for 21 sts, [k1 A, k1 B] 3 times, k1 A, k2tog A; on 2nd dpn, work rnd 3 of Chart C; on 3rd dpn, ssk A, [k1 A, k1 C] 3 times, k1 A; work rnd 3 of Chart C (beg with st 13 of chart) to end—101 sts. **Next rnd** Work 1 rnd even in pats as established. In same way, dec 2 sts every other rnd until all 9 sts of striped pat are used up—85 sts.

Foot Cont Chart C until foot is 2" less than desired length, end with rnd 6 or 12.

Toe **Rnd 1** Work Chart D around and dec 1 st—84 sts. Work through rnd 5 of Chart D. **Next rnd** Work striped pat: *K1 A, k1 C; rep from* across around. **Next rnd** On first dpn, work striped pat to last 3 sts, k2tog, k1; on 2nd dpn, k1, ssk, work striped pat to last 3 sts, k2tog, k1; on 3rd dpn, k1, ssk, work pat to end—80 sts. **Next rnd** Work even. Rep last 2 rnds until 28 sts rem. K sts from first dpn to 3rd dpn. Graft rem 14 sts from each dpn tog.

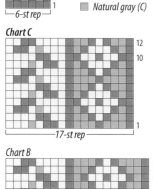

Chart D

Color Key
- ■ Natural black (A)
- □ Natural white (B)
- ▨ Natural gray (C)

6-st rep

Chart C

17-st rep

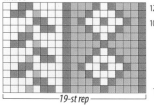

Chart B

19-st rep

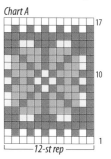

Chart A

12-st rep

Size Woman's medium.

Materials A Fingering-weight yarn: 1¾oz/50g (approx 220yds/201m) each in natural black (A), white (B), and gray (C). **B** Set of 4 double-pointed needles (dpn) size 0 (2mm) *or size to obtain gauge.*

Gauge 10 sts to 1" (2.5cm) over Chart pat using size 0 (2.mm) dpn.

Wedgwood Socks

INTERMEDIATE LEVEL

MARY KAISER

BIRMINGHAM, ALABAMA

"This sock is based on a 1789 Wedgwood 'coffee can' (a straight-sided coffee cup) in the collection of the Birmingham Art Museum. I was intrigued by its unusual green and violet color scheme, and its precise grid pattern reminded me of a Faroese pattern."

Note If you prefer, use a provisional cast-on for leg and after working Chart A, with MC k 3 rnds, fold hem, and on next rnd, k each st tog with a st from cast-on.

Leg With MC, cast on 80 sts and divide over 3 dpn: 26 sts on first and 3rd dpn, 28 sts on 2nd dpn. Place marker, join and k 9 rnds. **Rnd 10 (picot rnd)** *K2tog, yo; rep from* around. K 2 rnds. Work 5 rnds of Chart A. With MC, k 4 rnds. Work 16 rnds of Chart B a total of 3 times, then rep rnds 1–3 once.

Heel Sl 7 sts from first and 6 sts from 3rd dpn to 2nd dpn. Sl rem 20 sts from 3rd dpn to first dpn. Divide 41 sts from 2nd dpn onto 2 empty dpn. Work back and forth in rows on 39 sts of first dpn only: **Row 1** (RS) Sl 1, k2; [p1, k3] 9 times. **Row 2** Sl 1, p2; [k1, p3] 9 times. Rep last 2 rows until heel measures 2¼", end with a WS row.

Turn heel Cont on 39 sts of first dpn: **Row 1** (RS) K 26, ssk; turn. **Row 2** Sl 1, p13, p2tog; turn. **Row 3** Sl 1, k13, ssk; turn. **Row 4** Sl 1, p13, p2tog; turn. Cont to dec in same way, working 1 more st between decs on each row until 15 sts rem, end with a RS row. Do not turn.

Gusset With empty dpn and MC, pick up and k 13 sts along side of heel, plus 1 more st into st below first st on next dpn; sl 41 sts of next 2 dpn onto one dpn and with 2nd dpn k across; with 3rd dpn, pick up and k 1 into st below last st on dpn just worked, then pick up and k 13 sts along other side of heel and k 15 heel sts—84 sts. Beg of rnd is at side of heel. **Next rnd** On first dpn, k to last 2 sts, k2tog; on 2nd dpn, k2, [work 8-st rep of rnd 5 of chart B] 4 times, then sts 1–5 once, k2 MC; on 3rd dpn, ssk, k to end—82 sts. **Next rnd** On first dpn, [work 4-st rep of rnd 6 of Chart C] twice, k5 MC; cont Chart B across 2nd dpn; on 3rd needle, k4 MC, [work 4-st rep of rnd 6 of Chart C] 6 times. **Next rnd** On first dpn, work pat to last 4 sts, k2tog, k2; cont pat across 2nd dpn; on 3rd dpn, k2, ssk, cont pat to end—80 sts. **Next rnd** Work even. Rep last 2 rnds twice more—76 sts.

Foot Work even in pat until foot is 3" less than desired length, end with rnd 3 or 11. With MC, k 4 rnds and dec 4 sts evenly in 4th rnd—72 sts. Work 5 rnds of Chart A. With MC, k 1 rnd.

Toe **Next rnd** *K6, k2tog; rep from* around. K 6 rnds. **Next rnd** *K5, k2tog; rep from* around. K 5 rnds even. Cont to dec as established, working 1 rnd less after every dec rnd, until 9 sts rem. Cut yarn, leaving a 6" tail. Draw tail through rem sts, pull tog tightly and secure. Fold hem at picot row and tack to WS.

Chart A

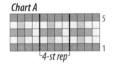

4-st rep

Chart B

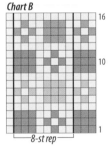

8-st rep

Chart C

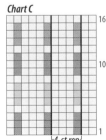

4-st rep

Color Key
- ☐ Cream (MC)
- ☐ Lavender (A)
- ☐ Mauve (B)
- ☐ Green (C)

Size Adult's medium.

Materials A Sport-weight yarn: 3½oz/100g (330yds/301m) in cream (MC); 1¾oz/50g each in lavender (A), mauve (B), green (C). **B** Set of 4 double-pointed needles (dpn) size 0 (2mm) or size to obtain gauge.

Gauge 9 sts to 1" (2.5cm) over Chart B pat using size 0 (2mm) dpn..

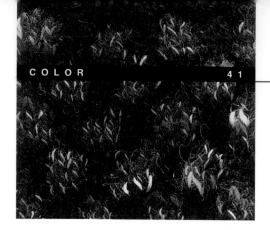

Stained Glass Bubble Socks

NANCY ERLANDSON

INTERMEDIATE LEVEL

EAST HAMPTON, CONNECTICUT

What looks like a complicated color pattern on the leg of this sock is really a slip stitch pattern that uses only a single color each round.
On four of every six rounds the bubbles are knit in contrast color and the black stitches are slipped. This causes the black lines to curve and the bubbles to pouf.
The effect is enhanced when the contrast yarn is textured, and it can even be a bit heavier than the black yarn.

Bubble Pat *(*Multiple of 6 sts) Slip all sts purlwise with yarn in back (wyib). **Rnds 1–2** With MC, knit. **Rnds 3–6** With CC, *k4, sl 2; rep from*. **Rnds 7–8** With MC, knit. **Rnds 9–12** With CC, k1, *sl 2, k4; rep from*, end sl 2, k3.

Leg With smaller needle and MC, cast on 48 sts and divide evenly over 3 dpn. Place marker, join and work 2" in k2, p2 rib. Change to larger needles and rep Rnds 1–12 of Bubble Pat until sock meas 8" from beg, end with rnd 2 or 8.

16 ╳ 16 / 16

Heel With larger dpn and MC, k first 12 sts onto first dpn, sl next 12 sts to 2nd dpn, next 12 sts to 3rd dpn, and last 12 sts to first dpn. Work back and forth in rows on 24 sts first dpn: **Row 1** (WS) Sl 1, p to end. **Row 2** *Sl 1, k1; rep from*. Rep last 2 rows 11 times more.

12 ╳ 12 / 24

Turn heel Cont on 24 sts of first dpn: **Row 1** (WS) Sl 1, p14, p2tog, p1, turn. **Row 2** Sl 1, k7, ssk, k1, turn. **Row 3** Sl 1, p8, p2tog, p1, turn. **Row 4** Sl 1, k9, ssk, k1, turn. Cont to dec in same way, working 1 more st between decs on each row until 16 sts rem, end with a RS row. Do not turn.

Gusset With empty dpn, pick up and k 12 sts along side of heel and sl to first dpn. With 2nd dpn, k 24 sts from next 2 dpn, then with 3rd dpn, pick up and k 12 sts along right side of heel, then k 8 rem heel sts—64 sts. Beg of rnd is at center of heel. **Rnd 1** Knit. **Rnd 2** On first dpn, k to last 3 sts, k2tog, k1; k across 2nd dpn; on 3rd dpn, k1, ssk, k to end—62 sts. Rep Rnds 1–2 until 48 sts rem.

24 / 20 ╲╱ 20

Foot Work even until foot is 2" less than desired length.

Toe Change to smaller needles and CC. **Rnd 1** On first dpn, k to last 3 sts, k2tog, k1; on 2nd dpn, k1, ssk, k to last 3 sts, k2tog, k1; on 3rd dpn, k1, ssk, k to end—4 sts dec. **Rnd 2** Knit. Rep Rnds 1–2 until 16 sts rem. K 4 sts from first dpn to 3rd dpn. Cut yarn, leaving a 20" tail. Graft rem 8 sts from each dpn tog.

24 / 12 ╲╱ 12

Size Woman's large, man's medium. Foot, from heel to toe, measures 10".

Materials A 3oz/85g (approx 240yds/219m) DK-weight yarn in black (MC). **B** 1¾oz/50g multi-colored novelty yarn of same or slightly heavier weight (CC). **C** Set of 4 double-pointed needles (dpn) size 4 and 5 (3.5mm and 3.75mm), *or size to obtain gauge.*

Gauge 5½ sts equal 1" (2.5cm) in MC over St st using size 5 (3.75mm) dpn.

Tile Socks

KATHY L. FRANTZ

BOULDER, COLORADO

INTERMEDIATE LEVEL

Leg With B, cast on 48 (56) stitches and divide evenly over 3 dpn. Place marker, join and work 2" in k2, p2 rib. With A, k 2 rnds. With A and B, work rnds 1–15 of Leg pat, and for size large only, inc 2 sts each on rnds 8 and 9—48 (60) sts. Change to larger dpn if necessary to maintain gauge when working checkerboard pat. Rep rnds 10–15 until sock measures 7½" from beg or to desired length of leg, end with rnd 12 or 15. With B, k 2 rnds and for size large only, dec 2 sts on each rnd—48 (56) sts.

Heel With B, k12 (14) sts on first dpn, sl next 12 (14) sts to 2nd dpn, sl next 12 (14) sts to 3rd dpn, then sl rem 12 (14) sts to first dpn. If desired, add reinforcing thread and/or change to smaller dpn. Work back and forth in rows on 24 (28) sts of first dpn only: **Row 1** (WS) Sl 1, purl across. **Row 2** *Sl 1, k1; rep from*. Rep last 2 rows 11 (13) times more.

Turn heel Cont on 24 (28) sts: **Row 1** (WS) P14 (16) sts, p2tog, p1, turn. **Row 2** Sl 1, k5, ssk, k1, turn. **Row 3** Sl 1, p6, p2tog, p1, turn. **Row 4** Sl 1, k7, ssk, k1, turn. Cont to dec in same way, working 1 more st between decs on each row until 14 (16) sts rem, end with a RS row. Cut reinforcing thread. Do not turn.

Gusset With empty dpn and A, pick up and k12 (14) sts along left side of heel and sl to first dpn; with 2nd dpn, k24 (28) sts from next 2 dpn; with 3rd dpn, pick up and k12 (14) sts along right side of heel, then k7 (8) rem heel sts—62 (72) sts. Beg of rnd is at center of heel. **Rnd 1** On first dpn, k to last 3 sts, k2tog, k1; k across 2nd dpn; on 3rd dpn, k1, ssk, k to end—60 (70) sts. **Rnd 2** Knit. Rep rnds 1–2 until 48 (56) sts rem.

One of the surprises of color pattern knitting is what happens when the chart grids take on the shape of knit stitches. The result can be quite fortuitous—check out the great little fleur-de-lis at the top of the leg.

Leg Pat

15
13
11
9
7
5
3
1

12-st rep

Toe Pat

18
17
15
13
11
9
7
5
3
1

4-st rep

☐ A   ▦ B

Foot Work even with A until foot is 4½" shorter than desired length. Work rnds 1–18 of Toe pat.

Toe Change to B. Add reinforcing thread and/or change to smaller dpn. **Rnd 1** On first dpn, k to last 3 sts, k2tog, k1; on 2nd dpn, k1, ssk, k to last 3 sts, k2tog, k1; on 3rd dpn, k1, ssk, k to end. **Rnd 2** Knit. Rep rnds 1–2 until 20 sts rem. K 5 sts of first dpn onto 3rd dpn. Cut yarn, leaving an 18" tail. Graft rem 10 sts from each dpn tog.

Size Adult small (large).

Materials **A** 1¾oz/50g (approx 175 yds/160m) sport-weight wool each in ivory (A) and black (B). **B** Set of 4 double-pointed needles (dpn) in size 4 (3.5mm) *or size to obtain gauge.* **C** Optional: size 5 (3.75mm) dpn if necessary to obtain gauge in color pat.

Gauge 6½ sts to 1" (2.5cm) over St st using size 4 (3.5mm) dpn.

Bob's Socks

EXPERIENCED LEVEL

CHARLENE ABRAMS
ST LOUIS, MISSOURI

With corrugated ribbing, fairisle patterning, plain bands, and pinstriped toe and heel, this sock is almost a colorwork sampler. "I used eight colors, divided into two groups: reds to yellows and blues to greens. Order each group from lightest to darkest or however it pleases you."
And Bob? Charlene made socks to thank him for mowing her lawn. When asked if he'd prefer wild or conservative socks, he said, "Wild!"

Leg With A, cast on 88 sts and divide over 3 dpn as foll: 29 sts each to first and 3rd dpns, 30 sts to 2nd dpn. Place marker, join, and work 1 rnd in k2, p2 rib. Using first color for k sts and 2nd color for p sts, work 4 rnds each in corrugated rib as foll: A and B; C and D; E and F; G and H; E and F; C and D; A and B.
Working 8-st rep around in colors as indicated, work 64 rnds of chart pat

Heel Sl next 44 sts to first dpn, next 22 sts to 2nd dpn, and next 22 sts to 3rd dpn. Work back and forth in rows on 44 sts of first dpn only: **Row 1** (RS) *Sl 1, k1 E; rep from* across. **Row 2** Sl 1, *p1 F, p1 E; rep from*, end p1 F. **Row 3** *Sl 1, k1 E; rep from* across, carrying F on WS by weaving in every other st. **Row 4** Rep row 2. Rep rows 3–4 until a total of 40 rows have been worked.

Turn heel Cont 2-color work as established over 44 sts of first dpn: **Row 1** (RS) Work 24 sts, ssk, k1, turn. **Row 2** Sl 1, p5, p2tog, p1, turn. **Row 3** Sl 1, pat 6, ssk, k1, turn. **Row 4** Sl 1, p7, p2tog, p1, turn. Cont to dec in same way, working 1 st more between decs on each row until 24 sts rem, end with a RS row. Do not turn.

Gusset With empty dpn and A, pick up and k 21 sts along side of heel and sl to first dpn; with 2nd dpn, k 44 sts from next 2 dpn; with 3rd dpn pick up and k 21 sts along other side of heel, then k 12 heel sts—110 sts. Beg of rnd is now at center of heel. **Next rnd** Knit. **Next rnd** On first dpn, k to last 2 sts, k2tog; k across 2nd dpn; on 3rd dpn, ssk, k to end—108 sts. Rep last 2 rnds once more. In same way, work 5 rnds each in B, C, D, E, then F, AT SAME TIME, cont to dec 2 sts every other rnd until 80 sts rem.

Foot Work even in colors as foll: 5 rnds each G, H, G, F, E, D, C.

Toe Sl 2 sts from beg of 2nd dpn to first dpn. Sl 2 sts from end of 2nd dpn to 3rd dpn—20 sts each on first and 3rd dpn, 40 sts on 2nd dpn. **Rnd 1** *K1 B, k1 A; rep from* around. **Rnd 2** Work colors as established: on first dpn, work to last 3 sts, k2tog, k1; on 2nd dpn, k1, ssk, work to last 3 sts, k2tog, k1; on 3rd dpn, k1, ssk, work to end. Rep last 2 rnds until 32 sts rem. K sts from first dpn to 3rd dpn. Graft rem 16 sts on each dpn tog.

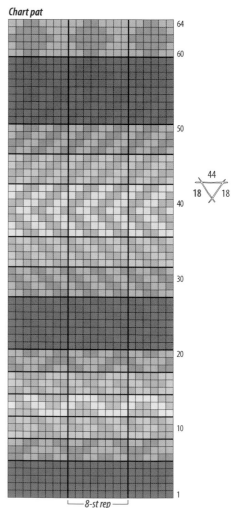

Chart pat

64
60
50
40
30
20
10
1

8-st rep

Size Man's medium.

Materials **A** Sock-weight yarn: 1oz/30g (approx 125yds/114m) each in navy (A), red (B), teal (C), orange (D), med. green (E), gold (F), blue (G), lt. yellow (H). **B** Set of 4 double-pointed needles (dpn) size 1 (2.25mm), *or size to obtain gauge.*

Gauge 10 sts to 1" (2.5cm) over Chart pat using size 1 (2.25mm) dpn.

■ Navy (A)   ■ Teal (C)   ■ Med. green (E)   ■ Blue (G)
■ Red (B)   ■ Orange (D)   ■ Gold (F)   □ Lt. yellow (H)

Salsa Socks

INTERMEDIATE LEVEL

ANN CARLILE

SALT LAKE CITY, UTAH

Leg With A, cast on 56 sts and divide over 3 dpn as foll: 16 sts each to first and 3rd dpn, 24 sts to 2nd dpn. Place marker, join and with B, k 1 rnd, then work 1 rnd in k2, p2 rib. With A, k 1 rnd, then work 10 rnds in k2, p2 rib as established. Working 8-st rep around, work 40 rnds of chart 1.

Heel Sl 2 sts each from first and 3rd dpn to 2nd dpn. With E, k across 14 sts from first dpn, sl sts from 3rd dpn to beg of first dpn. Divide rem 28 sts from 2nd dpn onto 2 dpn. Work back and forth in rows on 28 sts of first dpn as foll: Turn and with E, p 1 row. **Row 1** (RS) *Sl 1 knitwise, k1; rep from*. **Row 2** Sl 1, p across. Rep last 2 rows 13 times more.

Turn heel Cont to work on 28 sts of first dpn only: **Row 1** (RS) K16, ssk, k1, turn. **Row 2** Sl 1, p5, p2tog, p1, turn. **Row 3** Sl 1, k6, ssk, k1, turn. **Row 4** Sl 1, p7, p2tog, p1, turn. Cont to dec in same way, working 1 st more between decs on each row until 16 sts rem, end with a RS row. Do not turn.

Gusset With empty dpn and E, pick up and k 14 sts along side of heel and sl to first dpn; with 2nd dpn, k across 28 sts from next 2 dpn; with 3rd dpn, pick up and k 14 sts along other side of heel, then k 8 heel sts—72 sts. Beg of rnd is at center of heel. **Next rnd** With E, on first dpn, k to last 3 sts, k2tog, k1; k across 2nd dpn; on 3rd dpn, k1, ssk, k to end—70 sts. **Next rnd** On first dpn, k1 C; [k2 A, k2 C] 4 times; k3 A, k1 C; on 2nd dpn, k1 C, [k2 A, k2 C] 6 times, k2 A, k1 C; on 3rd dpn, k1 C, k3 A; [k2 C, k2 A] 4 times; k1 C. **Next rnd** Cont pat across first dpn to last 3 sts, k2tog A, k1 C; work pat across 2nd dpn; on 3rd dpn, k1 C, ssk A, cont pat around—68 sts. **Next rnd** Alternate A and C and work pat around. **Next rnd** On first dpn, work pat to last 3 sts, k2tog C, k1 A; work pat across 2nd needle; on 3rd dpn, k1 A, ssk C, cont pat around—66 sts. **Next rnd** On first dpn, k1 C; [k2 A, k2 C] 3 times; k3 A, k3 C; on 2nd dpn, k1 C, [k2 A, k2 C] 6 times, k2 A, k1 C; on 3rd dpn, k3 C, k3 A, [k2 C, k2 A]

3 times; k1 C. **Next rnd** On first dpn, work in pat to last 3 sts, k2tog C, k1 C; work pat across 2nd dpn; on 3rd dpn, k2 C, ssk C, cont pat around—64 sts. Working in colors as established, cont to dec 2 sts every other rnd twice more—60 sts. (16 sts each on first and 3rd needle; 28 sts on 2nd needle)

Foot Work 2 rnds even. Work 19 rnds of Chart 2. **Next rnd** With E, k and dec 4 sts evenly around—56 sts. Work 9 rnds of Chart 3. With E, k 2 rnds and dec 2 sts evenly in last rnd—54 sts.

Toe **Rnd 1** [K9 B, k9 C] 3 times. **Rnd 2** [Ssk B, k7; ssk C, k7] 3 times—48 sts. **Rnds 3, 5** Work even. **Rnd 4** [Ssk B, k6; ssk C, k6] 3 times—42 sts. Cont to dec 6 sts every other rnd as established twice more, then every rnd until 6 sts rem. Cut yarn, leaving a 6" tail. Draw tail through rem sts, pull tog and secure.

"Socks have long been a favorite project of mine. These socks were designed on the needles as I knit. Peruvian textiles intrigue me, so I am not surprised that this design found its way out of my subconscious."

Color emphasizes structure on the toes of these spicy socks. The stitches are divided into six segments, alternately knit in gold and purple.

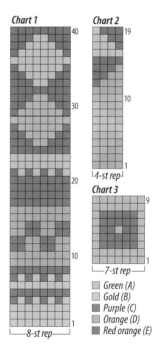

Chart 1 40 30 20 10 1 8-st rep

Chart 2 19 10 1 4-st rep

Chart 3 9 10 1 7-st rep

- Green (A)
- Gold (B)
- Purple (C)
- Orange (D)
- Red orange (E)

Size Medium woman's.

Materials **A** 1oz/28g sock-weight yarn (approx 100yds/91m) each in green (A), gold (B), purple (C), orange (D), red orange (E). **B** Set of 4 double-pointed needles (dpn) size 2 (2.75 mm), *or size to obtain gauge*.

Gauge 7 sts to 1" (2.5cm) over Chart pat using size 2 (2.75mm) dpn.

Chapter 5   Texture

9 PROJECTS

Ripple Socks **66**

The Ultimate Refootable Sock **67**

Austrian-Patterned Knee Socks **68**

Butterfly Bows **70**

Slouch Socks **71**

Dye-Your-Own Socks **72**

66   67   68   70

Aran Sandal Socks **74**

Ribble Socks **75**

Sideways Sox Supreme **76**

72

74

71

75

76

Texture Socks

Ripple Socks

EASY LEVEL

NADINE STEWART

NEW YORK, NEW YORK

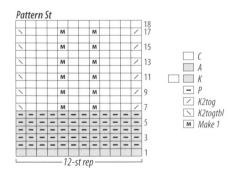

"Living in New York has changed the way I look at everything. I'm always on the lookout for a color combination that's just a bit offbeat or a texture that isn't like any other."

These socks show what can be done with a really simple 2-row pattern. On the cuff 12 rows of ripple alternate with reverse stockinette stitch welts in contrast color. On the foot, ripples with no welts continue on the top of the foot, changing to stockinette on the bottom of the foot.

Pattern St

												18
\			M		M					/		17
\			M		M					/		15
\			M		M					/		13
\			M		M					/		11
\			M		M					/		9
\			M		M					/		7
												5
												3
												1

— 12-st rep —

- ☐ C
- ☐ A
- ☐ K
- − P
- ◢ K2tog
- ◣ K2togtbl
- M Make 1

Size Woman's large.

Materials **A** Sock-weight yarn: 3½oz/100g (430yds/392m) in olive (A); small amount purple (B) for heel and toe; 1¾oz/50g (215yds/196m) multicolor (C). **B** Set of 4 double-pointed needles (dpn) size 2 (2.75mm) *or size needed to obtain gauge.*

Gauge 8 sts to 1" (2.5cm) over St st using size 2 (2.75mm) dpn.

Pattern Stitch Rnd 1 With A, knit. Rnds 2–6 With A, purl. Rnd 7 With C, *k2 tog, k3, M1, k2, M1, k3, k2tog through the back loop (tbl); rep from*. Rnd 8 Knit. Rnds 9–18 Rep Rnds 7 and 8. Rep Rnds 1–18 for pat.

Leg With A, cast on 84 sts and divide over 3 dpn. Place marker, join, and work 2" in k2, p2 rib. Work 5 reps of Pat st, then work Pat rnds 1–6. Fasten off.

Heel Sl next 19 sts onto first dpn, next 23 sts to 2nd dpn, next 23 sts to 3rd dpn, and next 19 sts to first dpn. Work back and forth in rows on 38 sts of first dpn only: Join B. Row 1 (RS) Sl 1, k across. Row 2 (WS) Sl 1, k5, *sl 1, p1; rep from* to last 6 sts, k6. Rep last 2 rows 20 times more.

Turn heel Cont on 38 sts: Row 1 (RS) Sl 1, k19, ssk, k1, turn. Row 2 Sl 1, p4, p2tog, p1, turn. Row 3 Sl 1, k5, ssk, k1, turn. Row 4 Sl 1, p6, p2tog, p1, turn. Cont to dec in same way, working 1 more st between decs on each row until 20 sts rem, end with a WS row. Join C and k 1 row. Do not turn.

Gusset With empty dpn, pick up and k 21 sts along side of heel and sl to first dpn. With 2nd dpn, k 46 sts of next 2 dpn. With 3rd dpn, pick up and k 21 sts along other side of heel flap, k 10 heel sts—108 sts. Beg of rnd is now at center of heel. **Rnd 1** On first dpn, k to last 2 sts, k2tog; on 2nd dpn k5, work Pat st rnd 7 over next 36 sts, k5; on 3rd dpn, ssk, k to end—2 sts dec. **Rnd 2** Work even in St st and Pat st rnd 8. Rep rnds 1 and 2 until 84 sts rem, working in col sequence as foll: 14 rows A, 4 rows C.

Foot Work even in pats as established until piece measures 2½" less than desired foot measurement (approx 3½" more), end with 4 rows C. Fasten off C, join B.

Toe Sl first 2 and last 2 sts of 2nd dpn onto first and 3rd dpn—21 sts on first dpn, 42 sts on 2nd dpn, 21 sts on 3rd dpn. **Rnd 1** On first dpn, k to last 3 sts, k2tog, k1; on 2nd dpn, k1, ssk, k to last 3 sts, k2tog, k1; on 3rd dpn, k1, ssk, k to end—4 sts dec. **Rnd 2** Knit. Rep rnds 1 and 2 until 24 sts rem. **Next rnd** K 6 sts from first dpn to 3rd dpn. Graft rem 12 sts from each dpn tog.

The Ultimate Refootable Sock

DEZ CRAWFORD

INTERMEDIATE LEVEL

BATON ROUGE, LOUISIANA

Abbreviations **Right Twist (RT)** Working in front of first st, k 2nd st on LH needle, k first st, sl both sts off needle.

Pattern Stitch Rnd 1 K1, *p2, RT; rep from* around, working last RT over first and last st of rnd. **Rnds 2–4** Work in k2, p2 rib as established. Rep rnds 1–4 for pat.

Leg Loosely cast on 60 sts and divide evenly over 3 dpn. Place marker, join and work 2″ in k2, p2 rib, beg and end with k1. Work in pat st until piece measures approx 8″ from beg, end with rnd 2.

Instep Sl next 30 sts to first dpn, next 15 sts to 2nd dpn, and next 15 sts to 3rd dpn. Working back and forth in rows and sl first st of each row, cont pat across 30 sts of first dpn only until piece measures approx 7″ or 2½″ less than desired foot measurement. Put sts on hold by placing point protectors each side of dpn.

Heel Sl 30 heel sts on hold to one dpn and work back and forth in rows: **Row 1** (RS) *Sl, k1; rep from* across. **Row 2** Sl 1, p across. Rep last 2 rows 14 times more.

Turn Heel Cont on 30 sts: **Row 1** (RS) K17, k2tog, k1, turn. **Row 2** Sl 1, p5, p2tog, p1. **Row 3** Sl 1, k5, k2tog, k1. Rep rows 2–3 until 8 sts rem, end with a WS row. K 1 row. Do not turn.

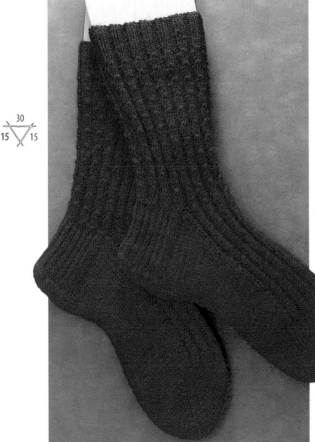

Gusset With empty dpn, pick up and knit 16 sts along side of heel with the last st picked up between the base of heel and the base of instep and sl to dpn with heel sts, turn. **Next row** P2tog, p across, pick up and purl 16 sts along other side of heel with the last st picked up between the base of heel and base of instep. Sl 4 heel sts to this dpn, turn. **Row 1** (RS) K2 tog, k to last 4 sts, k2tog, k2, pick up and k1 st from edge of instep, turn. **Row 2** P2tog, p across, pick up and p 1 st from edge of instep, turn. **Row 3** K2tog, k1, ssk (gusset dec), k to last 4 sts, k2tog (gusset dec), k2, pick up and k1 from instep edge. Rep last 2 rows 3 times more—31 sts counting last st picked up from instep. Turn.

Sole **Row 1** (WS) P2tog, p across, pick up and p 1 st from edge of instep, turn. **Row 2** (RS) K2tog, k across, pick up and k 1 from instep edge. Rep last 2 rows until end of instep is reached, end with WS row and do not pick up a st at end of last row. Turn and k15. Rearrange sts as foll: Sl first 15 sts to first dpn, next 30 sts to 2nd dpn, and next 15 sts to 3rd dpn. Beg of rnd is now at center of sole.

Toe **Rnd 1** On first dpn, k to 3 sts before end of dpn, ssk, k1; on 2nd dpn, k1, k2tog, k to last 3 sts, ssk, k1; on 3rd dpn, k1, k2tog, k to end—4 sts dec. **Rnd 2** Knit. Rep rnds 1–2 until 16 sts rem. With last dpn, k 4 sts from first dpn. Cut yarn, leaving an 18″ tail. Graft rem 8 sts from each dpn tog.

"You've seen refootable, reheelable and re-toe-able socks before. Elizabeth Zimmerman's moccasin socks are an old favorite of many knitters, as are her afterthought heels. Other refootable sock patterns have been published, but this is the first one I know of that looks like a perfectly ordinary sock. Bear in mind that this is not simply a sock pattern. It is a sock-making technique. If you follow the pattern and pay close attention to the technique, you'll be able to convert any standard sock pattern into a refootable version.

The idea came to me while my husband and I were visiting friends in a mountain valley in Tennessee. I was sitting on a rock at the edge of the Clinch River, enjoying the sunset, knitting a perfectly ordinary sock when I arrived at the dividing point for the heel and instep. I thought, 'what would happen if I knitted the instep *first* and then came back to knit the heel, sole and toe?' If I did this, and devised a means to dovetail top and bottom, I would have a refootable, but conventional-looking, sock. It worked, and here it is for you to try."

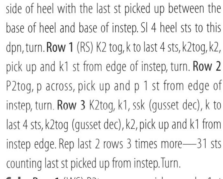

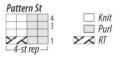

Pattern St

| | | | Knit |
| Purl |
| RT |

4-st rep

Size Woman's large.

Materials A 4oz/120g (approx 320yds/292m) DK-weight wool. **B** Set of 4 double-pointed needles (dpn) in size 2 (2.75mm) *or size needed to obtain gauge.* **C** Stitch holder.

Gauge 6 sts to 1″ (2.5cm) in St st using size 2 (2.75mm) dpn.

"I selected 6 patterns from Strickmuster—books 1 & 2 by Maria Erlbacher, separating each pattern with 4 sts. Pattern E will require the use of a cable needle for the 6-stitch twist; all the other twists were worked without a cable needle similar to the way the left and right twists are accomplished. For me this was my most difficult pattern, time consuming but rewarding! "

Size Woman's medium.

Materials **A** 5ozs/150g (approx 650yds/592m) sock-weight yarn. **B** Set of 4 double-pointed needles (dpn) in size 0 (2mm) *or size needed to obtain gauge*. **C** Stitch holder. **D** Cable needle. **E** Stitch marker. **F** Nylon sewing thread for reinforcement

Gauge 9 sts to 1" (2.5cm) in St st using size 0 (2mm) dpn.

Austrian-Patterned Knee Socks

EXPERIENCED LEVEL

Leg Hem Cast on 104 sts and divide evenly over 3 dpn. Place marker, join and k 11 rnds.

Next rnd (picot edge) *Yo, k2tog; rep from*. K 11 rnds more. Form hem by folding in half at picot edge and k 1 st from dpn tog with 1 cast-on st around. K 1 rnd and inc 32 sts evenly around—136 sts. Sl next 42 sts to empty dpn, next 55 sts to 2nd dpn, and next 39 sts to 3rd dpn. **Beg pats: Rnd 1** P1, k2tbl (through back loop), p1; Pat A (left) over next 5 sts; p1, k2tbl, p1; Pat B (center back) over next 16 sts; p1, k2tbl, p1, Pat A (right) over next 5 sts; p1, k2tbl, p1; Pat C (right) over next 5 sts; p1, k2tbl, p1; Pat D (right) over next 12 sts; p1, k2tbl, p1, Pat E (right) over next 10 sts; p1, k2tbl, p1; Pat F (center front) over next 16 sts; p1, k2tbl, p1; Pat E (left) over next 10 sts; p1, k2tbl, p1; Pat D (left) over next 12 sts; p1, k2tbl, p1; Pat C (left) over next 5 sts. Work in pats as established until piece measures approx 5½" from beg, end with rnd 2 of Pat B.

Shape Calf Cont pats and work from Calf Shaping chart, dec 38 sts evenly over 61 rows at center back and eliminating Pats A (each side) and B and the separating rib—98 sts. Rearrange sts on dpn as needed. Cont pats until piece measures approx 14" from beg, end rnd before 2nd Pat D.

Heel Sl next 46 to empty dpn; next 26 sts to 2nd dpn and rem 26 sts to 3rd dpn. Work back and forth in rows on 46 sts of first dpn only: k46 and dec 4 sts evenly spaced—42 sts. Join nylon sewing thread for reinforcement. **Row 1** (WS) Sl 1, p across. **Row 2** *Sl 1, k1; rep from* across. Rep last 2 rows 18 times more, then rep row 1.

Turn Heel Cont on 42 heel sts: **Row 1** (RS) K23, ssk, k1, turn. **Row 2** Sl 1, p5, p2tog, p1, turn. **Row 3** Sl 1, k6, ssk, k1, turn. **Row 4** Sl 1, p7, p2tog, p1, turn. Cont to dec in same way, working 1 st more between decs on each row until 24 sts rem, end with WS row. K 1 row.

Gusset With empty dpn, pick up tbl and k 18 sts along side of heel and sl to first dpn. With 2nd dpn, work 52 sts from next 2 dpn. With 3rd dpn, pick up tbl and k 18 sts along other side of heel, then k 12 heel sts—112 sts. Beg of rnd is at center of heel. **Rnd 1** On first dpn, k to last 3 sts, k2tog, k1; work pat across 2nd dpn; on 3rd dpn, k1, ssk, k to end—2 sts dec. **Rnd 2** Work even in pat. Rep rnds 1–2 until 88 sts rem.

Foot Work even for approx 4" more or until piece measures 1½" less than desired foot measurement.

Toe Rnd 1 K 1 rnd and dec 16 sts evenly spaced on 2nd dpn—72 sts. **Rnd 2** On first dpn, k to last 3 sts, k tog, k1; on 2nd dpn, k1, ssk, k to last 3 sts, k2tog, k1; on 3rd dpn, k1, ssk, k to end—4 sts dec. **Rnd 3** Knit. Rep rnds 2–3 until 32 sts rem. With 3rd dpn, k 8 sts from first dpn. Cut yarn, leaving an 18" tail. Graft rem 16 sts from each dpn tog.

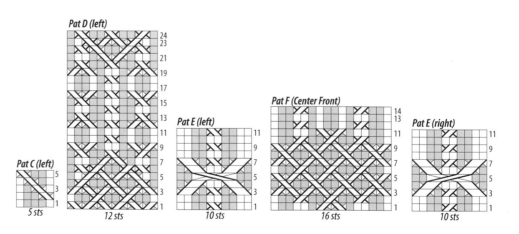

Pat D (left) — 12 sts

Pat C (left) — 5 sts

Pat E (left) — 10 sts

Pat F (Center Front) — 16 sts

Pat E (right) — 10 sts

Special Abbreviations *Note* All knit sts in pats are worked through the back loop (tbl). **RT** K 2nd st on LH needle in front of first st, do not sl off needle, then k first st; sl both sts off needle. **LT** With RH needle behind LH needle, k 2nd st on LH needle through back loop, do not sl off needle, then k into front of first st; sl both sts off needle. **1/1RPC** Sl 1 st to cable needle, hold to back, k1; p1 from cable needle. **1/1LPC** Sl 1 st to cable needle, hold to front, p1; k1 from cable needle. **1/1/1RC** Sl 2 sts to cable needle and hold to back, k1, then sl center st from cable needle to LH needle and k1; k1 from cable needle. **1/1/1LC** Sl 2 sts to cable needle and hold to front, k1, sl center st to LH needle and k1; k1 from cable needle. **2/1RPC** Sl 1 st to cable needle, hold to back, k2; p1 from cable needle. **2/1LPC** Sl 2 sts to cable needle, hold to front, p1; k2 from cable needle. **2/2/2RC** Sl 4 sts to cable needle and hold to back, k2, then sl 2 center sts from cable needle to LH needle and k2; k2 from cable needle. **2/2/2LC** Sl 4 sts to cable needle and hold to front, k2, sl 2 center sts to LH needle and k2; k2 from cable needle.

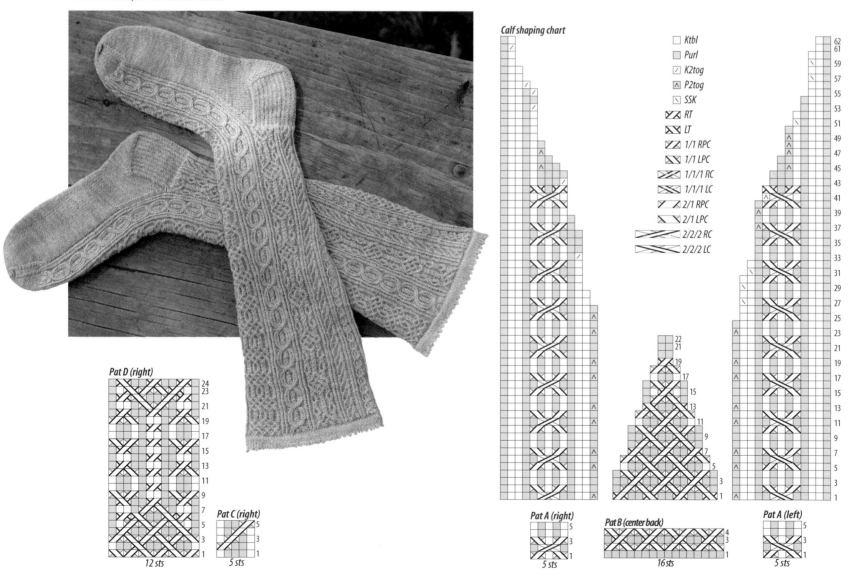

Calf shaping chart

Pat D (right)

Pat C (right)

Pat A (right)

Pat B (center back)

Pat A (left)

- ☐ Ktbl
- ▢ Purl
- ☑ K2tog
- ⬚ P2tog
- ◹ SSK
- RT
- LT
- 1/1 RPC
- 1/1 LPC
- 1/1/1 RC
- 1/1/1 LC
- 2/1 RPC
- 2/1 LPC
- 2/2/2 RC
- 2/2/2 LC

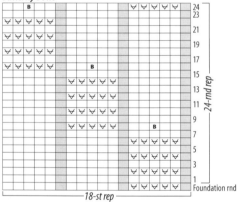

Butterfly Bows

JUDY GIBSON

INTERMEDIATE LEVEL

DESCANSO, CALIFORNIA

Butterfly Bows (Multiple of 18 sts) To gather bow: Insert tip of right-hand needle under the four long strands, then k the next stitch. **Note** At end of patterned portion of sock, gather bow as usual and work k5 instead of sl 5 sts with yarn in front (wyif) for last 4 odd rnds. **Foundation Rnd** *P1, sl 5 wyif, p1, k5, p1, k5; rep from*. **Rnd 1 and all odd rnds** *P1, k5; rep from*. **Rnds 2, 4, and 6** *P1, sl 5 wyif, p1, k5, p1, k5; rep from*. **Rnd 8** *P1, k2, gather bow, k2, p1, sl 5 wyif, p1, k5; rep from*. **Rnds 10, 12, and 14** *P1, k5, p1, sl 5 wyif, p1, k5; rep from*. **Rnd 16** *P1, k5, p1, k2, gather bow, k2, p1, sl 5 wyif; rep from*. **Rnds 18, 20, and 22** *P1, k5, p1, k5, p1, sl 5 wyif; rep from*. **Rnd 24** *P1, sl 5 wyif, p1, k5, p1, k2, gather bow, k2; rep from*. Rep rnds 1–24 for Butterfly Bows pat.

Leg Cast on 54 sts and divide evenly over 3 dpn. Place marker, join and work 1" in p1, k1 rib. **Next rnd** *P1, k5; rep from*. Beg with foundation rnd, work in Butterfly Bows pat until 5 sets of bows are completed, end with rnd 14. Remove marker; p1, k1.

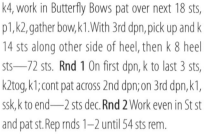

Heel Sl next 13 sts to empty dpn, next 14 sts to 2nd dpn, and next 27 sts to 3rd dpn. Work back and forth in rows on 27 sts of 3rd dpn only: **Rows 1, 3** (WS) Sl 1, p26. **Row 2** Sl 1, k15, gather bow, k to end. **Row 4** (RS) Sl 1, k26. Rep last 2 rows 12 times more, then rep row 1.

Turn heel Cont on 27 sts: **Row 1** (RS) Sl 1, k15, ssk, k1, turn. **Row 2** Sl 1, p6, p2tog, p1, turn. **Row 3** Sl 1, k7, ssk, k1, turn. **Row 4** Sl 1, p8, p2tog, p1, turn. Cont to dec in same way, working 1 more st between decs on each row until 17 sts remain. K 1 row.

Gusset With empty dpn, pick up and k 14 sts along side of heel and sl to first dpn. With 2nd dpn, work next 27 sts as foll: k4, work in Butterfly Bows pat over next 18 sts, p1, k2, gather bow, k1. With 3rd dpn, pick up and k 14 sts along other side of heel, then k 8 heel sts—72 sts. **Rnd 1** On first dpn, k to last 3 sts, k2tog, k1; cont pat across 2nd dpn; on 3rd dpn, k1, ssk, k to end—2 sts dec. **Rnd 2** Work even in St st and pat st. Rep rnds 1–2 until 54 sts rem.

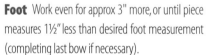

Foot Work even for approx 3" more, or until piece measures 1½" less than desired foot measurement (completing last bow if necessary).

Toe **Rnd 1** On first dpn, k to last 3 sts, k2tog, k1; on 2nd dpn, k1, ssk, k to last 3 sts, k2tog, k1; on 3rd dpn, k1, ssk, k to end—4 sts dec.

Rnd 2 Knit. Rep rnds 1–2 until 30 sts rem, then rep rnd 1 until 14 sts rem. K 4 sts from first dpn to 3rd dpn. Cut yarn, leaving an 18" tail. Graft rem 7 sts from each dpn tog.

Note To make the butterflies spiral the other direction on 2nd sock, read the chart rows from left to right.

"These socks were designed for my 10-year-old niece Sheri who says that socks with fold-over tops are for 'little kids.' This pair has stand-up cuffs at anklet length."

Butterfly Bows

24	
23	
21	
19	24-rnd rep
17	
15	
13	
11	
9	
7	
5	
3	
1	
Foundation rnd	

18-st rep

☐ K
▨ P
∨ Slip 1 wyif
B Gather Bow: With tip of right needle, pick up 4 long strands below and knit.

Size Child's medium.

Materials **A** 2oz/60g (approx 430yds/392m) cotton/synthetic sock-weight yarn. **B** Set of 4 double-pointed needles (dpn) in size 2 (2.75mm) *or size to obtain gauge*.

Gauge 7½ sts to 1" (2.5cm) in St st using size 2 (2.75mm) dpn; 8 sts to 1" (2.5cm) in Butterfly Bows pat.

Slouch Socks

INTERMEDIATE LEVEL

BETH MORGAN ADCOCK

WATERVLIET, NEW YORK

Right sock

Leg Using invisible cast-on shown on page 106, cast on 72 sts. Divide sts evenly over 3 dpn. Place marker and join. **Rnd 1** *K1, sl 1 with yarn in front; rep from*. **Rnd 2** *Sl 1 with yarn in back, p1; rep from*. Rep rnds 1–2 once. Work in k1, p1 rib until piece measures 2¼" from beg. Beg Slouch pat: **Rnds 1–3** *P3, k3; rep from*. **Rnds 4–6** Purl. **Rnds 7–9** *K3, p3; rep from*. **Rnds 10–12** Knit. Rep rnds 1–12 until piece measures 7" from beg.

Heel Sl first 36 sts to empty dpn, next 18 sts to 2nd dpn, and last 18 sts to 3rd dpn. Work back and forth in rows on 36 sts of first dpn: **Row 1** (RS) *Sl 1, k1; rep from*. **Row 2** Sl 1, p across. Rep last 2 rows 17 times more, then rep row 1 again.

Turn heel Cont on 36 sts: **Row 1** (WS) Sl 1, p22, p2tog, p1. **Row 2** Sl 1, k11, ssk, k1. **Row 3** Sl 1, p12, p2tog, p1. **Row 4** Sl 1, k13, ssk, k1. Cont to dec in same way, working 1 st more between decs on each row until 24 sts rem, end with a RS row.

Gusset With RS facing and empty dpn, pick up and k 18 sts along side of heel and sl to first dpn; with 2nd dpn, cont pat across 36 sts from next 2 dpn; with 3rd dpn, pick up and k 18 sts along other side of heel, then k12 heel sts—96 sts. **Rnd 1** On first dpn, k to last 3 sts, k2tog, k1; cont pat across 2nd dpn; on 3rd dpn, k1, ssk, k to end—2 sts dec. **Rnd 2** Work even. Rep rnds 1–2 until 72 sts rem.

Foot Work approx 3" more, or until piece measures 2½" less than desired foot measurement.

Toe **Rnd 1** On first dpn, k to last 4 sts, k2tog, k2; on 2nd dpn, k2, ssk, k to last 4 sts, k2 tog, k2; on 3rd dpn, k2, ssk, k to end—4 sts dec. **Rnd 2** Knit. **Rnd 3** On first dpn, k to last 4 sts, k2tog, k2; on 2nd dpn, k2, ssk, k to end of rnd—dec 2 on right side of foot only. **Rnd 4** Knit. Rep rnds 1–4 until 48 sts rem; then rep rnds 1 and 3 until 12 sts rem. With 3rd dpn, k 3 sts from first dpn. Cut yarn, leaving a 14" tail. Graft rem 12 sts tog. Fasten off. Remove waste yarn from invisible cast on.

Left sock Work as for right sock through rnd 2 of toe shaping. **Rnd 3** K across first dpn; on 2nd dpn, k to last 4 sts, k2tog, k2; on 3rd dpn, k2, ssk, k to end— 2 dec on left side of foot only. **Rnd 4** Knit. Complete as for right sock.

A simple, but highly-textured combination of knits and purls makes the cuffs slouch. Although the stitch continues on the top of the foot, it is flattened by the stockinette stitch worked on the bottom of the foot. This is a good one to try in a solid color, too.

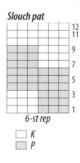

Slouch pat

6-st rep

☐ K
▨ P

Size Woman's medium.

Materials **A** 3½oz/100g (approx 430yds/392m) sock-weight yarn. **B** Set of 4 double-pointed needles (dpn) in size 1 (2.5mm), *or size needed to obtain gauge*. **C** Stitch marker. **D** Small amount of scrap yarn.

Gauge 7 sts to 1" (2.5cm) in slouch pat using size 1 (2.5mm) dpn.

Dye-Your-Own Socks

INTERMEDIATE LEVEL

Are you interested in dyeing your own yarn but don't want to invest in the equipment or are concerned about the safety?
Do you worry about making your socks too long and running out of yarn before you finish the second sock?
This is a safe and hassle-free dyeing method that requires no special materials or equipment. And since you knit the socks from the toe up, using one skein per sock, you can work the cuff until you run out of yarn, knowing that you have enough for the other sock.

"Using powdered drink mixes is a safe and fun way to dye yarn. You can use kitchen utensils without any safety concerns. This is a fun project to do with kids."

Size 7½ (8, 8½, 9)" around widest part of foot.
Materials A 3½oz/100g (approx 360 yds/328m) sport-weight wool, natural color. **B** Set of 4 double-pointed needles (dpn) in sizes 1 and 2 (2.5 and 3mm) *or size needed to obtain gauge and one size smaller.* **C** 2 stitch markers **D** Microwave and microwave-safe dish (8" x 8" glass dish is good size). **E** Powdered drink mixes: I used 1 package each of pink lemonade, lemon lime, cherry, black cherry, orange, and 2 lemonades. **F** Mixing containers (cups or yogurt containers). **G** Tools to apply dye: syringe, paintbrush, spray bottle, etc. **H** Vinegar. **I** Rubber gloves.
Gauge 7 sts to 1" (2.5cm) in St st using size 2 (3mm) dpn.

Dye the Yarn Put about 1" of warm water and a "glug" of vinegar in a microwave-safe dish. Using rubber gloves, put the 2 skeins (or balls) of yarn in the dish and gently push them down to get wet. Turn them and wet the other side. Let the yarn soak as you prepare the drink mixes. Using one container per flavor, empty the mixes into containers, add a little warm water and stir to dissolve. The more water you add, the more diluted the color will be. After preparing all of the colors that you want to use, gently squeeze the excess water out of the yarn. Empty the dish and put the yarn back in. Apply the drink mixes to the yarn any way you want. I like to use a syringe so I can squirt color inside the skeins and exert better control in placing the color. Pour, spray, or paint the drink mix onto the yarn. When finished, gently push down on the yarn so the inside and bottom of each skein will get dyed. You can turn the yarn over and apply more color. Place the uncovered dish in the microwave and "cook" on High for 2 minutes. Let sit for 2 minutes. Turn the skeins over and repeat cooking. If color comes out when you gently press on the yarn, cook some more. Let yarn sit in the dish until cool. Rinse by soaking yarn in water the same temperature as yarn. If the water is much hotter or colder than the yarn, it may felt. Repeat the rinsing process until all the excess drink mix (and smell!) is gone. If you have a washing machine, spin out excess water using the spin cycle. Set yarn on a towel to dry.

Knitting the Socks *Notes* **A** Socks are worked from toe to cuff. **B** If there is only one number given, use that number for all sizes.

Special Stitches Bar Increase K into front and back of st. **Lifted Increase** With RH needle, pick up the next st on LH needle 1 row below and place on LH needle. K the lifted st.

Faux Cable **Rnd 1** P2, work lifted increase, k4, ssk, k8, p2. **Rnd 2 and all even-numbered rnds** P2, k14, p2. **Rnd 3** P2, k1, lifted inc, k4, ssk, k7, p2. **Rnd 5** P2, k2, lifted inc, k4, ssk, k6, p2. **Rnd 7** P2, k3, lifted inc, k4, ssk, k5, p2. **Rnd 9** P2, k4, lifted inc, k4, ssk, k4, p2. **Rnd 11** P2, k5, lifted inc,

Ready for dyeing: Natural-colored wool and six flavors of drink mix to supply the color.

Apply the color to the skeins or balls, placing the colors as you wish.

After heating, rinsing, and drying, the yarn is ready to knit a pair of multi-colored socks.

Faux cable

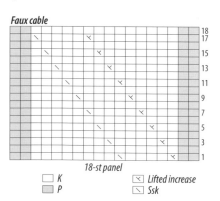

18-st panel

☐ K   ☒ Lifted increase
▨ P   ◹ Ssk

k4, ssk, k3, p2. **Rnd 13** P2, k6, lifted inc, k4, ssk, k2, p2. **Rnd 15** P2, k7, lifted inc, k4, ssk, k1, p2. **Rnd 17** P2, k8, lifted inc, k4, ssk, p2. **Rnd 18** P2, k14, p2. Rep Rnds 1—18 for pat.

Toe With larger dpn, cast on 4 sts. K into the front and back of each st—8 sts.

Next row *K1, sl 1 with yarn in front; rep from* across, turn and rep from* again. Pull dpn out. Sts will divide in half. Sl 1 dpn through 4 sts on one side, a 2nd dpn through 4 sts on other side. With 3rd dpn, k2—sts are now distributed on 3 needles: 2 sts on first dpn, 4 sts on 2nd dpn, 2 sts on 3rd dpn. Beg of rnd is at center of lower edge of toe.

Rnd 1 On first dpn, work bar inc, k1; on 2nd dpn, work bar inc, k to last 2 sts, work bar inc, k1; on 3rd dpn, work bar inc, k1—12 sts. **Rnd 2** On first dpn, k to last 2 sts, work bar inc, k1; on 2nd dpn, work bar inc, k to last 2 sts, work bar inc, k1; on 3rd dpn, work bar inc, k to end—16 sts. Rep rnd 2 until there are 24 (28, 32, 36) sts. K 1 rnd. **For first 3 sizes only** *Work rnd 2, then k 1 rnd; rep from* until there are 36 sts. **For all sizes** Work on 36 sts as foll: K across first dpn; on 2nd dpn, k1, p1, k 14, p1, k1; k across 3rd dpn.

Next rnd On first dpn, k to last 2 sts, work bar inc, k1; on 2nd dpn, work bar inc, p1, k14, p into the front and back of next st, k1; on 3rd dpn, work bar inc, k to end—40 sts.

Next rnd K to 2nd dpn, k1, place marker, work rnd 1 of Faux Cable pat, place marker, k1, k across 3rd dpn.

Next rnd On first dpn, k to last 2 sts, work bar inc, k1; on 2nd dpn, work bar inc, work rnd 2 of Faux Cable pat and inc 1 in last p st by p in the front and k in the back (move marker between these 2 sts), k1; on 3rd dpn, work bar inc, k to end—44 sts.

Cont to inc every other rnd (as in rnd 2 above) until there are 52 (56, 60, 64) sts, AT SAME TIME, work even in Faux Cable pat between markers until piece measures same as tip of toe to front of ankle bone. Beg heel shaping.

Heel shaping Work back and forth in rows: K13 (14, 15, 16), turn. **Row 1** Yo, p26 (28, 30, 32), turn. **Row 2** Yo, k25 (27, 29, 31). **Row 3** Yo, p24 (26, 28, 30). In same way, cont to yo at beg of row and work 1 less st until you have p10 (12, 14, 16). **Next row** Yo, k10 (12, 14, 16), k the yo and next st tog, turn. **Next row** Yo, p11 (13, 15, 17), sl next 2 sts (yo and next st) 1 at a time knitwise, then sl back onto left needle, p2 tog through the back loop (tbl), turn. **Next row** Yo, k12 (14, 16, 18), k3tog (both yo's and next st), turn. **Next row** Yo, p13 (15, 17, 19), sl next 3 sts (both yo's and next st) 1 at a time knitwise, then sl back onto left needle, p3tog tbl, turn. Cont working one more st each row and working yo's tog with next st until you have k26 (28, 30, 32). There should be 2 yo's left on each side of heel. Beg working in rnds again. **Next rnd** K3tog (both yo's and next st), k around to last st before other 2 yo's, sl 1, k2tog (both yo's), psso—52 (56, 60, 64) sts. K13 (14, 15, 16) to get to beg of rnd.

Leg Work in rnds for 2" and cont Faux Cable pat. Change to smaller dpn

Cuff Beg with k1, p2 (sizes S, L) or p1 (sizes M, XL), work in k2, p2 rib to marker; work Faux Cable pat; beg with k2, work in k2, p2 rib to end. Cont pats as established until piece measures desired length. Bind off loosely.

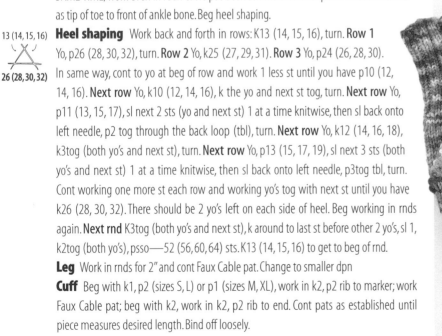

Aran Sandal Socks

LORI GAYLE

EXPERIENCED LEVEL

CAMBRIDGE, MASSACHUSETTS

These socks feature a cabled heel flap—extra patterning where it counts when wearing clogs or Birkies.

Pattern Stitches RT K 2nd st on LH needle in front of first st, do not sl off needle, then k first st; sl both sts off needle. LT With RH needle behind LH needle, k 2nd st on LH needle through back loop (tbl), do not sl off needle, then k into front of first st; sl both sts off needle. **1/2RC** Sl 2 to cn, hold to back k1; k2 from cn. *Cross Stitch Cable* (6 sts) **Rnd 1** P1, k4, p1. **Rnd 2** P1, k4 wrapping yarn twice around needle, p1. **Rnd 3** P1, sl 4 with yarn in back (wyib) and dropping extra wraps, pass the first 2 sts over second 2 sts and leave on LH needle, sl 2 sts on RH needle back to LH needle, k4, p1. **Rnd 4** P1, k4, p1. *Cable Rib* (5 sts) **Rnd 1** P1, 1/2 RC, p1. **Rnd**s 2–4 [P1, k1tbl] twice, p1. Rep rnds 1–4 for pat. *Mirror Cable* (8 sts). **Rnd 1** P3, k2, p3. **Rnd 2** K3, RT, k3. **Rnd 3** Rep rnd 1. **Rnd 4** K2, RT, LT, k2. **Rnds 5, 7** [P2, k1] twice, p2. **Rnd 6** Knit. **Rnd 8** K2, LT, RT, k2. **Rnds 9–12** Rep rnds 1–4. **Rnd 13** Rep rnd 1. **Rnd 14** K1, RT, k2, LT, k1. **Rnd 15, 19** P1, k6, p1. **Rnd 16** RT, k4, LT. **Rnd 17** Knit. **Rnd 18** LT, k4, RT. **Rnd 20** K1, LT, k2, RT, k1. **Rnd 21** Rep rnd 1. **Rnd 22** Rep rnd 8. Rep rnds 1–22 for pat. *Seed St* **Row 1** *K1, p1; rep from*. **Row 2** K the p sts and p the k sts. Rep row 2 for pat.

Leg Loosely cast on 56 sts and divide evenly over 3 dpn. Place marker, join and work 2" in k2, p2 rib. Knit 1 rnd and inc 4 sts evenly spaced—60 sts. Beg pats: **Rnd 1** *K1tbl, work 6 sts of Cross Stitch Cable, k1tbl, work 5 sts of Cable Rib, k1tbl, p1, work 8 sts of Mirror Cable , p1, k1tbl, work 5 sts of Cable Rib; rep from*. Work 43 rnds even in pats as established. Work 1 more rnd. Piece measures approx 6¾" from beg.

Heel *Note* Since heel is worked back and forth, even-numbered pat rows are worked as WS rows. K1tbl p1, k3 onto first dpn; sl next 14 sts onto 2nd dpn; sl next 14 sts onto 3rd dpn; sl rem 27 sts onto first dpn with first 5 sts. Work back and forth in rows on 32 sts of first dpn only: (WS) Work 3 sts in Seed st, k1, p1tbl, work pat across next 22 sts, p1tbl, k1, work 3 sts in Seed st, turn. Cont working back and forth on 32 heel sts in pat until end of Mirror Cable pat rep, work 1 more row, turn.

Turn heel Cont on 32 sts: **Row 1** (WS) P18, p2tog, p1, turn. **Row 2** Sl 1, k5, ssk, k1, turn. **Row 3** Sl 1, p6, p2tog, p1, turn. **Row 4** Sl 1, k7, ssk, k1, turn. Cont to dec in same way, working 1 st more between decs on each row until 18 sts rem, end with RS row. Do not turn.

Gusset With empty dpn, pick up and k 15 sts along side of heel and sl to first dpn. With 2nd dpn, work 28 sts of next 2 dpn in pat, beg and end with k1. With 3rd dpn, pick up and k15 sts along other side of heel, then k 9 heel sts—76 sts. **Rnd 1** On first dpn, k9, work in Seed st to last 2 sts, k2tog; on 2nd dpn, work in est pat; on 3rd dpn, ssk, work in Seed st to last 9 sts, k9—2 sts dec. **Rnd 2** On first dpn, k9, work in Seed st to last st, k1; on 2nd dpn, work in est pat; on 3rd dpn, k1, work in Seed st to last 9 sts, k1. Rep rnds 1–2 until 56 sts rem.

Foot Cont in pats, maintaining Seed st on sides of sole, to end of 2nd Mirror Cable rep (4 reps total from beg). Work 1 more rnd in pat. Work even in St st until piece measures 2" less than desired foot measurement (approx 7½" from back of heel).

Toe **Rnd 1** On first dpn, k to last 3 sts, k2tog, k1; on 2nd dpn, k1, ssk, k to last 3 sts, k2tog, k1; on 3rd dpn, k1, ssk, k to end—4 sts dec. **Rnd 2** Knit. Rep rnds 1 and 2 until 28 sts rem. Rep rnd 1 until 16 sts rem. With 3rd dpn, k 4 sts from first dpn. Cut yarn, leaving an 18" tail. Using tail, graft rem 8 sts from each dpn tog.

Cable rib

4
3
1

5 sts

Mirror cable

22
21
19
17
15
13
11
9
7
5
3
1

8 sts

□ K ☒ K1tbl
■ P
LT
or RT
1/2RC

Size Woman's medium.

Materials **A** 5¼ozs/150g (approx 330yds/301m) DK - weight wool. **B** Set of 4 double-pointed needles (dpn) in size 2 (2.75mm) *or size needed to obtain gauge*. **C** Cable needle (cn). **D** Stitch marker.

Gauge 6½ sts to 1" (2.5cm) over St st using size 2 (2.75) dpn.

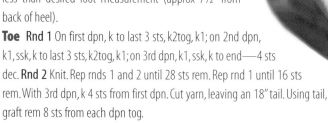

Ribble Socks

INTERMEDIATE LEVEL

KATHERINE MATTHEWS
TORONTO, ONTARIO, CANADA

Special Abbreviations **2/2 KPLC** Sl 2 sts to cable needle and hold in front, k1, p1, then k1, p1 from cable needle. **2/2 KPRC** Sl 2 sts to cable needle and hold in back, k1, p1, then k1, p1 from cable needle.

Pattern Stitch (Multiple of 8 sts) **Rnd 1** *[K1, p1] twice, 2/2 KPLC; rep from*. **Rnds 2-5** *K1, p1; rep from*. **Rnd 6** *2/2 KPRC, [k1, p1] twice; rep from*. **Rnds 7–10** Rep rnds 2–5. Rep rnds 1–10 for pat.

Leg With larger dpn, cast on 56 sts and divide evenly over 3 dpn. Place marker and work 6 rnds in k1, p1 rib. Work 3 reps of Pat st, end with Pat rnd 8. **Rnd 9** Ssk, *k1, p1; rep from* to last 2 sts, k2tog—54 sts. **Rnd 10** Ssk, *p1, k1; rep from* to last 2 sts, k2tog—52 sts. Change to smaller needles.

Heel (If adding reinforcement yarn, join here.) K next 14 sts onto first dpn; sl next 12 sts to 2nd dpn, next 12 sts to 3rd dpn, and next 14 sts to first dpn. Work back and forth in rows on 28 sts of first dpn only: **Row 1** (WS) Sl 1, p27. **Row 2** (RS) *Sl 1, k1; rep from*. Rep last 2 rows 14 times more, then rep row 1.

Turn heel Cont on 28 sts: **Row 1** (RS) K16, ssk, k1, turn. **Row 2** Sl 1, p5, p2tog, p1, turn. **Row 3** Sl 1, k6, ssk, k1, turn. **Row 4** Sl 1, p7, p2tog, p1, turn. Cont to dec in same way, working 1 more st between decs on each row until 16 sts rem. (If using reinforcement thread, cut here.) K 1 row.

Gusset With empty dpn, pick up and k 14 sts along side of heel and sl to first dpn. With 2nd dpn pick up and k 2 sts at beg of instep, work 24 sts of instep (2nd and 3rd dpn) in Pat row 1, pick up and k 2 sts at end of instep. With 3rd dpn, pick up and k 14 sts along other side of heel flap, then k 8 heel sts—72 sts. **Rnd 1** On first dpn, k to last 3 sts, k2tog, k1; on 2nd dpn work first and last 2 sts as k1, p1 and cont pat. On 3rd dpn, k1, ssk, k to end—2 sts dec. **Rnd 2** Work even in St st and Pat st. Rep rnds 1 and 2 until 56 sts rem.

Foot Work even in pat until piece measures 1½" less than desired foot measurement.

Toe (If adding reinforcement yarn, join here.) **Rnd 1** On first dpn, k to last 3 sts, k2tog, k1. On 2nd dpn, k1, ssk, k to last 3 sts, k2tog, k1. On 3rd dpn, k1, ssk, k to end—4 sts dec. **Rnd 2** Knit. Rep rnds 1 and 2 until 28 sts rem, then rep rnd 1 until 8 sts rem. Cut yarn, leaving an 8" tail. Run tail through rem sts, tighten and fasten off.

"One of my knitting inspirations is Lily Chin. When I took a reversible cable ('ribble') workshop with her, I knew that this would be a perfect technique to apply to socks. Ribbles have the illusion of being lacy, and because they are reversible, the sock can be worn with a cuff or without it! This sock is sized for my foot, size 8 and wide, especially over the instep."

A turned-down cuff reveals the reversibility of this cabled rib pattern.

Size Woman's medium.

Materials **A** 3½oz/100g (approx 230yds/210m) DK weight yarn. **B** Set of 4 double-pointed needles (dpn) in sizes 2 and 3 (2.75mm and 3.25mm) *or size needed to obtain gauge*. **C** Cable needle. **D** Optional reinforcement yarn for heels and toes.

Gauge 6½ sts to 1" (2.5cm) over St st using size 2 (2.75mm) dpn.

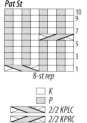

Pat St

10
9
7
5
3
1

8-st rep

☐ K
☐ P
⬜ 2/2 KPLC
⬜ 2/2 KPRC

**These socks are worked sideways and flat
on single-pointed needles with short row shaping
for heel, toe, and calf.
This pair is done in two-row stripes of color and
Seed stitch, with a small knit/purl band
and scalloped edging at the cuff.
The interplay between the color stripes
and the pattern stripes
in conjunction with the variegated yarn
creates a visually exciting design.**

Size Woman's medium.
Materials A 1¾oz/50g (approx 215yds/196m) merino wool sock yarn each: purple (MC) and multi-colored (CC). **B** One pair size 2 (2.75mm) needles *or size needed to obtain gauge.* **C** Stitch markers.
Gauge 6 sts and 11 rows to 1" (2.5 cm) over pat (2 rows St st, 2 rows seed st) using size 2 (2.75mm) needles.

Sideways Sox Supreme

INTERMEDIATE LEVEL

Note Cast on edge is from cuff to toe. Piece is worked flat, then cast-on edge is grafted to final row to form invisible seam that runs along side of sock.
Seed st (Over any number of sts) **Row 1** *K1, p1; rep from*. **Row 2 and all foll rows** K the purl sts and p the knit sts.
Sock Row 1 (RS) Using invisible cast-on and MC, cast on 80 sts over scrap yarn, leaving a tail. **Row 2** With MC, p37, place marker, p2 (heel), place marker, p across to last 7 sts, place marker; k1, p2, k2, yo, k2 (edging). **Row 3** With CC, k4, p1, k2, p1; work Seed st to next marker, k2 (heel), work Seed st to end. **Row 4** With CC, work Seed st to marker, p2, work Seed st to next marker; k1, p2, k2, yo, k3. **Row 5** With MC, k5, p1, k2, p1; k to last 14 sts, sl next st purlwise to right-hand needle, then with yarn in front (wyif) sl same st back to left-hand needle (1 st wrapped), turn. **Row 6** With MC, p to last marker; k1, p2, k2, yo, k4. **Row 7** With CC, k6, p1, k2, p1; work Seed st to marker, k2, work Seed st to wrapped st, work wrapped st and wrap tog, work 4 more sts, wrap next st, turn. **Row 8** With CC, work Seed st to marker, p2, work Seed st to last marker; k1, p2, k2, yo, k5. **Row 9** With MC, bind off 4 sts, weaving in CC between each st, k2, p1, k2, p1; k to wrapped st, then k wrapped st and wrap tog, k3, wrap next st, turn. **Row 10** With MC, p to last marker; k1, p2, k2, yo, k2. **Row 11** With CC, k4, p1, k2, p1; work Seed st to marker, k2, work Seed st to wrapped st, work wrapped st and wrap tog, work 2 more sts, wrap next st, turn. **Row 12** With CC, work Seed st to marker, p2, work Seed st to last marker; k1, p2, k2, yo, k3. **Row 13** With MC, k5, p1, k2, p1; k to wrapped st, then k wrapped st and wrap tog, k last st. **Rows 14–36** Work even in pats.
Cont chart pat, shaping as indicated, through row 96. Turn. With MC, bind off 4 sts for edging. Sl st on right-hand needle to left-hand needle. Leave rem sts on needle.
Side Seam Beg at toe with empty needle and pick up each MC st from cast-on edge, removing scrap yarn. With MC and RS facing, graft the cast-on edge to the last row.
Toe Thread tail from cast-on edge through the purl bumps at toe, pull tog tightly and fasten off.

LIZ CLOUTHIER
GROTON, CONNECTICUT

See page 109 for chart pat in written-out form.

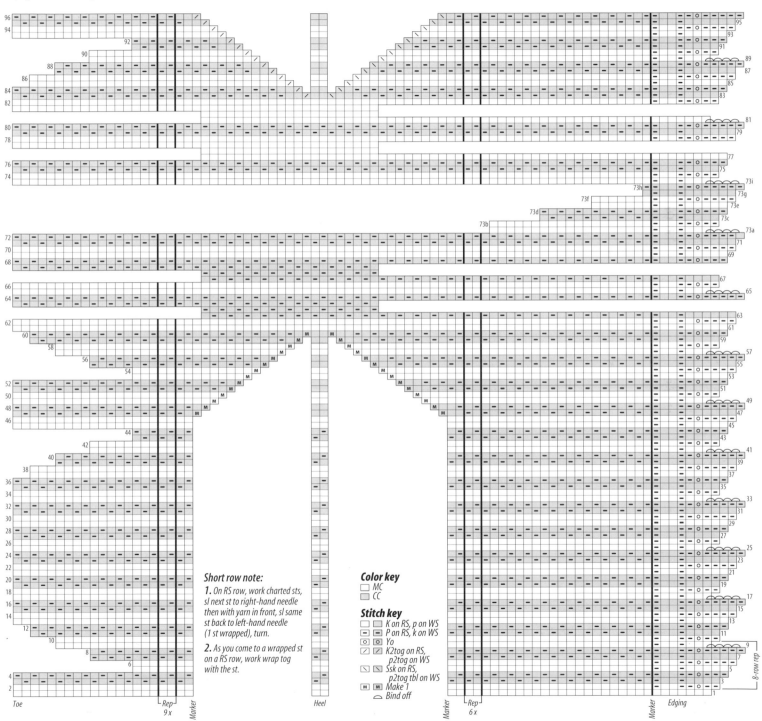

Short row note:

1. On RS row, work charted sts, sl next st to right-hand needle then with yarn in front, sl same st back to left-hand needle (1 st wrapped), turn.

2. As you come to a wrapped st on a RS row, work wrap tog with the st.

Color key
☐ MC
▨ CC

Stitch key
☐ K on RS, p on WS
− P on RS, k on WS
○ Yo
╱ K2tog on RS, p2tog on WS
╲ Ssk on RS, p2tog tbl on WS
M Make 1
⌒ Bind off

Toe · Rep 9 x · Marker · Heel · Marker · Rep 6 x · Marker · Edging · 8-row rep

Chapter 6   Whimsical

13 PROJECTS

Turn-of-the-Century Socks   **80**

Miniature Socks   **82**

Popcorn Panache   **83**

Sunrise Socks   **84**

Spring Fever   **87**

Little Piggy Toes   **88**

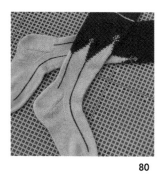

80

82

83

84

Maple Swirl Socks   **90**

Clock Socks   **92**

Watermelon Socks   **94**

Licorice Socks   **95**

Pearls of Wisdom   **96**

A Lilliputian Christmas   **98**

Boston Bulkies   **99**

95

94

88

90

92

Whimsical Socks

USA

96

98

99

"In the 1890's, black silk stockings enlivened by a bright color and embroidered silk flowers were very fashionable. This pattern uses flat intarsia knitting within the context of circular knitting. A stitch pattern down the back of the stockings conceals the short seam."

Size Woman's large.

Materials **A** Sock-weight yarn: 3½oz/100g (approx 435yds/396m) each in camel (A) and black (B). **B** Gold silk embroidery thread. **C** Optional: reinforcing yarn to match A. **D** Set of 4 double-pointed needles (dpn) in sizes 1 and 2 (2.25 and 2.75 mm) *or size to obtain gauge.* **E** One pair size 2 (2.75mm) needles. **F** Yarn bobbins.

Gauge 8 sts to 1" (2.5cm) over St st using size 2 (2.75mm) dpn.

Turn-of-the-Century Socks
INTERMEDIATE LEVEL

Leg With smaller dpn and A, cast on 88 sts and divide as foll: 27 sts each to first and 3rd dpn; 34 sts to 2nd dpn. Place marker, join and k 1 rnd, then p 1 rnd. **Border pat: Rnd 1** With B, *p1, k3; rep from*. **Rnd 2** *K3, p1; rep from*. Rep rnds 1–2 until piece measures 1¾" from beg. With A, rep rnds 1–2. Change to larger dpn and B. **Rnd 1** On first dpn, p1, k1, p1, k into back and front of next st, k across; k across 2nd dpn; on 3rd dpn, k to last 3 sts, p1, k2—89 sts. **Rnd 2** On first dpn, k2, p1, k across; k across 2nd dpn; on 3rd dpn, k to last 3 sts, p1, k1, p1. **Rnd 3** On first dpn, p1, k1, p1, k across; k across 2nd dpn, on 3rd dpn, k to last 3 sts, p1, k2. Rep rnds 2–3 until piece measures 4½" from beg, end with rnd 2.

Work chart Sl all sts to straight needles and work chart rows 1–64. Use separate strands for each area of color, twisting yarns on WS to prevent holes—71 sts. Rep last 2 rows until piece measures 15" from beg, end with a WS row. Turn.

Heel Change to larger dpn and A. K first 17 sts onto first dpn, sl next 37 sts to 2nd dpn, sl rem 17 sts to 3rd dpn. Turn. **Next row** Sl 1, p16, then p17 sts from 3rd dpn—34 sts on first dpn. If desired, join reinforcing yarn. Work back and forth on 34 sts of first dpn only: **Row 1** (RS) Sl 1, k33. **Row 2** Sl 1, p33. Rep last 2 rows 16 times more.

Turn heel Cont on 34 sts: **Row 1** (RS) K19, ssk, k1; turn. **Row 2** Sl 1, p5, p2tog, p1, turn. **Row 3** Sl 1, k6, ssk, k1, turn. **Row 4** Sl 1, p7, p2tog, p1, turn. Cont to dec in same way, working 1 st more between decs on each row until 20 sts rem, end with a RS row. Cut reinforcing yarn. Do not turn.

Gusset With empty dpn and A, pick up and k 17 sts along side of heel and sl to first dpn. With 2nd dpn, k next 37 sts (cont 1-st stripes in B as established). With 3rd dpn, pick up and k 17 sts along other side of heel, then k 10 heel sts— 91 sts. Beg of rnd is at center of heel. **Rnd 1** On first dpn, k to last 2 sts, k2tog; cont pat across 2nd dpn, on 3rd dpn, ssk, k to end—89 sts. **Rnd 2** Work even. Rep rnds 1–2 until 71 sts rem—17 sts on first and 3rd dpns, 37 sts on 2nd dpn.

Foot Sl 1 st each from 2nd dpn onto first and 3rd dpn—18 sts each on first and 3rd dpn, 35 sts on 2nd dpn. Work even as established until foot measures 6" from heel or 2" less than desired length, dec 1 st at beg of first dpn in last rnd—70 sts.

Toe Discontinue stripe pat and cont with A as foll: **Rnd 1** On first dpn, work to last 3 sts, k2tog, k1; on 2nd dpn, k1, ssk, k to last 3 sts, k2tog, k1; on 3rd dpn, k1, ssk, work to end—4 sts dec. **Rnd 2** Work even. Rep last 2 rnds until 30 sts rem. Dec every rnd until 18 sts rem. K sts from first dpn to 3rd dpn. Cut yarn, leaving a 12" tail. Graft 9 sts from each dpn tog.

Finishing Sew back seam. Work duplicate st with silk thread as indicated on chart.

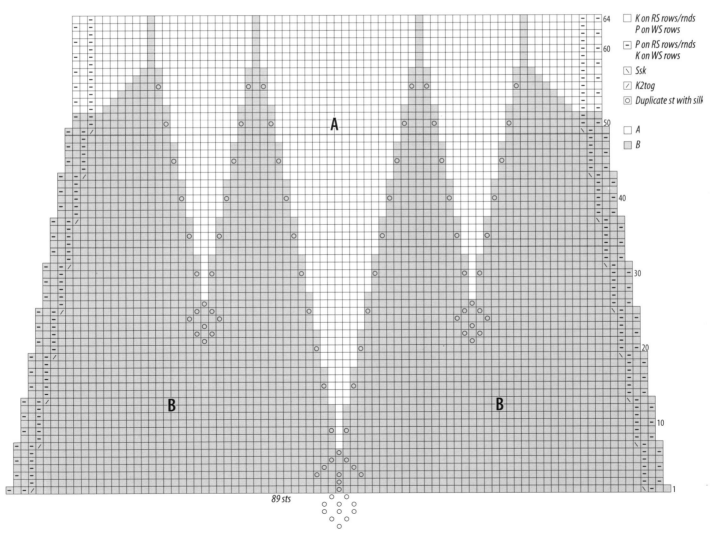

□ K on RS rows/rnds
  P on WS rows

⊟ P on RS rows/rnds
  K on WS rows

◣ Ssk

◢ K2tog

◎ Duplicate st with silk

□ A

▨ B

89 sts

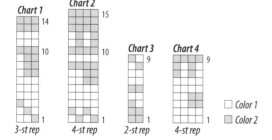

This basic sock pattern in miniature
shows beginning sock knitters how
to turn heels and weave toe stitches.
If it truly is your first sock, you may wish
to make a solid color one
before adding color patterns to the mix.

Miniature Socks

INTERMEDIATE LEVEL

DEBORAH FAYE WATSON

WARRENTON, VIRGINIA

Leg Cast on 20 sts and divide evenly over 3 dpn. Work 3 rnds in k1, p1 rib or seed st. Working 4-st rep around, work 15 rnds of Chart 2 (or inc 1 st on rnd 1 and, working 3-st rep around, work 14 rnds of Chart 1, dec 1 st on rnd 15).

Heel Sl next 10 sts to first dpn, next 5 sts to 2nd dpn, and next 5 sts to 3rd dpn. Work back and forth in rows on 10 sts of first dpn only: **Row 1** (RS) *Sl 1, k1; rep from* across. **Row 2** Sl 1, p across. Rep rows 1–2 until a total of 11 rows of heel have been worked.

Turn heel Cont on 10 sts: **Row 1** (WS) P 5, p2tog, p1, turn. **Row 2** Sl 1, k1, ssk, k1, turn. **Row 3** Sl 1, p2, p2tog, p1, turn. **Row 4** Sl 1, k3, ssk, k1—6 sts. Do not turn.

Gusset With empty dpn, pick up and k 4 sts along side of heel and sl to first dpn; with 2nd dpn, k 10 sts from next 2 dpn; with 3rd dpn, pick up and k 4 sts along other side of heel, then k 3 heel sts—24 sts. Beg of rnd is now at center of heel. **Next rnd** On first dpn, k to last 2 sts, k2tog; k across 2nd dpn; on 3rd dpn, ssk, k to end. **Next rnd** Knit. Rep last 2 rnds until 16 sts rem, AT SAME TIME, work 9 rnds of Chart 3 or Chart 4.

Foot Work even until foot measures 1½" from back of heel.

Toe Sl 1 st from beg of 2nd dpn to first dpn; sl 1 st from end of 2nd dpn to 3rd dpn—4 sts each on first and 3rd dpn, 8 sts on 2nd dpn. **Rnd 1** On first dpn, k to last 2 sts, k2tog; on 2nd dpn, ssk, k to last 2 sts, k2tog; on 3rd dpn, ssk, k to end. **Rnd 2** Knit. Rep rnds 1–2 until 8 sts rem. K sts from first dpn to 3rd dpn. Graft rem 4 sts on each dpn tog.

Twisted cord **Step ❶** Cut strands 6 times the length of cord needed. Fold in half and knot the cut ends together. **Step ❷** With knotted end in left hand and right index finger in folded end, twist clockwise until cord is tightly twisted. **Step ❸** Fold cord in half and smooth as it twists on itself; knot.

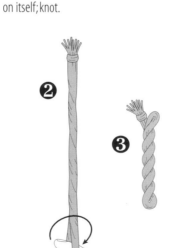

Chart 1
14
10
1
3-st rep

Chart 2
15
10
1
4-st rep

Chart 3
9
1
2-st rep

Chart 4
9
1
4-st rep

☐ Color 1
▨ Color 2

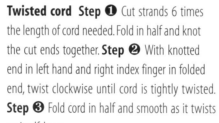

Size 2½ to 3" depending on yarn thickness.

Materials **A** Small amounts of fingering-weight to sport-weight yarn. **B** Set of 4 double-pointed needles (dpn) in size 0 (2mm), *or size to obtain gauge.* 4 to 5" dpn work well for this project.

Gauge 8 sts to 1" (2.5cm) over St st using size 0 (2mm) dpn.

Popcorn Panache

INTERMEDIATE LEVEL

KATHLEEN DAY

SANTA YNEZ, CALIFORNIA

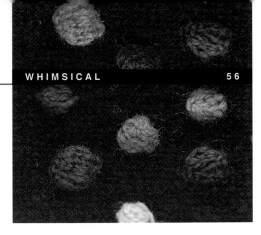
Make bobble K1-yo-k1-yo- k1 into the same st. Turn, p5, turn, work 4 (or 5, or 6) rows of St st. Sl the 2nd st, then 3rd, 4th, and 5th st over the first st. Sl the last bobble st to the left-hand needle and knit it through the back loop (tbl). If, on the next row, that st seems loose, knit it tbl.

Leg *Note:* Read through instructions before working bobbles. With MC, cast on 62 sts and divide evenly over 3 dpn. Place marker, join, and k 7 rnds, inc 2 sts on the last rnd—64 sts. Work 5 rnds in k2, p2 rib. **Rnds 1–4** Knit. **Rnd 5** K1, ssk, k to last 3 sts, k2tog, k1—2 sts dec. Rep rnds 1–5 until 52 sts rem. Work even until piece measures 8" from beg, AT SAME TIME, on the first knit row below the ribbing, use approx 1 yd of a colored yarn to make a bobble every 7th st around. Measure lengths of several colors before starting a bobble row. Knit approx 7 rnds between bobble rnds. Alternate the positions of the bobbles on subsequent rnds. Intermittently, make a 3-st bobble (k1-yo-k1; work 2, 3, or 4 rows of St st). You can even choose to have the purl side of some of the bobbles out.

Heel Sl next 26 sts to first dpn, next 13 to 2nd dpn, and next 13 to 3rd dpn. Change to a bright color. Work back and forth in rows on 26 sts of first dpn only: **Row 1** (RS) K3, *sl 1, k1; rep from* across to last 3 sts, k3. **Rows 2, 4** K3, p20, k3. **Row 3** K3, *k1, sl 1; rep from* to last 3 sts, k3. Rep last 4 rows 9 times more.

Turn heel **Row 1** K18, ssk, turn. **Row 2** Sl 1, p10, p2tog, turn. **Row 3** Sl 1, k10, ssk, turn. Rep Rows 2–3 until 12 sts rem, end with RS row. Do not turn.

"I like to use the five-inch needles by Brittany. They come in sets of five. I have two sets of the same size and routinely knit socks on six needles. That way I can easily try on the socks as I knit."

Gusset Change to MC. With RS facing and empty dpn, pick up and k 18 sts along side of heel and sl to first dpn. With 2nd dpn, k 26 sts from next 2 dpn. With 3rd dpn, pick up and k 18 sts along other side of heel, then k 6 heel sts—74 sts. Beg of rnd is now at center of heel. **Rnd 1** On first dpn, k to last 3 sts, k2tog, k1; k across 26 sts of 2nd dpn; on 3rd dpn, k1, ssk, k to end—2 sts dec. **Rnd 2** Knit. Rep rnds 1–2 until 52 sts rem.

Foot Work even until foot measures 2" less than desired length.

Toe Change to a bright color. **Rnd 1** On first dpn, k to last 3 sts, k2tog, k1; on 2nd dpn, k1, ssk, k to last 3 sts, k2tog, k1; on 3rd dpn, k1, ssk, k to end. **Rnd 2** Knit. Rep rnds 1–2 until 16 sts rem. K 4 sts of first dpn onto 3rd dpn. Graft rem 8 sts from each dpn tog.

Finishing Finish ends of bobbles: Gently pull on each end of yarn to tighten, knot, then pull each end through to front so as to come through the bobble at a different spot. Weave back into bobble (over one strand of a st) and out at another spot. Cut the yarn close to the bobble. This leaves the inside of the sock clean and beautiful.

Size Woman's medium.

Materials **A** 3½oz/100g (approx 375yds/342m) sock-weight yarn in black (MC). Several yards each of lime, purple, pink, dark pink, turquoise; allow extra yarn for heel and toe color. **B** Set of 4 double-pointed needles (dpn) size 0 (2mm), *or size to obtain gauge.*

Gauge 7 sts to 1" (2.5cm) over St st using size 0 (2mm) dpn.

WHIMSICAL 57

Sunrise Socks

EXPERIENCED LEVEL

MARILYN BUSTER
TULSA, OKLAHOMA

"I've named this heel The Skinny Ankle Heel. It's similar to a commercial heel and a neat fit if you have slim ankles."

"Work the foot of the sock until you can just see the web between your big toe and second toe when you try it on."

Size Woman's medium.

Materials A 3½oz/100g (approx 435yds/397m) sock-weight yarn in dark blue (MC); small amounts in white, medium blue, magenta, dark pink, light pink, dark lavender, light lavender, yellow orange, medium yellow, light yellow, and medium green. **B** Set of 4 double-pointed needles (dpn) in size 1 (2.5 mm), *or size to obtain gauge.* **C** One pair size 1 (2.5mm) straight needles. **D** Bobbins.

Gauge 8½ sts to 1" (2.5cm) in St st using size 1 (2.5mm) dpn.

Note Socks are worked back and forth in rows on straight needles from cast-on edge to beg of heel, then joined and worked on dpns to end.

First Sock - *Tulsa Skyline*

With MC and straight needle, cast on 72 sts. Work 1¼" in k2, p2 rib. Work rows 1–84 of Tulsa Skyline chart. Rearrange sts as foll: Sl first 18 sts to dpn, next 36 sts to 2nd dpn, and rem 18 sts to 3rd dpn. Place marker, join, and with MC, k 2 rnds, ending last rnd after working 2nd dpn.

Heel K across 18 sts from first dpn, sl 18 sts from 3rd dpn to beg of first dpn—36 sts. Divide rem 36 sts from 2nd dpn onto 2 empty dpn and leave on hold. Work back and forth in rows on 36 sts of first dpn only: **Row 1** (RS) K35, turn. **Row 2** P34, turn. Rep rows 1–2, working 1 st less at end of every row until 12 sts are left in center, end with a WS row. **Next row** (RS) K12, with tip of left-hand needle, pick up 2 sts along the edge between the needles, k3tog through the back loop (tbl). Turn. **Next row** P13, pick up 2 sts along the edge between the needles, p3tog , turn. Cont in this manner until all sts are used up, end with a WS row. Turn.

Foot Sl 36 sts on hold to empty dpn. K 18 heel sts onto 3rd dpn and leave rem 18 heel sts on first dpn—72 sts. Work even in rnds until foot measures 4" or 2" less than desired length from heel.

Toe Rnd 1 K to last 2 sts on first dpn, sl 2 tog knitwise to right-hand (RH) needle, k1 from 2nd dpn and p2sso; k to last 2 sts on 2nd dpn, sl 2 tog knitwise to RH needle, k1 from 3rd needle and p2sso— 68 sts. **Rnd 2** Knit. Rep last 2 rnds until 24 sts rem. K 6 sts from first dpn onto 3rd dpn. Cut yarn, leaving a 12" tail. Graft rem 12 sts from each dpn tog. Sew leg seam.

Second sock - *Bristol Head Mountain*

Work as for first sock, working Bristol Head Mountain chart (see page 86).

Tulsa Skyline

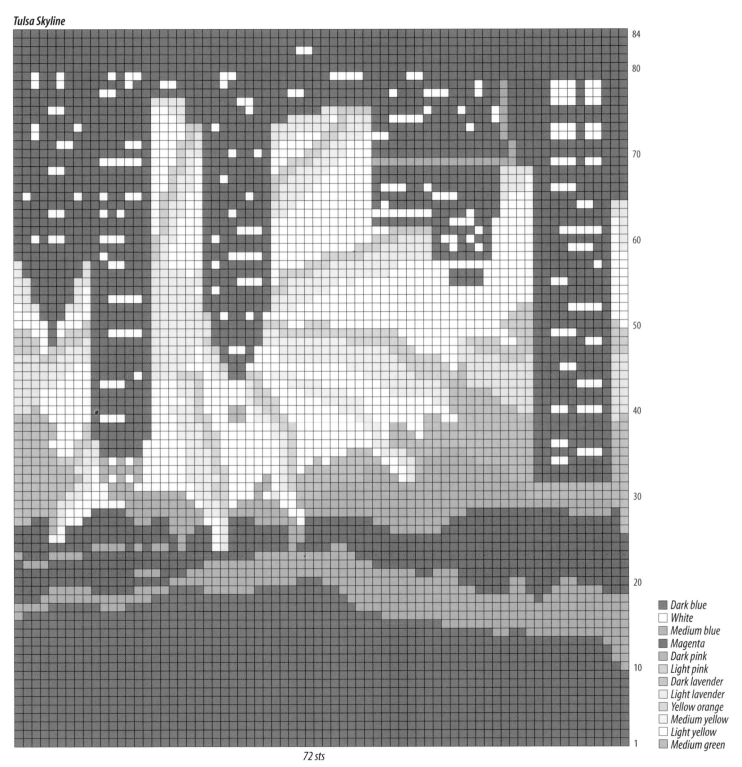

84
80
70
60
50
40
30
20
10
1

72 sts

■ Dark blue
□ White
■ Medium blue
■ Magenta
■ Dark pink
■ Light pink
■ Dark lavender
□ Light lavender
■ Yellow orange
□ Medium yellow
□ Light yellow
■ Medium green

Bristol Head Mountain

72 sts

■ Dark blue
☐ Medium blue
■ Magenta
☐ Light pink
☐ Dark lavender
☐ Light lavender
☐ Yellow orange
☐ Medium yellow
☐ Light yellow

Spring Fever

EXPERIENCED LEVEL

RITA GARRITY KNUDSON
GOLDEN VALLEY, MINNESOTA

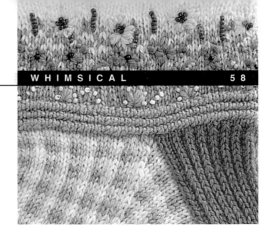

Note Instruction is written for one sock; brackets indicate changes for second sock.

Leg With scrap yarn, cast on 67 sts. With A, k 4 rnds. **Rnd 5** (picot rnd) K1, *yo, k2tog; rep from* across. **Rnds 6–11** Knit. **Rnd 12** Knit and inc 13 sts evenly across—80 sts. Work 8-st rep of rnds 1–15 of Chart 1. **Next rnd** (WS) With MC, knit and dec 8 sts evenly across—72 sts. Work ridges: **Rnds 1–3** Knit. **Row 4** With spare needle and working on WS, pick up the loops of the purl sts from 3 rows below. *K2tog (a picked-up loop and next st on left-hand needle). Rep from* across until all sts are worked. Rep last 4 rows twice more.

Heel K first 18 sts to first dpn, sl next 18 sts to 2nd dpn, next 19 sts to 3rd dpn, and rem 17 sts to first dpn. Work back and forth in rows on 35 sts of first dpn only: **Row 1** (RS) With C [D], k1; *sl 1, k1; rep from* across. **Row 2** (WS) P35. Rep last 2 rows until heel measures 2¾", end with a WS row.

Turn heel Cont on 35 sts: **Row 1** (RS) K19, ssk, k1, turn. **Row 2** Sl 1, p4, p2tog, p1; turn. **Row 3** Sl 1, k 5, ssk, k1; turn. **Row 4** Sl 1, p6, p2tog, p1; turn. Cont to dec in same way, working 1 more st between decs, until 19 sts rem, end with a RS row. Do not turn.

Gusset With empty dpn and MC, pick up and k 24 sts along side of heel and sl to first dpn; with 2nd dpn, k across 37 sts on next 2 dpn; with 3rd dpn, pick up and k 24 sts along other side of heel, then k 9 heel sts—104 sts. Beg of rnd is at center of heel. **Beg Chart 2: Rnd 1** Work 4-st rep around. **Rnd 2** On first dpn, work chart pat to last 2 sts, k2tog; cont pat across 2nd dpn; on 3rd dpn, ssk, cont pat around—102 sts. Cont chart pat and dec 2 sts every other rnd as in rnd 2 until 76 sts rem. Work even in chart pat until foot measures 6½" or 2" less than desired length, end with rnd 2 or 4.

Toe Sl 1 st from first dpn onto 2nd dpn—19 sts each on first and 3rd dpns; 38 sts on 2nd dpn. **Rnd 1** With E [F], knit. **Rnd 2** On first dpn, k to last 2 sts, k2tog; on 2nd dpn, k1, ssk, k to last 3 sts, k2tog, k1; on 3rd dpn, ssk, k around—72 sts. Cont to dec every other rnd until 48 sts rem. Dec every rnd until 32 sts rem. K 8 sts from first dpn to 3rd dpn. Cut yarn, leaving a 16" tail. Graft 16 sts on each dpn tog.

Finishing Fold hem at picot row, remove scrap yarn, and sew hem loosely to inside. With F [C], work Chart 3 in duplicate st on toe. With C [E], embroider flower above the 'i'. Using photos as guide, embroider flowers, using lazy daisy and straight sts plus French knots; sew on beads.

Rita is in a fever to work on three more pair—
summer, fall, and winter, of course.

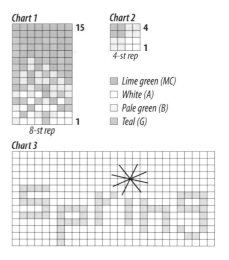

Chart 1 15 ... 1

8-st rep

Chart 2 4 ... 1

4-st rep

- ■ Lime green (MC)
- □ White (A)
- □ Pale green (B)
- ■ Teal (G)

Chart 3

Lazy daisy stitch

French knot stitch

Size Woman's medium.

Materials A 1¾oz/50g (approx 215yds/196m) sock-weight yarn: 1 ball each in lime green (MC), white (A), pale green (B); small amounts each in magenta (C), purple (D), blue (E), yellow (F), and teal (G). Scrap yarn. **B** Set of 4 double-pointed needles (dpn) in size 1 (2.5 mm), *or size to obtain gauge*. **C** Straight needles in size 1 (2.5mm). **D** Tapestry needle, embroidery needle, stitch holders and markers. **E** Seed beads (size 11/0), multicolor.

Gauge 8 sts to 1" (2.5cm) in St st using size 1 (2.5mm) needles.

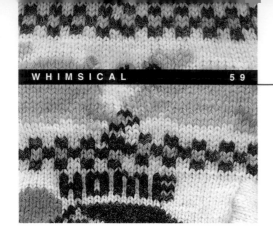

Little Piggy Toes
EXPERIENCED LEVEL

If you feel toes should be given a choice,
individually,
—to go to market, or to stay home,
to have roast beef, or to have none—
these 'gloves' for feet are the answer.
And you don't have to decide how many pigs
are enough until after the socks are knit.
The pigs on feet and legs
are added in duplicate stitch.

Left Sock

Note Pigs on legs and feet are duplicate stitched after the socks are knit.

Leg With A and larger dpn, cast on 66 sts. Divide sts evenly over 3 dpn. Change to smaller dpn, place marker, join and work 7 rnds in k1, p1 rib, inc 2 sts evenly on each dpn—72 sts. With larger dpn and MC, k 1 rnd. Work 4-st rep of 6 rnds of Chart 1. With MC, k 21 rnds. Work Chart 1 once more.

Heel Rearrange sts: first 36 sts on first dpn, next 18 sts on 2nd dpn, and next 18 sts on 3rd dpn. Working back and forth on 36 sts of first dpn only, work rows 1–28 of Chart 2.

Turn heel Cont on 36 sts: **Row 1** (RS) K20, ssk, k1; turn. **Row 2** Sl 1, p5, p2tog, p1; turn. **Row 3** Sl 1, k6, ssk, k1; turn. **Row 4** Sl 1, p7, p2tog, p1; turn. Cont to dec in same way, working 1 st more between decs, until 20 sts rem, end with a RS row. Do not turn.

Gusset With empty dpn and MC, pick up and k 20 sts along side of heel and sl to first dpn; with 2nd dpn, k across 36 sts from next 2 dpn; with 3rd dpn, pick up and k 20 sts along other side of heel, then k 10 heel sts—96 sts. **Next rnd** On first dpn, k to last 3 sts, k2tog, k1; k across 2nd dpn; on 3rd dpn, k1, ssk, k to end—94 sts. **Next rnd** Knit. Rep last 2 rnds until 76 sts rem. Work Chart 1 once, AT SAME TIME, cont decs until 72 sts rem.

Foot With MC, k 21 rnds. Work Chart 1 once. With MC, k 1 rnd. With C, k 3 rnds.

Toes Work toes with C. Sl sts from 3rd and first dpn to spare dpn. Sl sts from 2nd dpn to 2nd spare dpn—36 sts on first dpn for bottom of toes and 36 sts on 2nd dpn for top of toes.

Little Toe Sl last 6 sts from bottom dpn to empty dpn; first 6 sts from top dpn to 2nd dpn; cast on 4 sts onto 3rd dpn—16 sts. Join and k 6 rnds. **Next rnd** K1; [k2tog, k1] 5 times—11 sts. K 1 rnd. **Next rnd** K2tog, [k1, k2tog] 3 times—7 sts. K 1 rnd. Cut yarn, leaving a 4" tail. Thread yarn through rem sts, pull tightly and fasten off. Pick up and k 4 sts along 4-st cast-on from little toe, k across rem sts from top and bottom of toes—64 sts. K 1 rnd.

2nd Toe Sl last 6 sts from bottom of toes to empty dpn; next 10 sts to 2nd dpn; cast 4 sts onto 3rd dpn—20 sts. Join and k 11 rnds. **Next rnd** K2, [k2tog, k1] 6 times—14 sts. K 1 rnd. **Next rnd** K2tog, [k1, k2tog] 4 times—9 sts. K 1 rnd. Cut yarn and complete as

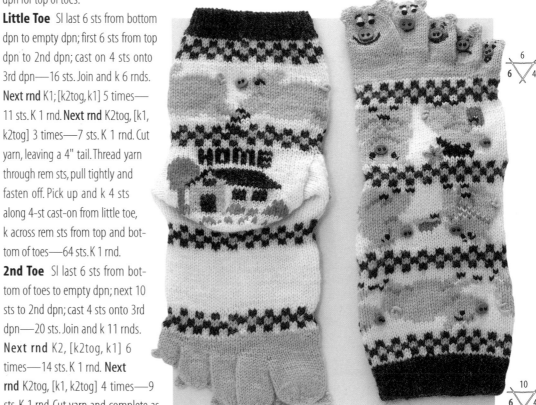

Size Woman's medium.

Materials A 1¾oz/50g (approx 215yds/196m) sock-weight yarn: 1 ball each in white (MC), in charcoal (A), light pink (B), and pink (C). Small amounts of dark pink, medium blue, light green, bright green, and brown. Small amounts of embroidery thread in black, white, blue, and red. **B** Set of 4 double-pointed needles (dpn) in sizes 0 and 1 (2 and 2.5 mm), *or size to obtain gauge.* 2 spare dpns in size 1 (2.5mm). **C** Tapestry needle, embroidery needle. **D** Glass seed beads in black. **E** Pig noses in rose: 4 large (1cm), 16 medium (¾cm), and 4 small (½cm).

Gauge 8 sts to 1" (2.5cm) in St st, using size 1 (2.5mm) dpn.

for Little Toe. Pick up and k 4 sts along 4-st cast-on from 2nd Toe, k across rem sts from top and bottom of toes—52 sts.

Middle Toe SI last 6 sts from bottom of toes to empty dpn; next 10 sts to 2nd dpn; cast on 4 sts onto 3rd dpn—20 sts. K 20 rnds. **Next rnd** K2, [k2tog, k1] 6 times—14 sts. K 1 rnd. **Next rnd** K2tog, [k1, k2tog] 4 times—9 sts. K 1 rnd. Cut yarn and complete as for Little Toe. Pick up and k 4 sts along 4-st-cast-on from Middle Toe, k across rem sts from top and bottom of toes—40 sts.

4th Toe Work as for Middle Toe. Pick up and k 4 sts along 4-st-cast-on from 4th Toe, k across rem sts from top and bottom of toes—28 sts.

Big Toe K 14 rnds. **Next rnd** *K1, k2tog, k2, k2tog; rep from* around—20 sts. K 1 rnd. **Next rnd** K2tog, [k1, k2tog] 6 times—13 sts. K 1 rnd. Cut yarn and complete as for Little Toe.

Finishing Using photo as guide, foll charts and duplicate st Pig #1 (the wee, wee, wee pig) on upper MC section 3 times; Pigs #2 and #3 (the pigs with and without roast beef) on middle MC section once; and Pigs #4 and #5 (the market pig and the stay-home pig) on lower MC section once. Use boullion stitch for tails. Attach noses plus 2 black seed beads for nostrils. Embroider faces on toes, using satin, lazy daisy and outline stitches.

Ears Big toe With smaller dpn, pick up and k 7 sts along upper shaped side of big toe. Work in rev St st as foll: *2 rows even, then dec 1 st each side of next row—5 sts. Rep from* once—3 sts. Work 1 row even, then k3tog. Fasten off. Rep for 2nd ear.

2nd, Middle and 4th Toes Pick up and k 5 sts. In rev St st, work 2 rows and dec 1 st each side on 2nd row. Work 1 row over 3 sts, then k3tog. Fasten off.

Little Toe Pick up and k 3 sts. Work 2 rows in rev St st. K3tog. Fasten off.

Right Sock Work as for Left Sock, reversing pig placement and toe shaping.

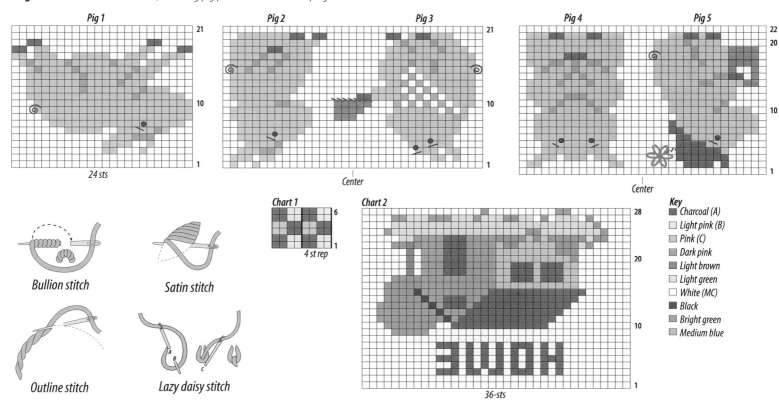

Pig 1 — 24 sts

Pig 2 — Center

Pig 3

Pig 4

Pig 5 — Center

Bullion stitch

Satin stitch

Outline stitch

Lazy daisy stitch

Chart 1 — 4 st rep

Chart 2 — 36-sts

Key
Charcoal (A)
Light pink (B)
Pink (C)
Dark pink
Light brown
Light green
White (MC)
Black
Bright green
Medium blue

Maple Swirl Socks

ADVENTUROUS LEVEL

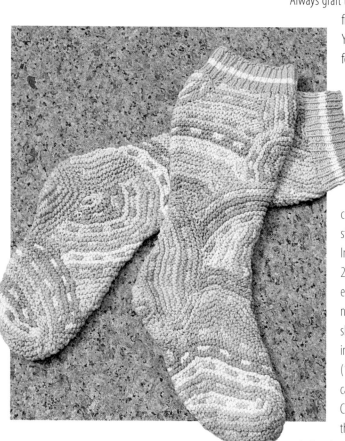

"I have been developing a technique for knitting in swirls which weave about each other. Since a sock is a relatively complex sculptural form, and quite small, it was challenging to design. I have had to come up with a new system of graphing and notation."

"This is a garter stitch pattern so it lies flat in all directions. That makes it quite thick and I didn't want too hot a sock, so I used cotton. I have designed them to avoid joins as much as possible. These are grafted for smoothness. Each piece is picked up from a previous one to avoid making a jigsaw sock."

Suggestions Colors Colors A and B are changed from band to band. To reduce the number of ends, carry one of the colors up to next segment. Knitting with one color in each hand works well with this pattern. **Ends** Weaving in ends as you go is highly recommended. **Markers** These are vital for following the graph and should be placed between segments. **Increases** Always inc on a RS row by k into front and back of a st, preferably not over contrasting color. **Grafting** Always graft top or bottom edge of pattern over a selvedge. Graft knitwise through selvedge (i.e., down to back, up to front) and purlwise through pattern edge (i.e., up to front, down to back). **Casting on and binding off** Your usual cast-on and bind-off may produce extra ridges and add bulk when seamed or grafted. Try the foll: *For edges to be grafted later,* use a loose backward-loop cast-on in first WS row or bind off by putting last RS row on holding thread. *For edges to be picked up and knitted later,* use loose backward-loop cast-on in first RS row (when casting on after picked-up sts) or use long-tail cast-on in first WS row (when casting on before picked-up stitches) or bind off by putting last WS row on holding thread. **Holders** You will have lots of sts on holders. Use a contrasting yarn threaded through.

First sock

Work in chart pat throughout, foll diagram and accompanying notes for shaping. **A** Note the direction arrow and remember that each band consists of 6 rows. The first small band consists of 2 triangles, with a +1 and a +2 in them. These represent increases at an edge and, in this case, start from 0 stitches. You could work them as: **Row 1** Make a loop. **Row 2** Inc—2 sts. **Row 3** Knit. **Row 4** Inc in first st—3 sts. **Row 5** Knit. **2nd band** Change colors and work in chart pat. Place a marker after the 2nd st and work an inc in each segment in every RS row (4 +5 sts). **3rd band** Inc 3 sts at the left-hand edge, then separate them with a marker to make 3 segments (8+7+3 sts). **5th band** Note that there are now 3 incs within all 3 segments as well as 3 edge incs on the left. **6th band** The 3 decs on the right should occur more at the beginning than at the end to give the shaping shown. On the left there is first one inc, then 4 decs. **8th band** The dec on the right occurs late in the band. **9th band** Cont to work on the (13+11) sts on the right and 6 sts on the left. Place rem 7 sts on a holding thread. The last row of section A can be bound off normally. It will be ribbed later. **B** 16 sts are picked up from A (see diagram). **5th band** Cast on (8 +16) sts on the right to be used for later pick-up. Leave a 24" end, work the 11 picked-up sts, then use the end for a long-tail cast-on at the end of the next WS row. At the end of the band, k10, cut a 24" end and use it for grafting piece B over piece A (see diagram). **C** Pick up 50 sts from A and B. In the last row, k2tog while binding off. **D** Note the direction arrow. This piece starts from the outside of the coil and decreases in. Pick up 65 sts from A and B, then cast on 8 by the loop method for later pick up. Cast on the 20 sts for later grafting at beg of first WS row by the loop method. Leave a 20" end for later grafting. In the last row, the first 7 segments disappear. You could work 4 decs at the beginning of the last RS row, then graft D over A and D, then draw the last 4 sts tog with the grafting thread. **E** Pick up 7 from D, 4 from B, 25 from A, 11 from D. Cast on 14 for later grafting by the loop method at beg of first WS row. After the last RS row of band 1, leave 10 sts on thread for grafting. After the last RS row of band 3, put the first 35 sts on a holding thread, leave a 3 foot end and cont to work on rem (12 +9) sts. Sew the open ends of E tog. **F** In the 3rd band all decs are on the right. Most need to be done by casting off. Graft D over F. **G** Leave a 24" end, pick up

Size Women's medium. Adjust size with needle size.
Materials A A total of 7½ozs/210g (approx 425yds/387m) worsted-weight cotton in 7 colors. **B** Knitting elastic for ribbed cuff (optional). **C** 24" (60cm) circular needle in size 6 (4mm), *or size to obtain gauge.*
Note Socks can be knitted on straight needles.
Gauge 5¼ sts to 1" (2.5cm) over chart pat using size 6 (4mm) needle.

23 sts from F and E, use the tail to cast on 25 sts at end of first WS row. **H** The last row will later be grafted under piece E. **I** The center 8-st pick up takes 4 from G and 4 from H. **J** Pick up from F and most of G. (K will need to pick up 6 from G also.) Now graft E over J, then E over H and I, and the last bit of I over J. **K** Pick up from J, G, I, and J again. Cast on 8 for grafting. After band 2, cast on 10 for grafting. Graft K to itself. **L** Pick up 18 from K, using diagram as guide. After completing L, try sock on, fit comfortably, and tack in position. If socks are to fit either foot, try it on both and compromise. Graft L in place.

Second sock

Work graph in reverse. Read pattern as if it refers to reverse side of work (read it with WS of work facing you).

Finishing Sew in ends. With smaller needles, pick up and k 56 sts evenly around top edge. Work 18 rows of k1, p1 rib with yarn and knitting elastic held tog. Bind off in rib.

Chart pat

☐ Color A
▨ Color B

6-st rep

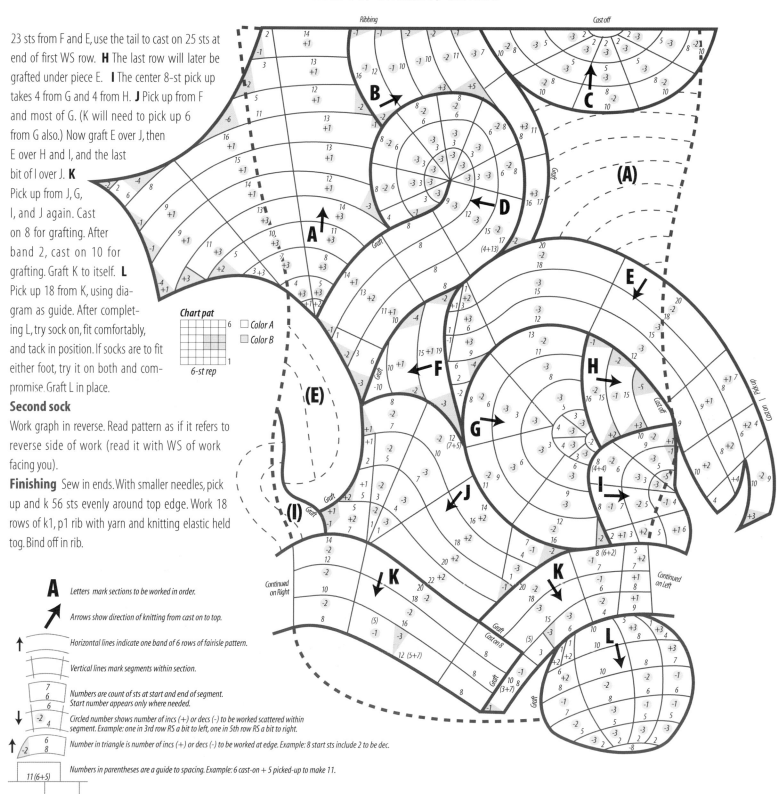

A Letters mark sections to be worked in order.

↗ Arrows show direction of knitting from cast on to top.

Horizontal lines indicate one band of 6 rows of fairisle pattern.

Vertical lines mark segments within section.

Numbers are count of sts at start and end of segment. Start number appears only where needed.

Circled number shows number of incs (+) or decs (−) to be worked scattered within segment. Example: one in 3rd row RS a bit to left, one in 5th row RS a bit to right.

Number in triangle is number of incs (+) or decs (−) to be worked at edge. Example: 8 start sts include 2 to be dec.

Numbers in parentheses are a guide to spacing. Example: 6 cast-on + 5 picked-up to make 11.

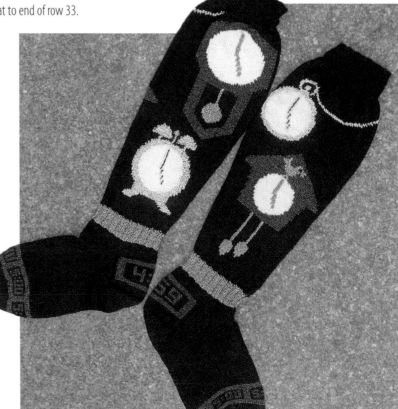
Clock Socks

PATRICIA BRUNNER

SEATTLE, WASHINGTON

EXPERIENCED LEVEL

These socks celebrate clocks that have marked time throughout Patricia's life: ". . . my Dad's silver pocket watch from the 1930s; the pesky two-bell alarm that drove me nuts at college in the 50s; the cuckoo my husband brought home from Germany in the 60s; the quirky clock I bought in the 80s which signals the hour with a wimpy boink; the wrist watch awarded me for 30 years of faithful service; and the digital LEDs that glow on all the 90s electronics I can't live without. Most of the clocks are set at 5:00, that favorite hour which a former co-worker referred to as 'go-home time.' The clock on the heel is like me— always a little behind."

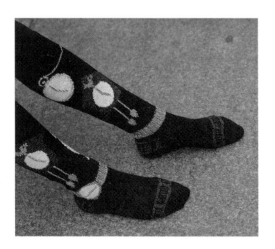

Size Woman's medium.

Materials **A** Sock-weight yarn: 4oz/115g (approx 490yds/447m) in black (MC); 1oz/30g in white. **B** ¾oz/25g lurex yarn each in copper, silver, and gold; 75 yds lurex yarn in red. **C** Optional: 75 yds spool of fine polyester in rainbow. **D** Set of 4 double-pointed needles (dpn) in sizes 0 and 1 (2 and 2.5mm) *or size to obtain gauge.*

Gauge 9 sts to 1"(2.5cm) over St st using size 1 (2.5mm) dpn.

Notes 1 Socks are knit circularly, working intarsia in the round. If you prefer, work back and forth in rows from cast-on edge to beg of heel, then join and work on dpns to end. *2 Work intarsia circularly as foll:* K the first rnd from right to left using standard intarsia technique. At end of first rnd, drop last working yarn and with a new strand of same color, beg 2nd rnd by knitting back from left to right. At the end of 2nd rnd, drop working yarn and pick up yarn from first rnd under yarn from 2nd rnd. In same way, cont to alternate rnds, crossing yarns at end of each rnd. Hold needles parallel and close tog to regulate tension at join. *3 Work decs as foll:* At beg of rnd, k1, ssk, cont pat around to last 3 sts, end k2tog, k1. *4* Embroider clock hands, bird's eye and numerals when socks have been knit. *5* If you do not want to knit from left to right, turn at end of rnd and purl back on alternate rnds, remembering to cross yarns and keeping colors correct. Dec on RS as above. *Dec on WS as foll:* At beg of rnd, p1, p2tog through the back loop, cont pat around to last 3 sts, end p2tog, p1. *6* Use optional strand rainbow polyester with white sock yarn on clock and watch faces.

Left Sock

Leg With smaller dpn and MC, cast on 100 sts and divide over 3 dpn as foll: 34 sts each on first and 3rd dpns and 32 sts on 2nd dpn. Place marker, join and work 22 rnds in k1, p1. Change to larger dpns. Work rnds 1–171 of Chart 1, working decs as indicated, ending last rnd 20 sts before end—72 sts.

Heel K across 20 sts from first dpn and sl sts from 3rd dpn onto beg of first dpn—40 sts. Divide rem 32 sts on 2nd dpn to 2 empty dpn and leave on hold. Work back and forth in rows on 40 sts of first dpn only: **Row 1** Work 40 sts of Chart 2. Sl first st of every row and cont in chart pat to end of row 33.

Turn heel Cont on 40 sts of first dpn: **Row 1** (WS) With MC, p24, p2tog, p1, turn. **Row 2** Sl 1, k9, ssk, k1. **Row 3** Sl 1, p10, p2tog, p1. **Row 4** Sl 1, k11, ssk, k1. Cont to dec in same way, working 1 st more between decs on each row until 24 sts rem, end with a RS row. Do not turn.

Gusset With empty dpn and MC, pick up and k 17 sts along side of heel, M1 in loop of st below first instep st and sl to first dpn; with

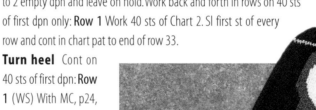

Chart 2

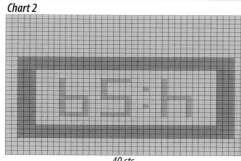

40 sts

Chart 3

72 sts

Chart 1

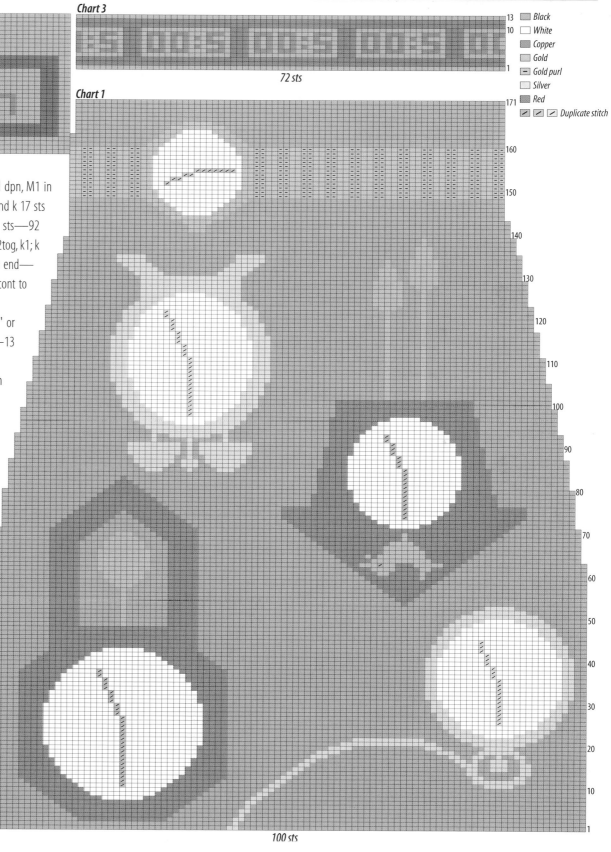

13 ◼ Black
10 ◻ White
◼ Copper
◻ Gold
– Gold purl
◻ Silver
171 ◼ Red
⟋ ⟋ ⟋ Duplicate stitch

2nd dpn, k across next 2 dpn; with 3rd dpn, M1 in loop of st below last instep st, pick up and k 17 sts along other side of heel, then k 12 heel sts—92 sts. **Rnd 1** On first dpn, k to last 3 sts, k2tog, k1; k across 2nd dpn; on 3rd dpn, k1, ssk, k to end—90 sts. **Rnd 2** Work even. In same way, cont to dec every other rnd until there are 72 sts.

Foot Work even until foot measures 4" or 2" less than desired length. Work rnds 1–13 of Chart 3.

Toe Sl 2 sts each from first and 3rd dpn to 2nd dpn (18 sts each on first and 3rd dpn, 36 sts on 2nd dpn). Work with MC and reinforcing yarn as foll: **Rnd 1** On first dpn, cont pat to last 3 sts, k2tog, k1; on 2nd dpn, k1, ssk, cont pat to last 3 sts, k2tog, k1; on 3rd dpn, k1, ssk, cont pat to end—4 sts dec. **Rnd 2** Work even. Rep last 2 rnds until 40 sts rem. Dec every rnd until 24 sts rem. K 6 sts from first dpn to 3rd dpn. Cut yarn, leaving a 12" tail. Graft rem 12 sts from each dpn tog.

Finishing Duplicate st clock hands, bird's eye, and numerals using colors as indicated on charts. *Note* Use single strand of red lurex for numerals on toe, double strand on heel.

Right Leg Work as for Left Leg, reversing clock placement.

100 sts

Watermelon Socks

SHARON PHILBRICK

EASY LEVEL

CRESCENT CITY, CALIFORNIA

As these two socks show,
whimsy can be as simple as the selection and
placement of color (red socks with white and
green bands to suggest watermelon rind and
black stitches for seeds) or the material used
(consider anything that is the shape of yarn,
even string licorice!).

Leg With green, cast on 44 sts and divide over 3 dpn as foll: 12 sts on first dpn, 16 on 2nd dpn, and 16 on 3rd dpn. Place marker, join and knit 6 rnds. Work 2 rnds in k2, p2 rib. Change to white and knit 1 rnd. Work 4 rnds in k2, p2 rib. Leaving 10" tail when ending old color or joining new color, change to red and k every rnd for 1½."

Heel Sl next 22 sts to first dpn, next 11 sts to 2nd dpn, and next 11 sts to 3rd dpn. Work back and forth in rows on 22 sts of first dpn only: **Row 1** (RS) Sl 1, k21. **Row 2** *Sl 1, p1; rep from* across. Rep last 2 rows 6 times more.

Turn heel Cont on 22 sts: **Row 1** Sl 1, k15, ssk, turn. **Row 2** Sl 1, p10, p2tog, turn. **Row 3** Sl 1, k10, ssk, turn. Rep rows 2–3 until 12 sts rem, ending with WS row, turn. **Next row** Sl 1, k11.

Gusset With RS facing and empty dpn, pick up and k 14 sts along side of heel and sl to first dpn. With 2nd dpn, k 22 sts from next 2 dpn. With 3rd dpn, pick up and k 14 sts along other side of heel, then k 6 heel sts—62 sts. Beg of rnd is now at center of heel. **Rnd 1** Knit. **Rnd 2** On first dpn, k to last 3 sts, ssk, k1; k 22 sts of 2nd dpn, on 3rd dpn, k1, k2tog, k to end —2 sts dec. Rep rnds 1—2 until 44 sts rem.

Foot K every rnd for 4" or until 2" less than desired length.

Toe **Rnd 1** On first dpn, k to last 3 sts, k2tog, k1; on 2nd dpn, k1, ssk, k to last 3 sts, k2tog, k1; on 3rd dpn, k1, ssk, k to end—4 sts dec. **Rnd 2** Knit. Rep rnds 1—2 until 16 sts rem. K 4 sts of first dpn onto 3rd dpn. Graft rem 8 sts from each dpn tog.

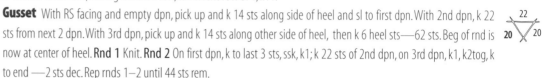

Finishing Weave all 10" ends through to outside of sock at rib. Tie into bows. Add optional small bows to ends of toes. With black, embroider straight-stitch seeds around leg by stitching over 3 rows in every 4th stitch.

Size Adult's small.

Materials **A** 2ozs/56g (approx 135yds/123m) worsted-weight yarn in red (MC); small amounts green, ecru, and black . **B** Set of 4 double-pointed needles (dpn) in size 5 (3.75mm), *or size to obtain gauge.*

Gauge 4½ sts to 1" (2.5cm) over St st using size 5 (3.75mm) dpn.

Licorice Socks

INTERMEDIATE LEVEL

DEBBIE NEW

WATERLOO, ONTARIO, CANADA

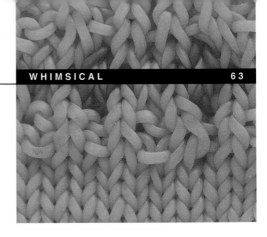

Technical suggestions Licorice laces are remarkably easy to knit with if not too cold, but they won't tolerate much stretching. If unpicking, you need to support the remaining stitches while easing out the unwanted ones. (It is best to eat these rather than reuse them!) My laces came in 18" lengths which means lots of bulky joins. Near the ribbed tops where they show, I found it best to weave in ends as you go. Inside, I left knots with short ends. Longer laces would be nice.

Leg Using MC, cast on 24 sts and divide evenly over 3 dpn. Place marker, join and work 2 rnds in k1, p1 rib. Join A and work 3 rnds of any 2-color, 4-st pattern. Cut A. With MC, k 1 rnd; work 2 rnds k1, p1 rib; and k 8 rnds.

Heel Rnd 1 K 17 sts in MC; join A and k 7 sts. Rnd 2 K 6 sts in A. Carefully thread a separate lace through the next 11 sts to hold them without stretching. Work back and forth in rows on 13 sts only: Row 1 (WS) Sl 1, p to end. Row 2 Sl 1, *k1, sl 1 with yarn in front; rep from* to last 2 sts, k2. Rep last 2 rows 4 times, then rep row 1 once.

Turn heel Cont on 13 sts: Row 1 Sl 1, k8, ssk, turn. Row 2 Sl 1, p5, p2tog, turn. Row 3 Sl 1, k5, ssk, turn. Rep rows 2 and 3 once, then rep row 2 once. Row 7 K2tog, k3, ssk. Change to MC.

Gusset With RS facing and empty dpn, pick up and k 7 sts along side of heel. Sl 11 instep sts back onto 2nd dpn and k. With 3rd dpn, pick up and k 7 sts along other side of heel, then k 3 heel sts—30 sts. Sl 2 rem heel sts to first dpn; beg of rnd is now at center of heel. Rnd 1 On first dpn, k to last 2 sts, k2tog; k 11 sts of 2nd dpn; on 3rd dpn, ssk, k to end. Rnd 2 Knit. Rep rnds 2–3 twice more—24 sts.

Foot K 11 rnds. Change to A.

Toe Rnd 1 Knit. Rnd 2 On first dpn, k to last 3 sts k2tog, k1; on 2nd dpn, k1, ssk, k to last 3 sts, k2tog, k1; on 3rd dpn, k1, ssk, k to end—4 sts dec. Rep rnds 1–2 until 12 sts rem. Thread lace through rem sts and fasten off. Eat leftovers.

"These socks are for grandmothers who love
to make hand-knit socks for grandchildren
who hate to wear them.
As with any knitting project,
choice of yarn is vital.
My first efforts totally self-destructed one night.
I have now found this superior knitting licorice at
Woolworths (in England where I am at present).
What makes a licorice suitable for knitting?
The strands are finer
and more flexible than most.
They don't dry out, crack, or break as easily."

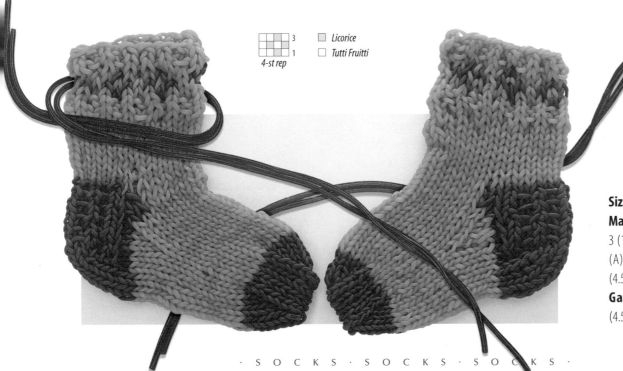

| | 3 | Licorice |
| | 1 | Tutti Fruitti |
4-st rep

Size Finished length, from heel to toe, is 6".

Materials A Woolworth's Bag of Fun licorice bootlaces: 3 (120g) bags of Tutti Fruitti (MC); 1 bag of Black Licorice (A). **B** Set of 4 double-pointed needles (dpn) size 7 (4.5mm), *or size to obtain gauge.*

Gauge 3½ sts to 1" (2.5cm) over Sts using size 7 (4.5mm) dpns.

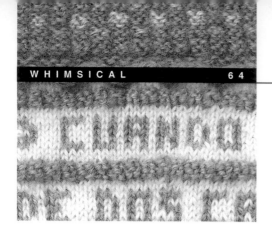

"In 'Ode to my socks,'
the Chilean poet Pablo Neruda
tells of receiving a pair of handknit wool socks
and wearing them with
an almost magical sense of joy.
In the last stanza is the moral of this tale:
as translated by poet Robert Bly,
'Beauty is twice beauty and what is good
is doubly good' (right sock)
'When it is a matter of two socks
made of wool in winter' (left sock).
I felt honor-bound to use the original Spanish
and two Andean knitting techniques—
a shell-like edge called *puntas*
and a purled check pattern."

Size Woman's large.

Materials **A** Sport-weight yarn: 6oz/165g (approx 265yds/242m) in white (MC); 4oz/115g in plum (A); 3oz/85g in violet (B); ¾oz/25g each in light green (C) and medium green (D). *(Spinner's note* English Teeswater wool, spun worsted, 3 ply, at approx 1600yds/lb; dyed with Gaywool plum, violet, and lucerne dyes.) **B** Set of 4 double-pointed needles (dpn) in size 2 (2.75 mm) *or size to obtain gauge.* **C** One straight knitting needle size 2 (2.75mm). **D** One size F/5 crochet hook. **E** 27 small pearls and one beading needle.

Gauge 7 sts to 1"(2.5cm) in chart pat using size 2 (2.75mm) dpn.

Pearls of Wisdom

EXPERIENCED LEVEL

Notes 1 Read charts from right to left only. *2* Instructions are for right sock: changes for left sock are in brackets. *3* Embroider diagonal lines in the letters M and N.

Cuff With crochet hook and A, chain 113 sts. Cut yarn. **Make first punta** Inserting dpn into back loops of crochet chain, k 1 st in each of next 8 chains, do not turn. Slide these 8 sts back to right end of dpn. Using dpn as left-hand needle and straight needle as right hand (RH) needle, sl first st to straight needle and with 2nd ball of A (do not cut first ball), k4, sl last 2 sts just worked back to dpn and k2tog; k1 from dpn; sl next 2 sts from RH needle over last st worked (3 sts now on RH needle); k2 from dpn; (5 sts on RH needle). **2nd punta** *With dpn, pick up 7 sts from chain loops, do not turn. Slide sts back to right end dpn; k4, sl last 2 sts just worked back to dpn; k2tog; k1 from dpn; sl next 2 sts from RH needle over last st worked; k2 from dpn;* (9 sts now on RH needle). Rep from* to * until all chain sts have been worked and 16 puntas are on RH needle—65 sts.

Rearrange sts as foll: Sl 22 sts each to first and 3rd dpns, and 21 sts to 2nd dpn. Place marker, join and k 1 rnd, then p 1 rnd. K 1 rnd and inc 15 sts evenly around—80 sts.

Work Check pat from chart or as foll: **Rnd 1** *K2 A, k2 D; rep from* around. **Rnds 2–3** Purl in colors as established. **Rnd 4** *K2 B, k2 A; rep from*. **Rnds 5–6** Rep rnd 2. **Rnd 7** *K2 A, k2 C; rep from*. **Rnds 8–9** Rep rnd 2. **Rnd 10** *K2 D, k2 A; rep from*. **Rnds 11–12** Rep rnd 2. **Rnd 13** *K2 A, k2 B; rep from*. **Rnds 14–15** Rep rnd 2. **Rnd 16** *K2 C, k2 A; rep from*. **Rnds 17–18** Rep rnd 2.

Work turning ridge: With A, k 1 rnd, p 1 rnd, then k 1 rnd.

Work 10 rnds in k1, p1 rib as foll: 3 rnds A, 7 rnds MC. Turn work inside out.

Leg With MC, k 14 rnds. Rep rnds 13–15 of Check pat. Work 9 rnds of Chart 1 [Chart 6]. Rep rnds 10–12 of Check pat. Dec 4 sts evenly in first rnd and work Chart 2 [Chart 7]—76 sts. Rep rnds 13–15 of Check pat. Dec 4 sts evenly in first rnd and work Chart 3 [Chart 8]—72 sts. Rep rnds 16–18 of Check pat. Dec 4 sts evenly in first rnd and work Chart 4 [Chart 9]—68 sts. Rep rnds 13–15 of Check pat. Dec 4 sts evenly in first rnd and work Chart 5 [Chart 10]—64 sts. Rep rnds 10–12 of Check pat.

With MC, k 5 rnds, dec 4 sts evenly in 2nd rnd, ending last rnd 14 sts before end—60 sts.

Heel Sl next 29 sts onto first dpn, divide next 31 sts onto 2 empty dpn and leave on hold. Work back and forth in rows on 29 sts of first dpn only: **Row 1** (RS) K4 B; [k1 A, k1 B] 10 times; k1 A; k4 B. **Row 2** [K1 B, p1 B] twice; [p1 A, p1 B] 10 times; p1 A; [p1 B, k1 B]

21
22 \/ 22

26
27 \/ 27

15 \/ 16
29

JEAN NEWSTED

CALGARY, ALBERTA, CANADA

twice. **Row 3** [K1 B, p1 B] twice; [k1 A, k1 B] 10 times; k1 A; [p1 B, k1 B] twice. Rep last 2 rows 9 times more, then rep row 2 once.

Turn heel Cont on 29 sts: **Row 1** (RS) K17 B, ssk, k1, turn. **Row 2** Sl 1, p6, p2tog, p1. **Row 3** Sl 1, k7, ssk, k1. **Row 4** Sl 1, p8, p2tog, p1, turn. Cont to dec in same way, working 1 st more between decs on each row until 17 sts rem, end with a RS row. Do not turn.

Gusset With empty dpn and MC, pick up and k 13 sts along side of heel, k 1 st from next dpn, and sl sts to first dpn; with 2nd dpn, k across next 2 dpn, with 3rd dpn, pick up and k 13 sts along other side of heel, then k 9 heel sts—74 sts. Beg of rnd is at center of heel. K 3 rnds. **Next rnd** On first dpn, k to last 3 sts, k2tog, k1; k across 2nd dpn; on 3rd dpn, k1, ssk, k to end—72 sts. **Next rnd** Knit. Rep last 2 rnds until 60 sts rem—15 sts each on first and 3rd dpn; 30 sts on 2nd dpn.

Foot (When working Check pat, k sts from first and 3rd dpn instead of purling.) K 2 rnds. Rep rnds 7–9 of Check pat. ****Next 9 rnds** Work your name or initials and date [city and province or state] over 30 sts of 2nd dpn and work rem sts as foll: **Rnds 1–2, 8–9** K with MC. **Rnds 3–7** On first dpn, k1 MC, k2 B, [k2 MC, k2 B] 3 times; on 3rd dpn, [k2 B, k2 MC] 3 times, k2 B, k1 MC.** Rep rnds 4–6 of check pat. Rep from** to **. Rep rnds 1–3 of Check pat. With MC, k until piece measures 6" from heel or 2" less than desired length.

Toe Change to A. **Rnd 1** On first dpn, k to last 4 sts, k2tog, k2; on 2nd dpn, k2, ssk, k to last 4 sts, k2tog, k2; on 3rd dpn, k2, ssk, k around—4 sts dec. K 1 rnd. Rep last 2 rnds until 16 sts rem. K 4 sts from first dpn to 3rd dpn. Cut yarn, leaving a 12" tail. Graft rem 8 sts from each dpn tog.

Finishing With B, embroider diagonal lines in letters M and N. Sew on pearls. Fold cuff at turning ridge.

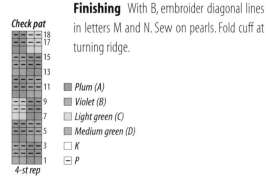

Check pat

Plum (A)
Violet (B)
Light green (C)
Medium green (D)
☐ K
⊟ P

4-st rep

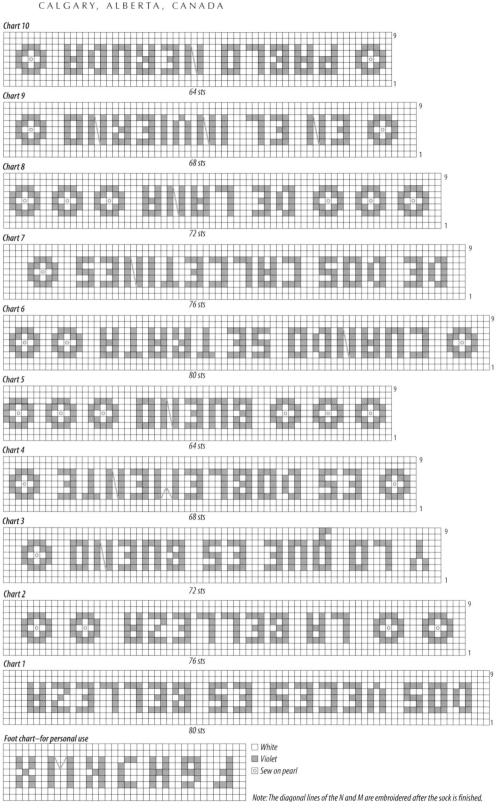

Chart 10 — 64 sts

Chart 9 — 68 sts

Chart 8 — 72 sts

Chart 7 — 76 sts

Chart 6 — 80 sts

Chart 5 — 64 sts

Chart 4 — 68 sts

Chart 3 — 72 sts

Chart 2 — 76 sts

Chart 1 — 80 sts

Foot chart—for personal use

☐ White
■ Violet
⊙ Sew on pearl

Note: The diagonal lines of the N and M are embroidered after the sock is finished.

A Lilliputian Christmas

ADVENTUROUS LEVEL

BETTY SALPEKAR

EDISON, NEW JERSEY

This most amazing pair is a really basic 48-stitch sock worked at a gauge of 38 stitches to the inch! It can be done. For Christmas on a more human scale, try worsted-weight yarn at 5 stitches to the inch. In either case, cast on 48 sttiches and follow Claire Kellogg's socks on page 12 for numbers for heel and toe shapings.

Actual size

Christmas stockings in 1/12 scale

"These stockings are meant to hang in a miniature (1 inch=1 foot, or 1/12 scale) Christmas room. I knitted them in the round on needles that I made from piano wire in two thicknesses: 0.019" in diameter and 0.024" in diameter. Since everyone's Christmas stocking, whether miniature or full-size, ought to be a little bit different from everyone else's, I made these two with analogous designs rather than identical ones. They are larger than what would fit a 1/12 scale foot because a Christmas stocking, in any scale, ought to be ample!

"I started each sock with a temporary cast-on using the smaller needles and finer thread for the hem (I used fine machine embroidery thread). Beginning with the turning row, I changed to the larger needles and thicker thread (regular machine embroidery thread) and worked the rest of the sock at a gauge of 38 stitches and 42 rows to the inch. I turned the hem under and attached it at the appropriate time by knitting the stitches from the cast-on together with the working stitches from the sock itself. For the rest of the sock, I generally followed the conventional precepts for top-down sock architecture. I twisted the colors on each carry longer than about 7 stitches. To avoid the inherent 'pattern jog' of stranded knitting in the round, I tried working the first and last stitches of appropriate rounds together, then making one stitch. It was moderately successful."

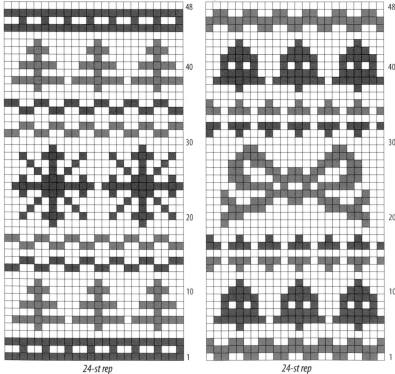

Leg pat 1

48
40
30
20
10
1

24-st rep

Leg pat 2

48
40
30
20
10
1

24-st rep

Foot chart

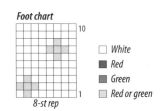

10

1

8-st rep

□ White
■ Red
▨ Green
▨ Red or green

Boston Bulkies

INTERMEDIATE LEVEL

PATRICIA TONGUE EDRAOS
BOSTON, MASSACHUSETTS

Double knitting A tube is formed when working back and forth in rows on two needles by slipping every other st on one row, then knitting (or purling) them on the next row. After two rows, each stitch has been worked once. Work a test piece as foll: Cast on 10 sts. **Tubular rib row 1** *Sl 1 with yarn in front (wyif), p1; rep from*—5 sts purled. Turn. **Tubular rib row 2** Rep row 1. Notice that you are slipping the purled sts and purling the slipped sts from row 1. Rep last 2 rows 7 times more. Sl all sts from needles and gently pull apart. The 5 sts worked on each row form two sides of a tube. **Notes 1** When working socks, take care not to close up the tube by keeping yarn outside sts at all times. Yarn should not 'cross' over between the 2 rows of sts at any time. **2** When working short rows, only 'worked' sts of that row (either knits or purls) are wrapped; slipped sts are never wrapped to avoid closing up the tube. **3** Keep careful track of short rows when shaping heel.

Left Sock Cast on 26 sts. Work Tubular rib rows 1–2—13 purl sts each side.

Toe **Short row 1** *Sl 1 wyif, p1; rep from* 6 times more—7 sts purled. Sl next st, then wrap 8th purl st as foll: bring yarn to back, sl p st to right-hand (RH) needle, bring yarn to front, sl same p st to left-hand (LH) needle; turn. **Complete short row** Sl 1 with yarn in back (wyib), *k1, sl 1 wyib; rep from* 6 times more—same 7 sts purled from short row 1 have been knit. Turn. Work 2 rows on other side to balance: **Short row 2** *K1, sl 1 wyib; rep from* 6 times more. Wrap 8th knit st by bringing yarn to front, sl k st to RH needle, bring yarn to back, sl same k st to LH needle; turn. **Complete short row** *Sl 1 wyif, p1; rep from* 6 times more—same 7 sts knitted from short row 2 have been purled. Turn. In same way, rep short rows 1 2, working 9 sts (wrapping 10th), then 11 sts (wrapping 12th) on each side.

Foot Work approx 4" to 5" even, or until desired length of foot.

Heel Work short rows in same way as for toe. **Short row 1** *Sl 1 wyif, p1; rep from* 12 times more, turn and rep from* twice—15 sts worked (13 across first side, or sole, and 2 on 2nd side, or top of foot). Wrap and turn. **Next row** Sl the slipped sts and work 17 knit sts—2 from top of foot, 13 from sole, then 2 from top of foot. Wrap and turn. In same way, work 12 more short rows, working 1 st less each row—5 sts worked on 12th short row.

Turn heel: Work 22 sts on next row, then 9 sts on next row. Work 13 more short rows, beg with 5 sts and working 1 st more on each row—17 sts worked on 13th row. Work 2 sts of final short row.

Finishing Working back and forth on 13 sts each side, work approx 2" even, or desired length to cuff. Work 2" in k1, p1 rib. Separate front and back of tube, placing sts on separate needles. Cut yarn, leaving a 6" tail. Work tubular bind-off.

Right Leg Cast on 26 sts. Work Tubular rib rows 1–2—13 purl sts each side. Work as for Left leg through foot.

Heel Reverse heel shaping as foll: Work 2 sts on first short row. Wrap and turn. Work 13 more short rows, beg with 17 sts and working 1 st less on each row—5 sts worked on 13th row. Work 9 sts on next row, then 22 sts on next row. Work 13 more short rows, beg with 5 sts and working 1 st more on each row—17 sts worked on 13th row. Work 15 sts of final short row. Complete as for Left leg.

If you've tried double knitting before and found the knitting tedious, give Patricia's purl-side-out version a try!

"These socks start at the toe and all shaping is done by short rows. I developed them to wear with clogs and sandals. When felted, they make wonderful boot liners. "

Size Woman's large.

Materials A 7oz/200g (approx 230yds/210m) bulky-weight yarn. **B** Size 10½ (6½mm) knitting needles, *or size to obtain gauge.*

Gauge 3 sts to 1" (2.5cm) over double knitting using size 10½ (6½mm) needles.

Chapter 7   Icelandic

4 PROJECTS

Socks for Troll Children   **102**

Snowflake Slippers   **103**

SOS! Special Occasion Slippers   **104**

Building Blocks   **105**

102   103   104

Icelandic Socks

Socks for Troll Children

ÁSTHILDUR THORSTEINSSON

INTERMEDIATE LEVEL   HURÐARBAK, REYKHOLTSDALUR, ICELAND

Note These garter stitch heels are quite shallow and rounded. Numbers for a more standard, square heel are given in brackets.

Leg With straight needles and MC, cast on 40 sts. K 7 rows. *Work 10 rows of chart pat, working 8-st rep 5 times. With MC, k 4 rows. Rep from* once. With dpn and MC, k 1 row as foll: 20 sts on first dpn, 10 sts each on 2nd and 3rd dpns. Place marker, join and k 13 rnds more.

Heel Work back and forth in rows on 20 sts of first dpn only: K 14 [40] rows.

Turn heel Cont on 20 sts: **Row 1** K14, k2tog, turn. **Row 2** Sl 1, k8, k2tog, turn. Rep last row until 10 sts rem. K 1 row.

Gusset With MC and empty dpn, pick up and k 9 [20] sts along side of heel; with 2nd dpn, k across 20 sts of next 2 dpn; with 3rd dpn, pick up and k 9 [20] sts along other side of heel, then k 5 heel sts—48 [70]sts. Beg of rnd is at center of heel. **Row 1** Knit. **Row 2** K to last 3 sts of first dpn, k2tog, k1; k across 2nd dpn; on 3rd dpn, k1, ssk, k to end. Rep last 2 rows 3 [14] times more—10 sts each on first and 3rd dpn, 20 sts on 2nd dpn.

Foot K every rnd until foot measures 2" less than desired length.

Toe **Rnd 1** On first dpn, k to last 3 sts, k2tog, k1; on 2nd dpn, k1, ssk, k to last 3 sts, k2tog, k1; on 3rd dpn, k1, ssk, k across. **Rnd 2** Knit. Rep last 2 rnds until 16 sts rem (4 sts each on first and 3rd dpns, 8 sts on 2nd dpn). K 4 sts from first dpn to 3rd dpn. Weave 8 sts from each dpn tog. With MC and CC, make a braid with tasselled edges. Using photo as guide, sew to slipper opening, beg at back of heel and leaving 4" at each end. Sew decorative button at front of leg opening.

Ásthildur is a farmer in western Iceland. She loves knitting and spinning and uses mainly wool and horse hair. The buttons are made from sheep horn.

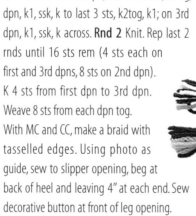

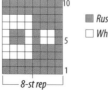

Rust
White

8-st rep

Size Child's large.

Materials A 1¾oz/50g (approx 160yds/146m) chunky-weight yarn in cream (MC), ¾oz/25g in burgundy (CC). **B** Set of 4 double-pointed needles (dpn) in size 7 (4.5mm) *or size to obtain gauge.* **C** One pair size 7 (4.5mm) straight needles. **D** 1½" decorative button. **Gauge** 4½ sts to 1" (2.5cm) with MC over St st using size 7 (4.5mm) dpn.

Snowflake Slippers

INTERMEDIATE LEVEL

HÓLMFRÍÐUR ÓFEIGSDÓTTIR
BÚASTAÐIR, VOPNAFJÖRÐUR

Note Slip all sts knitwise.

Sole With MC and circular needle, cast on 3 sts. **Shape heel: Row 1** (RS) K1, M1, k to last st, M1, sl 1. **Row 2** K to last st, sl 1. Rep last 2 rows 7 times more—19 sts. Cont selvage as established (k first st, sl last st) and k 72 rows more (36 ridges). **Shape toe: Row 1** (RS) K1, k2tog, k to last 3 sts, k2tog, sl 1. **Row 2** K to last st, sl 1. Rep last 2 rows until 5 sts rem, end with a WS row. Place sts on hold.

Foot band With RS facing, circular needle, and MC, beg above the 5th ridge from cast-on edge and pick up and k 1 st between the ridges along the right edge of sole as foll: Insert the needle from *front to back* and draw the yarn through, then insert the needle from *back to front* and draw the yarn through; do not pick up a st between the last 2 ridges—44 sts. K across 5 sts on hold, marking the center st. Pick up and k 44 sts along the left edge of the sole in the same way—93 sts. K 11 rows (6 ridges).

Top of foot **Row 1** (RS) K to center st of toe, k center st, k1, k2tog, k1, turn. **Row 2** K5, k2tog, k1, turn. **Row 3** K to center st, k center st, k2, k2tog, k1, turn. **Row 4** K7, k2tog, k1, turn. **Row 5** K to center st, k3, k2tog, k1, turn. **Row 6** K9, k2tog, k1, turn. Work 4 rows more in same way, adding 1 st each side. **Row 11** K to center st, k center st, k6, k2tog, k1, turn. **Row 12** K15, k2tog, k1, turn. Rep rows 11–12 until 48 sts rem.

Leg Divide sts evenly on 3 dpn. **Rnds 1, 3** Knit and at each side, k 1 st of foot band and 1 st of top of foot tog. **Rnds 2, 4** Purl. Work 8 more ridges on 44 sts. Work 14 rnds in k1, p1 rib. Turn sock inside out. Cont in garter st and inc 4 sts evenly spaced across first row (to 48 sts) in colors as foll: *1 ridge C, 1 ridge MC; rep from* 5 times, work 1 ridge more in C—7 stripes in C. Bind off in C.

Finishing Sew heel flap to heel. With A, B and C, work cross-stitch snowflake on top of foot.

In Iceland, the custom is for children to place a shoe on the windowsill in their room before going to sleep the days before Christmas (from December 12th through December 24th). If they have been nice during the day, they get candy, fruit or a toy in their shoe; if they have been naughty, they get a potato. In Hólmfríðr's family, a red version of this slipper has replaced the shoe.

Cross-stitch

A cross-stitch is made in two steps: a diagonal stitch to the right crossed by a diagonal stitch to the left. Work each cross-stitch over one knit stitch.

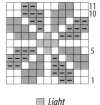

	Light
	Medium
	Dark

Size Woman's medium.

Materials **A** 3½oz/100g (approx 230yds/210m) worsted-weight yarn in cream (MC). **B** Small amounts of 3 contrasting colors in light (A), medium (B), and dark (C) burgundy. **C** Size 7 (4.5mm) circular needle, 24" (60cm), *or size to obtain gauge.* **D** Size 7 (4.5mm) double-pointed needles (dpn).

Gauge 5 sts to 1" (2.5cm) over garter st using MC and size 7 (4.5mm) dpn.

Johanna is a knitwear designer. Some of her Icelandic circular yoke sweaters and jackets have become classics. Since she doesn't like to work ribbings, she uses garter stitch on her slippers.

SOS! Special Occasion Slippers

JÓHANNA HJALTADÓTTIR

EASY LEVEL

REYKIAVÍK, ICELAND

Lace Panel (15 sts) **Rnd 1** K5, k2tog, yo, k1, yo, ssk, k5. **Rnd 2 and all even rnds** Knit. **Rnd 3** K4, k2tog, yo, k3, yo, ssk, k4. **Rnd 5** K3, k2tog, yo, k5, yo, ssk, k3. **Rnd 7** K2, k2tog, yo, k7, yo, ssk, k2. **Rnd 9** K1, k2tog, yo, k2, k2tog, yo, k1, yo, ssk, k2, yo, ssk, k1. **Rnd 11** K4, k2tog, yo, k3, yo, ssk, k4. **Rnd 13** K6, yo, sl2-k1-p2sso, yo, k6.

Slipper With straight needles, cast on 31 sts and k 24 rows. Do not turn work. Beg working in St st and divide sts over 3 dpn as foll: k 8 sts onto one dpn, k 8 sts onto next dpn, k 7 sts onto next dpn, place marker. **Next rnd** With empty dpn k7, k2tog (last st from straight needle and first st from dpn), k7; k to end of rnd—30 sts arranged as foll: 15 sts on first dpn, 8 on 2nd dpn, and 7 on 3rd dpn. Work 14 rnds of 15-st lace panel on first dpn, working all other sts in St st..

Toe Rnd 1 On first dpn, k1, ssk, k to last 3 sts, k2tog, k1; on 2nd dpn, k1, ssk, k to end; on 3rd dpn, k to last 3 sts, k2tog, k1—4 sts dec. **Rnd 2** Knit. Rep last 2 rnds until 10 sts rem. K sts of 3rd dpn onto 2nd dpn on last rnd. Cut yarn, leaving 12" tail. Graft 5 sts from each dpn tog. Fold foot in half and sew heel tog.

$$\begin{matrix} 8 & & 7 \\ & \diagdown\!\diagup & \\ & 15 & \end{matrix}$$

Lace Panel

□	K
⊙	Yo
⁄	K2tog
＼	Ssk
△	Sl2-k1-p2sso

— 15-st panel —

Size Woman's small.

Materials A 1¾oz/50g (approx 115yds/105m) worsted-weight yarn in cream. **B** Set of 4 double-pointed needles (dpn) in size 7 (4.5mm) *or size to obtain gauge.* **C** One pair size 7 (4.5mm) straight needles. **D** Stitch markers.

Gauge 4½ sts to 1" (2.5cm) in garter st using size 7 (4.5mm) dpn.

Building Blocks

EASY LEVEL

HILDUR HALLDÓRSSON

GILHAGI, ÖXARFJÖRÐUR, ICELAND

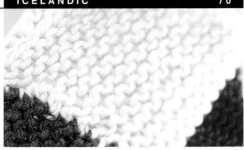

With A, cast on 12 sts and k 24 rows A, 48 rows C, 24 rows B, 24 rows A, 24 rows C. Bind off loosely. With RS facing, pick up and k sts along top of 24 rows of C as foll: 12 sts with B along top of rows 25–48, 12 sts with A along rows 1–24. K 24 rows, twisting colors at each color change. Bind off loosely. Fold piece foll diagram and sew seams.

Hildur was born in Norway. She is a farmer on the northeastern coast of Iceland. An old Icelandic woman taught her how to knit these slippers. The knitting is simple; the assembly is ingenious.

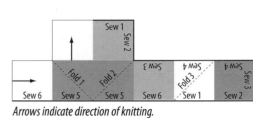

Arrows indicate direction of knitting.
Fold along dotted lines then sew matching solid lines together.

Size Woman's small or child's large.

Materials A 1oz/25g (approx 65yds/59m) each worsted-weight yarn in cream (A), blue (B) and red (C). **B** One pair size 9 (5.5mm) needles *or size to obtain gauge.*

Gauge 4 sts to 1" (2.5 cm) over garter st using size 9 (5.5mm) needles.

Backward loop cast-on

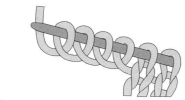

Chain cast-on

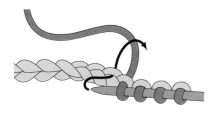

Invisible cast-on

❶

❷

Long tail cast-on

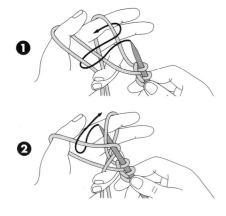

❶

❷

Backward loop cast-on *Uses* To cast on a few sts for a buttonhole or the start of a sleeve. Form required number of backward loops.

Chain cast-on *Uses* As a temporary cast-on.
Chain desired number with scrap yarn. With main yarn, knit up 1 stitch in each chain, inserting needle into back loops of crochet.

Invisible cast-on *Uses* As a temporary cast-on, when access to the bottom loops is needed: to knit, graft, attach a border, or for an elastic hem.
1 Knot working yarn to contrasting scrap yarn. With needle in right hand, hold knot in right hand. Tension both strands in left hand; separate the strands with fingers of the left hand. Yarn over with working yarn in front of scrap strand.
2 Holding scrap strand taut, pivot yarns and yarn over with working yarn in back of scrap strand.
3 Each yarn over forms a stitch. Alternate yarn over in front and in back of scrap strand for required number of stitches. For an even number, twist working yarn around scrap strand before knitting the first row. Later, untie knot, remove scrap strand, and arrange bottom loops on needle.

Long tail cast-on Make a slip knot for the initial stitch, at a distance from the end of the yarn (about 1½" for each stitch to be cast on).
1 Arrange both ends of yarn in left hand as shown. Bring needle under front strand of thumb loop, up over front strand of index loop, catching it . . .
2 . . . and bringing it under the front of the thumb loop. Slip thumb out of loop, and use it to adjust tension on the new stitch. One stitch cast on.

3-needle bind-off *Uses* Instead of binding off sts and sewing them together.
Seam effect. Place right sides together, back stitches on one needle and front stitches on another. *K2tog (1 from front needle and 1 from back needle). Rep from* once. Bind first stitch off over 2nd stitch. Continue to k2tog (1 front stitch and 1 back stitch) and bind off across.
Ridge effect. Place wrong sides together, then work as above.

Bind off in pattern As you work the bind-off row, knit or purl the stitches as the pattern stitch requires. Try the same technique on cast-on rows.

Tubular bind-off *Uses* Produces an invisibly-secured edge. The ribs flow smoothly from RS to WS.
Thread a blunt needle with matching yarn. Assuming the first st on LH needle is a knit st, bring yarn through first st as if to purl, leave st on needle.
1 Take needle behind knit st, between first 2 sts, and through purl st as if to knit. Leave sts on needle.

3-needle bind-off

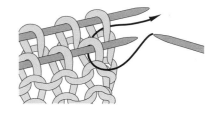

Tubular bind-off

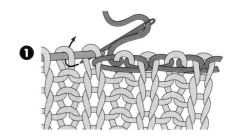

❶

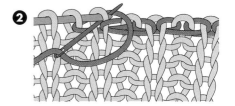

❷

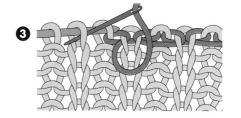

❸

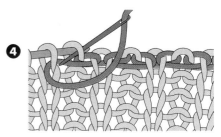

❹

Make 1

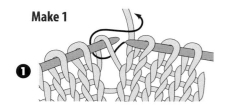

➊

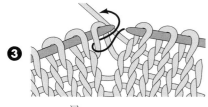

➋

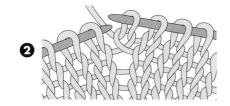

➌

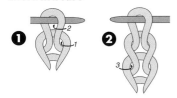

➍

Lifted increase

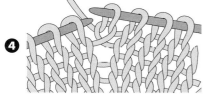

➊   ➋

SSK

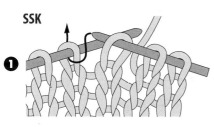

➊

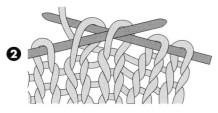

➋

2 Bring yarn to front, then through the same knit st as if to knit. Slip st off needle.

3 Take needle in front of purl st and through the next knit st as if to purl. Leave sts on needle.

4 Bring yarn through purl st as if to purl and slip off needle.

5 Adjust tension. Repeat Steps 1–4. If you find it easier, slip knit stitches to one needle and purl stitches to another needle, then work stockinette graft.

Make 1 (Single increase, M1.)

1. With right needle from back of work, pick up strand between last st knitted and next st. Place on left needle and knit through back (or purl through back for M1 purlwise).

2. This increase can be used as the left increase in a paired increase (M1L).

3. For the right paired increase, with left needle from back of work, pick up strand between last stitch knitted and next stitch. Knit twisted.

4. This is a right M1 (M1R).

Lifted increase For a right increase, knit into right loop of next st in the row below (1), knit into next st (2). For a left increase, knit into left loop of last st knitted in the row below (3).

SSK *Uses* SSK is a left-slanting single decrease.

1 Slip 2 sts separately to right needle as if to knit.

2 Knit these 2 sts together by slipping left needle into them from left to right. 2 sts become one.

S2KP2, SSKP, sl2-k1-p2sso *Uses* A centered double decrease.

1. Slip 2 sts together to right needle as if to knit.

2. Knit next st.

3. Pass 2 slipped sts over knit st and off right needle.

4. Completed: 3 sts become 1; the center st is on top.

Short rows wrap *Uses* Each short row adds two rows of knitting across a section of the work. Since the work is turned before completing a row, stitches must be wrapped at the turn to prevent holes.

Work a wrap as follows:

1 With yarn in back, slip next stitch as if to purl. Bring yarn to front of work and slip stitch back to left needle as shown. Turn work.

2 When you come to the wrap on a right-side row, make it less visible by working the wrap together with the stitch it wraps.

S2KP2, SSKP, sl2-k1-p2sso

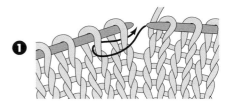

➊

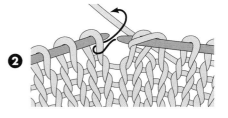

➋

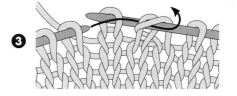

➌

➍

Short rows wrap

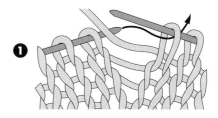

➊

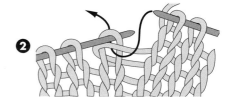

➋

Grafting Stockinette graft

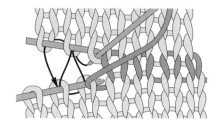

Grafting Garter st graft

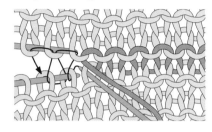

Knitting in reverse

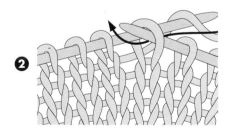

❶

❷

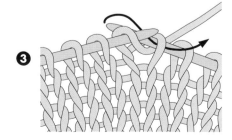

❸

Grafting

Uses An invisible method of joining knitting horizontally: row to row. Useful at shoulders; underarms; tips of mittens, socks, and hats.

Stockinette graft:

1 Arrange stitches on two needles.

2 Thread a blunt needle with matching yarn (approximately 1" per stitch).

3 Working from right to left, with right sides facing you, begin with steps 3a and 3b:

  3a Front needle: yarn through 1st stitch as if to purl, leave stitch on needle.

  3b Back needle: yarn through 1st stitch as if to knit, leave on.

4 Work 4a and 4b across:

  4a Front needle: through 1st stitch as if to knit, slip off needle: through next st as if to purl, leave on needle.

  4b Back needle: through 1st stitch as if to purl, slip off needle: through next st as if to knit, leave on needle.

5 Adjust tension to match rest of knitting.

Garter st graft:

1 Arrange stitches on two needles so stitches on one needle come out of purl bumps (lower needle) and stitches on the other needle come out of smooth knits (upper needle).

2–4 Work as for Stockinette graft except: on 3b, go through the stitch as if to *purl*. On 4b, go through 1st stitch as if to *knit*, and through next st as if to *purl*.

Knitting in reverse

1 To knit in reverse, enter back loop with left needle tip.

2 Wrap yarn from back to front over left needle tip.

3 While lifting right needle tip, draw wrap through and onto left needle to form new stitch.

3-st I-cord   I-cord is a tiny tube of stockinette stitch, made with 2 double-pointed needles.

1 Cast on 3 sts.

2 *Knit 3. Do not turn work. Slide stitches to right end of needle. Rep from *.

Duplicate stitch   Duplicate stitch (also known as Swiss darning) is just that: with a blunt tapestry needle threaded with a length of yarn of a contrasting color, cover a knitted stitch with an embroidered stitch of the same shape.

3-st I-cord

Duplicate stitch

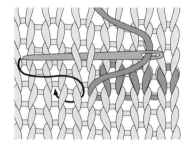

Metrics

To convert inches to centimeters, multiply the inches by 2.5. *For example:* 4" x 2.5 = 10cm

To convert feet to centimeters, multiply the feet by 30.48. *For example:* 2' x 30.48 = 60.96cm

To convert yards to meters, multiply the yards by .9144. *For example:* 4 yds x .9144 = 3.66m

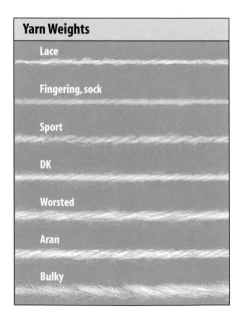

Yarn Weights
Lace
Fingering, sock
Sport
DK
Worsted
Aran
Bulky

Sideways Sox Supreme
Written-out instructions for chart on p. 77

Note On rows 1–46 and 61–82, work heel sts in pat (2 rows St st, 2 rows Seed st). On rows 47–60 and 83–96, work heel sts in St st. **Row 1** With MC, cast on 80 sts. **Row 2** (WS) With MC, p37, place marker (pm), p 2 sts for heel, pm, p to last 7 sts, pm, k1, p2, k2, yo, k2. **Row 3** With CC, k4, p1,k2, p1, work to end in Seed st. **Row 4** With CC, work to 3rd marker in Seed st, k1, p2, k2, yo, k3. **Row 5** With MC, k5, p1, k2, p1, k to last 14 sts, then work short row wrap: sl next st purlwise to right-hand (RH) needle, bring yarn forward, sl st back to left-hand (LH) needle, turn. **Row 6** With MC, p to last marker, k1, p2, k2, yo, k4. **Row 7** With CC, k6, p1, k2, p1, work to wrapped st in Seed st, work wrapped st and wrap tog, work 4 more sts, wrap next st, turn. **Row 8** With CC, work across in Seed st to 3rd marker, k1, p2, k2, yo, k5. **Row 9** With MC, bind off 4 sts, weaving-in CC between each st, k2, p1, k2, p1, k across to wrapped st, k wrapped st and wrap tog, k3, wrap next st, turn. **Row 10** With MC, p to last marker, k1, p2, k2, yo, k2. **Row 11** With CC, work in pat to wrapped st, work wrapped st and wrap tog, work 2 sts, wrap next st, turn. **Row 12** with CC, work in pat. **Row 13** With MC, work in pat to wrapped st, k wrapped st and wrap tog, k last st. **Rows 14–36** Work even in pat. **Rows 37, 38** Work in pat to last 2 sts, wrap next st, turn, work across (Row 38). **Rows 39, 40** Work across to last 5 sts, wrap next st, turn, work across (Row 40). **Rows 41, 42** Work across to last 9 sts, wrap next st, turn, work across. **Rows 43, 44** Work across to last 14 sts, wrap next st, turn, work across. **Row 45** Work to end, knitting wrapped sts and wraps tog. **Rows 46** Work even in pat. **Rows 47–52** Work to heel marker, M1, work 2 sts, M1, work to end. **Row 53** Work to heel marker, M1, work 2 sts, M1, work in pat to last 14 sts, wrap next st, turn. **Row 54** Work to heel marker, M1, work 2 sts, M1, work to end in pat. **Row 55** Work to heel marker, M1, work 2 sts, M1, work to wrapped st, work wrapped st and wrap tog, work 4 sts, wrap next st, turn. **Row 56** Rep row 54. **Row 57** Work to heel marker, M1, work 2 sts, M1, work to last 5 sts, knitting wrapped st and wrap tog, wrap next st, turn. **Row 58** Rep Row 51. **Row 59** Work to heel marker, M1, work 2 sts, M1, work to last 2 sts, working wrapped st and wrap tog, wrap next st, turn. **Row 60** Rep row 54. **Row 61** Work in pat to end, working wrapped st and wrap tog. **Row 62** Work in pat to end. **Row 63** Work in pat to 13 sts past 2nd heel marker, wrap next st, turn. Work 21 sts in seed st, wrap next st, turn, work to end, working wrapped st and wrap tog. **Row 64** Work in pat to end, working wrapped st and wrap tog. **Row 65, 66** Work even in pat. **Row 67, 68** Cont in pat, rep rows 63, 64. **Rows 69–72** Work even in pat. **Rows 73a–73h** With MC work 19 sts past first marker, wrap next st, turn. Work to end. With CC, work in established pat to 13 sts past first marker, turn, work to end in pat. With MC, work in pat to 7 sts past first marker, wrap next st, turn, work in pat to end. With CC, work in pat to 1 st past marker, wrap next st, turn, work to end. **Row 73i** With MC, work across, working wrapped st and wraps tog. **Row 74–76** Work in pat. **Row 77** With MC, work 13 sts past 2nd heel marker, wrap next st, turn. Work 6 sts past 2nd heel marker, wrap next st, turn. Work to end. **Row 78–80** Work in pat. **Rows 81, 82** Rep rows 77, 78. **Row 83** Work to 2 sts before first heel marker, ssk, k2, k2tog, work to end. **Row 84** Work to 2 sts before heel marker, p2tog, p2, p2tog tbl, work across in pat. **Rows 85–93** Rep heel shaping of previous 2 rows and short row shaping of rows 37–45 (working to last 2 sts, then 5, then 9, then 14, then to end). **Rows 94–96** Cont in pat, working heel shaping. Turn, with MC, bind off 4 sts for edging.

Abbreviations
approx approximate(ly)
beg begin(ning)(s)
CC contrasting color
cn cable needle
cm centimeter(s)
cont continu(e)(ed)(es)(ing)
dec decrease(e)(ed)(es)(ing)
dpn double pointed needle(s)
foll follow(s)(ing)
g gram(s)
" inch(es)
' foot(feet)
inc increas(e)(ed)(es)(ing)
k knit(ting)(s)(ted)
lb pound(s)
m meter(s)
mm millimeter(s)
MC main color
oz ounce(s)
p purl(ed)(ing)(s)
pat(s) pattern(s)
pm place marker
psso pass slipped stitch(es) over
rem remain(s)(ing)
rep repeat(s)
rev reverse(d)
RS right side(s)
rnd round(s)
sl slip(ped)(ping)
SSK slip, slip, knit 2tog
st(s) stitch(es)
St st stockinette stitch
tog together
WS wrong side(s)
wyib with yarn in back
wyif with yarn in front
yd(s) yard(s)
yo yarn over

Colophon

THE MAKING OF SOCKS, SOCKS, SOCKS

Three judges and a roomful of socks—(from left) Nancy Bush, Anna Zilboorg, and Priscilla Gibson-Roberts with hundreds of pairs.

Judgment Day Imagine being one of the judges of *Knitter's Magazine* Sock Contest. You pick up a pair of socks and see—not lace, colorful, oddball, handspun, or any of the nine or so other categories—but licorice!

"Whenever I got to a mistake, it wasn't really a problem, because I'd just have to eat it!" says Debbie New (Waterloo, Ontario) of her whimsical entry. "I rather like black licorice more than green, so I found I used up about six bags of black—even though the pattern calls for only one!"

Debbie's was one of hundreds of pairs of socks that XRX Books Editor Elaine Rowley had placed on the carpeted floor of the Presidential Suite at Stitches '96. And the Queens of Socks—authors Anna Zilboorg (*Fancy Feet*), Nancy Bush (*Folk Socks*), and Priscilla Gibson-Roberts (*Ethnic Socks and Stockings*) were about to rule.

"There we were, the three of us," Anna says, "surrounded by hundreds of socks. My first impression was, 'Wow, how wonderful!' And then, of course, we got into judgment mode, and we started looking at them with a jaundiced eye. When three judges come together they have to one-up one another: 'There's a mistake…' 'This toe is not…' 'This heel will never fit!'"

Andreas Doxas filtering the bright Mediterranean sun.

"It was so overwhelming, so exciting, to see so many wonderful, exceptional socks," says Nancy. "There was something special about every pair that was entered; it was tough for us to narrow it down."

"We had a wonderful, rewarding day!" says Priscilla. "All these absolutely glorious socks…"

"It really was quite remarkable," Anna says, "because Nancy and Priscilla and I come from very different visions and very different practices—and very different criteria of judgment… When it came down to my three favorites, I might rank them one, two, three; Nancy might rank them two, three, one; Priscilla three, one, two—but those were the three that we *all* liked! The socks we chose are various. What they have in common is that they're beautifully done, well conceived—whether they're peaceable and quiet, witty and whimsical, or even conventional—you see a conception, a vision. And they're excellently worked."

Studio shots Now that the judges had spoken we were ready for the next step—photography. Betty Salpekar's unbelievable 'A Lilliputian Christmas' sock only needed a sense of scale: a penny? A pair of needles? A stamp? We settled on a "Love" stamp picturing two doves in a basket of roses to underscore just how tiny these delightful miniatures really are. "Can you believe that someone did that?" Anna says. "Look, there's an initial inside! Like all the finest products of the human spirit, it leaves you speechless."

Would anything other than a kid taking a bite from Debbie New's licorice yummies do justice to her inventiveness? But we did not succumb to this temptation, leaving the socks whole so one of Debbie's grandchildren might have the pleasure. As Debbie says, "After all if they're not going to wear them, they can eat them!"

For Cindy Walker's (Davis, California) 'Leaf Socks,' only a session with my large-format Sinar 4 x 5 would do: the camera's super-sharp Zeiss lenses and large film format bring every tiny lace stitch to the printed page (*see details upper left and opposite page, right*).

Sock accessories But sooner or later Photo Stylist Carla Fauske knew we would need the ultimate sock accessory: feet. First to model Jóhanna Hjaltadóttir's (Reykjavik, Iceland) 'Lace Socks' was Circulation Director Ruth Dunham's young daughter Colleen, while her older brother Travis wore his overalls, a big smile, and Anna Lubiw's (Kitchener, Ontario, Canada) 'Dragon Socks.'

Then it was time to move our photo shoot, and my Hasselblad, across the street to Dave and Debbie Hoffman's Victorian, where their children, niece, and neighborhood friends made their modeling debuts. But how to show the socks and also get those angelic faces into the picture? Voilà! Our series of sock portraits (right): Elizabeth Hoffman, Seth Allen, and the Hoffman children: Pierce, Mollie, Spencer, and Heidi. Their modeling fee? An afternoon at Gigglebee's, the neighborhood pizza-and-bumper-car arcade.

Knitter's crew cooling their heels in Lake Michigan.

Photographing our older models took us to the Falls of the Big Sioux River, where Demetri Sengos and friend Michelle Jones spent an afternoon fishing and playing with XRX mascots, Yorkies Violetta and Leonora, to a *Knitter's Magazine* photo shoot in Chicago: that's our crew (*left*) cooling their heels in Lake Michigan.

And when a business trip took me to Greece, I tucked a few pairs into my suitcase—to photograph against the azure blue of the Mediterranean: that's my boyhood friend Andreas Doxas (holding a scrim to filter the bright Greek sun) with his twin daughters Angelikí and Iríni (*opposite page*).

Knitting it all together Graphic Designer Bob Natz worked his usual magic, knitting together all the various elements: images, text, and charts. "Given the subject matter," Bob says, "It was decided early on to handle the materials in a visually fun manner. And given the variations of the projects, instructions, charts, and details, it was important to bring them all together in a positive, pleasing, whole.

"Close-ups were placed, in a series of 3 sizes, as a design element to provide necessary details and to also give the book the look and feel of a knitter's notebook. Project photos are shown as large as possible and sometimes nearly actual size. This combination provides a window to the amazing colors, texture, details and complements the all-necessary instructions. Headlines are Avant Garde, 18 point, upper and lower case. Contestants and knitting skill level information is Optima book, caps, 8 point. These elements provide a soft contrast to the text, which is Myriad light, condensed, 10 point, on 14.5 leading. The intent was to provide the maximum readability while accommodating various text lengths. Subheads are bold for accent and reference, and intros are Futura, condensed, bold, and red for variety."

This book was completed in our spacious, bright, new quarters using Macintosh Power PCs, and QuarkXpress, Adobe Illustrator, and Adobe Photoshop. Digital color layouts and proofs were printed on an Epson Rip Station 5000 ink-jet printer under the watchful eye of Publishing Services Director David Xenakis and our dedicated staff: Book Production Manager Debbie Gage, Digital Color Specialist Daren Morgan, Production Chief Carol Skallerud, and Production Artists Jay Reeve and Lynda Selle.

—*Alexis Yiórgos Xenakis*
Sioux Falls, South Dakota

AN INDEX OF THE SOCK KNITTERS

Charlene Abrams — St. Louis, Missouri
Bob's Socks **62**
Experienced

Lynn Adamick — Redondo Beach, California
Dad's Easy Cable Socks **13**
Intermediate

Beth Morgan Adcock — Watervliet, New York
Slouch Socks **71**
Intermediate

Diane N. Ballerino — Supply, North Carolina
After Bertha **11**
Easy

Judith C. Black — Sloansville, New York
Lined Sandal Socks **19**
Intermediate

Beverly Brookhart — Broadway, North Carolina
Heart to Heart **17**
Easy

Patricia Brunner — Seattle, Washington
Clock Socks* **92**
Experienced

Shirley Bryan — Tacoma, Washington
Baby Socks **22**
Easy

Traci Bunkers — Lawrence Kansas
Dye-Your-Own Socks **72**
Intermediate

Nell Bushby — Salt Spring Island, BC, Canada
Austrian-Patterned Knee Socks **68**
Experienced

Marilyn Buster — Tulsa, Oklahoma
Sunrise Socks **84**
Experienced

Nancy Byers — Kenosha, Wisconsin
Retro Anklets **10**
Easy

Ann Carlile — Salt Lake City, Utah
Salsa Socks **63**
Intermediate

Liz Clouthier — Groton, Connecticut
Sideways Sox Supreme **76**
Intermediate

Dez Crawford — Baton Rouge, Louisiana
The Ultimate Refootable Sock **67**
Intermediate

Cynthia Dahl — Olathe, Kansas
False Flame Crew Socks **55**
Intermediate

Kathleen Day — Santa Ynez, California
Popcorn Panache **83**
Intermediate

Debbie Drechsler — Santa Rosa, California
Best Of Show Socks* **58**
Experienced

Patricia Edraos — Boston, Massachusetts
Boston Bulkies **99**
Intermediate

Lorraine Ehrlinger — Cleveland Heights, Ohio
Slip-st Cuffs That Won't **15**
Intermediate

Dennis Elmer — Portland, Oregon
Turn-Of-The-Century Socks **80**
Intermediate

Nancy Erlandson — East Hampton, Connecticut
Stained Glass Bubble Socks **60**
Intermediate

Beverly Francis — Wellington, New Zealand
First Lace **26**
Intermediate

Kathy L. Frantz — Boulder, Colorado
Tile Socks **61**
Intermediate

Sheri Franz — Pittsburgh, Pennsylvania
Purl Lace Socks **40**
Intermediate

Kathy Garguilo — Salem, Oregon
Vine Lace Socks **43**
Intermediate

Lori Gayle — Cambridge, Massachusetts
Aran Sandal Socks **74**
Experienced

Judy Gibson — Descanso, California
Butterfly Bows **70**
Intermediate

Dorothy S. Grubbs — Lebanon, New Hampshire
Golf Socks **16**
Intermediate

Lisa Gwinner — Rochester, New York
Brendan's Vine Socks **31**
Intermediate

Hildur Halldórsson — Gilhagi, Öxarfjörður, Iceland
Building Blocks **105**
Easy

Jóhanna Hjaltadóttir — Reykjavík, Iceland
Shell Lace **28**
Intermediate

Jóhanna Hjaltadóttir — Reykjavík, Iceland
SOS! Special Occasion Slippers **104**
Easy

Darcy Hobgood — North Berwick, Maine
Autumn Leaves **14**
Easy

Darlene Joyce — Des Plaines, Illinois
My Little Angel* **29**
Intermediate

Mary Kaiser — Birmingham, Alabama
Wedgwood Socks* **59**
Intermediate

Claire Kellogg — Beavercreek, Oregon
My Christmas Stocking* **12**
Easy

Rita Garrity Knudson — Golden Valley, Minnesota
Spring Fever **87**
Experienced

Rita Garrity Knudson — Golden Valley, Minnesota
Little Piggy Toes **88**
Experienced

Megan Lacey — Courtice, Ontario, Canada
2 Socks, 2 Ways **46**
Intermediate

Anna Lubiw — Kitchener, Ontario, Canada
Dragon Socks* **32**
Intermediate

Katherine Matthews — Toronto, Ontario, Canada
Tipsy Knitter Socks **41**
Intermediate

Katherine Matthews — Toronto, Ontario, Canada
Ribble Socks **75**
Intermediate

Marilyn Morgan — Olathe, Kansas
Tweed Socks **49**
Intermediate

Lucy Neatby — Dartmouth, Nova Scotia, Canada
Travelling Socks **52**
Experienced

Debbie New — Waterloo, Ontario, Canada
Free-Form Socks **53**
Adventurous

Debbie New — Waterloo, Ontario, Canada
Maple Swirl Socks* **90**
Adventurous

Debbie New — Waterloo, Ontario, Canada
Licorice Socks* **95**
Intermediate

Jean Newsted — Calgary, Alberta, Canada
Pearls of Wisdom* **96**
Experienced

Hólmfríður Ófeigsdóttir — Búastaðir, Vopnafjörður
Snowflake Slippers **103**
Intermediate

Lisa Parker — Monterey, California
Crazy Crayons **24**
Intermediate

Guðlaug Pétursdóttir — Þórshöfn, Iceland
Slipper Socks **30**
Beginner

Sharon Philbrick — Crescent City, California
Watermelon Socks **94**
Easy

Maureen Pratt — Radnor, Pennsylvania
Gray Progression **48**
Intermediate

Margaret Radcliffe — Blacksburg, Virginia
Tiger Eyes **42**
Intermediate

Leslie Rehfield — Juneau, Alaska
Ragg Time **18**
Easy

Camille Remme — Etobicoke, Ontario, Canada
Rainbows **51**
Intermediate

Betty Salpekar — Edison, New Jersey
A Lilliputian Christmas* **98**
Adventurous

Vivienne Shen — Houston, Texas
Gull Wings **39**
Intermediate

Kim Slad — Ramona California
Toe-tally Reversible Toasty Toes **54**
Experienced

Maude Smith — San Francisco, California
Multicolored Sockies **27**
Easy

Vickie Starbuck — Columbus, Ohio
Entrelac Socks* **56**
Experienced

Vickie Starbuck — Columbus, Ohio
Harry's Socks* **57**
Experienced

Nadine Stewart — New York, New York
Ripple Socks **66**
Easy

Judith Sumner — Knoxville, Tennessee
Feather & Fan **38**
Intermediate

Mary Anne Thompson — Boise, Idaho
Gumball Boot Socks **23**
Beginner

Ásthildur Thorsteinsson — Reykholtsdalur, Iceland
Socks for Troll Children **102**
Intermediate

Cindy Walker — Davis, California
Leaf Socks* **36**
Experienced

Deborah Faye Watson — Warrenton, Virginia
Miniature Socks **82**
Intermediate

Tricia Weatherston — East Stroudsburg, Pennsylvania
Harlequin Socks **50**
Experienced

This alphabetical listing of the knitters gives a detail of the sock, its name, the suggested skill level, and, in bold, the page on which it is found.

*Prize winners in the sock contest.

XRX Books would like to hear from you!

We can't publish all the knitting books in the world—only the finest.

We are knitting enthusiasts and book lovers. Our mission is simple: to produce quality books that showcase the beauty of the knitting and give our readers inspiration, confidence, and skill-building instructions.

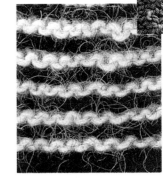

Publishing begins as a partnership between author and publisher. XRX Books attracts the best authors and designers in the knitting universe because we share their passion for excellence. But books also require a shared vision: photographer Alexis Xenakis and his team bring the garments and fabrics to glorious life. This is where our journey begins.

Cutting-edge computer technology allows us to focus on editing and designing our publications. XRX Books Editor Elaine Rowley can exchange files from South Dakota with our knitting editor in New York or our authors, wherever they happen to live, within a matter of minutes. Our digital consultant, David Xenakis, and his team insure accuracy of color and texture in our images. Graphic Artist Bob Natz, believing that design is not good unless it functions well, produces beautiful, easy-to-read pages.

Now those pages are in your hands and your journey begins.

Tell us what you think:

- **by mail**
  XRX Books
  PO Box 1525
  Sioux Falls, South Dakota
  57101-1525

- **by phone**
  605-338-2450

- **by fax**
  605-338-2994

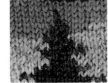

- **by e-mail**
  erowley@xrx-inc.com

- **on xrx-inc.com**
  You may visit our XRX Books site
  on the World Wide Web: www.xrx-inc.com

- **On our Knitter's OnLine forums:**
  Join the conversation and post your reactions and comments in our book discussion bulletin boards:
  www.knittinguniverse.com/script/webx.dll?knitalk

We look forward to hearing from you. New journeys are under way.

other publications from XRX, Inc.

Sally Melville Styles
Sally Melville

Magnificent Mittens
Anna Zilboorg

Ethnic Socks and Stockings
Priscilla A. Gibson-Roberts

The Great American Afghan

Knitter's Magazine

Weaver's Magazine

 BOOKS